Feminism, Young Women, and Cultural Studies

Feminism, Young Women and Cultural Studies

Birmingham Essays from 1975 Onwards

Angela McRobbie

Goldsmiths
Press

Copyright © 2024 Goldsmiths Press
First published in 2024 by Goldsmiths Press
Goldsmiths, University of London, New Cross
London SE14 6NW

Printed and bound by Short Run Press Limited, UK
Distribution by the MIT Press
Cambridge, Massachusetts, USA and London, England

Text copyright © 2024 Angela McRobbie

A CIP record for this book is available from the British Library

ISBN 978-1-913380-45-8 (pbk)
ISBN 978-1-913380-44-1 (ebk)

www.gold.ac.uk/goldsmiths-press

Goldsmiths
UNIVERSITY OF LONDON

Contents

Preface

What prompted me to gather this collection of articles and essays in September 2020 as I prepared to leave my full-time teaching and research post at Goldsmiths, University of London, to become an emeritus professor was a number of interrelated factors. For the last few years before the pandemic, I had been doing talks and lectures at a range of sixth-form colleges and London comprehensives. Whilst talking about my own earliest works on a range of topics, it was interesting to see that four – nearly five – decades later, they still had relevance to the young people in the secondary-school system and across three A-level courses: sociology, media studies and English literature. This was confirmed when, returning to teach first-year BA students at Goldsmiths after a period of research leave, I found the same thing: enthusiasm to discuss magazines in the digital age, the question of subcultures, pop music, sexuality and gender, all through the prism of race, class and sex. Even though my own current research was not engaging with the most recent topics of interest, such as TikTok and Instagram, it seemed that the foundations provided across these early essays still resonated – for example, the 'out of date' concepts of 'bedroom culture' and of 'teenybopper culture' seemed to have new meanings for tweens and young teenagers nowadays socialising by social media from their bedrooms with their friends after school, marking indeed the end of 'street corner society'. It was also apparent that the rise of vintage styles, with their environmentally friendly image, fitted well with students committed to climate crisis activism. For all of these reasons, I embarked in September 2021 on a project of writing four new essays and an introduction to map the field, which hopefully would bridge the gap between the early work and the current sociological realities. This new work comprises Section 1 of the book. Section 2 includes seven essays from the Birmingham years, or perhaps I should say in the orbit of the Birmingham Centre for Contemporary Cultural Studies, for two reasons: first, because there was always rich interaction and collaboration with scholars in other universities at that time (in this case with Simon Frith, who was then a lecturer at Warwick University), and second, because two of the later pieces – on vintage dress and on rethinking moral panic (the latter co-authored with Sarah Thornton, then a lecturer at Sussex University) – extended the field of youth cultures in new directions while also reflecting back sociologically on the key concepts from that time in the Birmingham School. It is important for me to acknowledge the real value of collaboration and co-authorship. Especially in the very early days of the mid-1970s, young feminist graduate students like myself really did not have a clear idea of what kind of career lay ahead or what sort of value may or may not attach itself to what at the time felt like rather half-baked ideas. It was for this very reason of uncertainty and a sense of marginality of gender issues, especially the topic of girls' culture, in the academy that the work undertaken during these early years did not quite mount up to a PhD submission. Factors in my family life also intervened, and so instead I found myself, like a few others from the Birmingham years, out on the academic labour market with a master's in research from Birmingham and publications and even post-graduate research grants based on the topics of girls' magazines, but without that formal doctoral qualification. Eventually, this was put right when I submitted an entirely new body of work (on fashion designers and creative labour) as a doctoral dissertation to Loughborough University in 1998, and then in 2019, to my delight, Glasgow University (where I had undertaken my first degree in English literature and sociology) awarded me an honorary doctorate on the basis of this now quite extensive field of research that started so hesitatingly with the 'girls work'.

I would therefore like to express my warm thanks to the co-authors, Jenny Garber, Simon Frith and Sarah Thornton; to my colleagues at Goldsmiths University, especially Sarah Kember, Julian Henriques, Daniel Strutt, Sarah Cefai, Catherine Rottenberg and Des Freedman (all of us in the 'teaching machine'). Finally, to my fellow students at Birmingham: Paul Gilroy, Charlotte Brunsdon and Lucy Bland.

PART 1

The Contemporary Field of 'Feminism for Girls'

1

Young Women, Feminist Cultural Studies, Then and Now

The Birmingham Centre for Contemporary Cultural Studies

This book is something of a hybrid. In this first part, there is a series of essays which sketch out the parameters for more up-to-date considerations of the topics which were the focus of my attention as a graduate student in the mid-1970s. The second part comprises the reprinted essays, most of which were written between 1976 and 1984, except for the last essay, which, although published in 1995, is also included because its contents and the framing reflect so many of the themes from the late 1970s. This period that I refer to is the time of what has come to be known as the Birmingham School, that is, a body of research associated with the Centre for Contemporary Cultural Studies (CCCS) at the University of Birmingham, under the leadership of Professor Stuart Hall. Cultural studies, as it developed during this period, was itself something of a hybrid. It stood in a kind of middle ground between sociology and English literature. It was also informed by what was then referred to as 'European Marxism' or 'continental philosophy', and this was expanded to include structuralism, Barthesian semiology and Saussure-influenced linguistics. And while in the UK in other universities and institutes (for example, at Leicester and Glasgow) there was, at the time, a growing body of work on the sociology of media and communications, the work carried out at the Birmingham CCCS carved a different pathway from the then dominant political economy of media approach Indeed, there were quite frequent and lively altercations as to which of these paradigms were the most academically (and politically) valid.[1] A further feature of that moment in Birmingham was that the graduate student body itself tilted towards the preference for 'theory', with a much smaller cohort, led by the ethnographer Paul Willis, that was interested in documenting the everyday lives of different social groups such as low-achieving working-class boys at school, or housewives as audiences for TV soap operas. I found myself, as a graduate student arriving in October 1974, somewhere in the middle of these two camps. The world of girls' magazines and the values they promoted formed a core interest, but alongside this, there was the question, not so much of readers of magazines (which would have entailed a reception study), as of the wider everyday lives of girls and young women, especially those from poor or disadvantaged communities. This led to some periods of observation in two youth centres, which I refer to below. But those visits did not quite qualify as an ethnography – it was more like a tentative attempt to tune into the key interests of girls at school and in the home and to listen to what they had to say. The focus was on working-class girls, and this not only reflected the wider emphasis on class at that time in the CCCS (as I discuss below), but it also emerged from a feminist perspective that recognised the disparity of life chances for girls in the mid-1970s depending on their social class. For middle-class young women this was a period influenced by what was then called women's liberation, and with those second-wave feminist struggles, suddenly things were changing, especially in education and then at work. But for working-class and for many ethnic minority young women, change was a lot slower and new job opportunities were more limited, since without higher education qualifications, the labour market remained restricted to traditionally feminine sectors such as retail, and other spheres characterised by low pay and few career prospects. The focus on working-class girls was also underpinned by the attention a cultural studies perspective would give to questions of struggle, resistance and community in the face of perceived inequality.[2]

As the articles that are reprinted in part 2 suggest, it was the choice of subjects for research that was a defining feature of the Birmingham Centre since these were, at that point, not considered legitimate in the wider fields of sociology and English Literature.[3] Despite the years that have passed, the topics have found a new relevance. For example, the question of girls' and women's magazines today is thrown into the spotlight with the shift to digital media and the decline of the familiar print copy. How do we gauge the kind of influence new digital magazine formats have? The other topics that were within my horizon nearly 50 years ago were those of youth subcultures and the media-led 'moral panics' that arose when groups of usually working-class teenage boys got caught up in ritualistic skirmishes during bank holidays with some other group of adversaries, with both being identifiable through their distinctive styles of dress and objects such as motor bikes or scooters. My questions were, inevitably, about the seeming invisibility of girls and, alongside this, the permutations of representation when they became visible.

When I first thought to investigate the lives of ordinary or working-class girls and young women in the mid-1970s, in conjunction with the magazines they read and the pop culture that surrounded them, it was from a city location that was completely new to me, i.e. Birmingham in the West Midlands. As a post-graduate student and a young mother, I was living in the predominantly white and poor working-class neighbourhood of Selly Oak. I had decided upon a two-prong course of study: a textual analysis of the magazine *Jackie* alongside a period of observation involving the kinds of girls who were the main target readership for a magazine like this, i.e. 14-15-year-olds. Inevitably, I looked around locally, and the girls in the neighbourhood all attended a local comprehensive a couple of miles away. There was a youth centre attached to the school, and this, along with another school and youth centre, a bit farther away on the outer reaches of Kings Heath, became the location for this part of my research.

Having come recently from Glasgow, from a middle-class background but having grown up in this staunchly working-class city, it was difficult for me to get a grip on the class politics in Birmingham, including the families of the girls in question. There did not seem to be a radical or left-wing ethos, or the kind of class pride and humour found in Glasgow. It was perhaps instructive then that within a few years, the girls I had got to know had become the consorts to groups of right-wing racist skinheads and football thugs, which, among other things, forced the hasty departure of my small family from the area. The second group, based in the youth centre a few miles away, were also all white and working class – a friendship group of about six, aged around 15. Over a period of a couple of years, they gravitated, in complete contrast, to the punk and reggae scene that was happening in nearby Moseley in South Birmingham. They got to know some of us middle-class feminists and left-wing young men involved in various campaigns, including Rock against Racism and the Anti-Nazi League. They formed bands and helped in the setting up of a couple of independent record labels, and their lives from then on took an entirely different direction from what their original white working-class location would have suggested. Anthropologists would surely point out that the second group, possibly already alienated from the school and its low expectations for working-class girls, and due to other precipitative factors at home, were poised to latch onto the middle-class feminists who arrived at the youth centre with the idea of setting up 'girls' groups'. They were, in effect, looking for the ways and means of exiting the claustrophobia of heterosexuality, early marriage and the ensuing babies that they saw their older sisters disappear into.

Class and Culture

In the CCCS, most of the research that was being undertaken was underpinned by a concern with class both as lived experience and as an abstract category within Marxist thought. Class domination and the ensuing inequality were considered from two vantage points. One followed the course of classical Marxism, with class as a motor force for historical change and a concept for struggle and conflict. This analysis provided a vector for understanding how power and domination operate, how capitalism has to ensure that its workforce remains servile and subordinate and in need of forms of employment within its industries and in its post-industrial service sector in order to ensure its own reproduction. The working class was formed out of these relations of struggle, exploitation and oppression. In this equation, the working class is the instrument through which capital leverages its profits by extracting the surplus value from labour. It is a tool for the political economy, and for this reason working-class people must be kept in a relation of subordination and dependency. But there was always scope for resistance. Class was then a category formed through the struggle for domination. It was from this understanding of class that further work in cultural studies developed along more theoretical lines, first with the concepts of ideology and hegemony and then through psychoanalysis, representation, language and difference, all of which permitted the analysis of how power operated in the wider social and cultural world, particularly in representations and media forms. Even though many major social institutions operated with a degree of independence or autonomy, their key function as 'ideological state apparatuses', such as the media, was to ensure the passivity of working people (including young people) so that they did not organise and make demands that would challenge the existing social order (Althusser 1971).

The other approach that informed the research at Birmingham was more directly derived from Richard Hoggart (the author of *The Uses of Literacy*) and Raymond Williams (*Culture and Society* being one of his most famous books) (Hoggart 1957; Williams 1957). For each of these writers (Richard Hoggart was actually the original founder of the CCCS), the lived experience of class domination and the forms of coherent activities and practices that emerged (e.g. music hall, the pub, bingo, gossip) gave meaning and identity to working-class people. It was this second approach that informed the sociological and historical studies of distinctive class groupings, such as Willis's influential study of white working-class boys in a Midlands comprehensive school (Willis 1978). This approach was also associated with the growth of local oral histories and with the importance of documenting lives that were otherwise forgotten, overlooked or absent from the archives. Over the years that followed, socialist-feminist researchers from a range of different universities looked to institutions including the home, the school, the youth clubs and the factory floors. Distinctive forms of class culture were documented which showed complex patterns of resistance to and compliance with the capitalist and the patriarchal forces which limited ambition and trapped young women into motherhood and typically part-time or low earnings. Some of the CCCS feminist researchers pursued this line of study, and this in turn gave rise to lively sociological discussions (also being conducted elsewhere at the time) about accessing the fields of ordinary women's lives, entering their homes and using them as the subjects of academic research (Hobson 1982). Then, through the 1980s, there were various research projects with teenage working-class girls often carried out in youth centres and set up with local authority support on the basis that girls had in the past been poorly served (Nava 1982). These were explicitly defined as feminist (and also lesbian) projects.

During this period of time, Stuart Hall made the important argument that for black people race was the 'modality' through which class was lived (Hall et al. 1978). Endemic racism across British society meant that economic hardship and marginalisation in the labour market were experienced as primarily, if not exclusively, the outcome of racial discrimination. Through the 1990s, class came increasingly to be understood as interwoven with race, ethnicity, gender and sexuality. Class was no longer the sole determination for understanding social structure. And this corresponded with changes taking place in and across 'class society' at large. When viewed through the lens of gender, the centrality of class in fact began to fade through the 1990s. It is not so much that class inequalities had reduced significantly, but more that the power of ideology, as manifest through popular culture and the media, ramped up so that there was a negation of class as a point of community and belonging, and this was especially true for women. Women were increasingly expected to be socially mobile, to be aspirational. With the rise of neoliberal society,[4] young women were encouraged to become more self-responsible and to undertake all sorts of forms of self-improvement.[5] Working-class identity in this context was antithetical to 'female success'. The wider social institutions, such as the schools and the employers and the media, looked to girls and young women to achieve, to do better in life than their parents, to improve themselves and to leave the old idea of working-class culture behind them (McRobbie 2008).

Young Women in the 2000s: The Myth of Social Mobility

By the late 1990s, sociologists like Zygmunt Bauman were providing an account of the unfolding of the neoliberal society (Bauman 1999, 2001). *Liquid Modernity* in effect marked the transition away from a society of classes to one of individuals, where so much more emphasis was put on the self. Feminists such as myself and others tracked this process through the early 2000s and the period of the New Labour Blair government, where the female individualisation process became a significant project of the government, a kind of undertaking, or what Foucault would call a *dispositif,* i.e. a converged way of managing this population of young women with various attractive enticements to achieve, but with certain terms and conditions. This period of 'post-feminism' cast a negative shadow over the idea of feminism, making it somehow unpalatable. Girls were encouraged instead to think about their own personal achievements. The magazines and media advocated all sorts of self-monitoring and the 'must try harder' ethos. At the same time, various steps were taken by the government to cut back on the welfare state and to put limits of public spending on facilities like libraries and youth centres. Failure came to be seen as a personal matter and nothing to do with government policies. Demeaning images of working-class life also began to circulate in popular culture and the media. 'Chavs' and single mothers were demonised as living off the state on 'handouts', and low-income young women were instructed by their middle-class counterparts on prime time makeover TV on 'what not to wear' (McRobbie 2008, 2020).

Britain was becoming a much more divided society, with a kind of aspirational middle classification process (as Stuart Hall also noted) masking the downward push which affected so many people who might previously have been securely working-class in more social democratic times – but with welfare so reduced, with social housing a matter of rundown dangerous estates and with the labour market now a place of low-paid casualised jobs, they had become the 'working poor' or even the 'underclass'. The shaming of people on benefits and the reform of the welfare system impacted on disadvantaged women, including young women. If they did not have the level of qualifications which might lift them into more secure employment, they got stuck in routine low-paid jobs, such as in supermarkets, call centres or in packaging for distribution and fulfilment centres. With little wider attention being paid to this low-wage economy and the overall 'degradation of labour', and with an assumption that it was somehow the person's own fault for ending up in this kind of work, the neoliberal revolution had quietly squeezed out of the picture the importance of labour organisation and union representation.[6] These changes are discussed in recent feminist work that focuses on the degradation of labour along with wage stagnation and the hollowing out of the welfare state giving rise to new levels of female poverty and hardship (Cooper 2017; Brown 2015; McRobbie 2020).

The impact of long-term low wages and the way in which the benefits system in the UK is now providing (minimal and ever-decreasing) support, not to the unemployed but to those whose wages are so low that they are forced to rely on additional 'top-up' benefits in order to survive, have eventually been acknowledged in political culture. Suddenly, the 'myth of the meritocracy' and the idea of the 'personal-choice society' have been exposed, and the feminist question is how the end of this dream of mobility now impacts on women, and in our case young women (Littler 2017). Overall the shallowness of the appeal to individual pathways has become apparent, and there is perhaps some grudging recognition on the part of the political parties that social structures (such as housing and accommodation, childcare, equal pay, wages and flexible working) do need to be addressed. This shift of attention back to the key institutions, such as the National Health Service and the housing provision in the UK, is, especially since the pandemic, the outcome of campaigns, protests and strikes, as well as reports and investigative journalism, often led by women. (The nursing profession offers a good example of many of the above points.) A vocabulary of care has reentered the field of public debate (The Care Collective 2020; Dowling 2021). The difficult circumstances experienced by even those 'good girls' who have gained the qualifications and found their way into the labour market but who are still saddled with student debt and who are finding it almost impossible to get a foothold in the housing market, never mind consider having children, mean that the upbeat image of neoliberal society, with its ethos of competition and entrepreneurship, is now, perhaps fatally, dented. The individualised society no longer resonates, and meanwhile new forms of solidarity that fit with the times are in the process of being invented. It is as if the very idea of 'the social' is by sheer necessity once again in view.

Girlhood Studies: Race and Ethnicity

The girl is an assemblage of social and cultural issues and questions rather than a field of physical facts, however much the girl's empirical materiality is crucial to that assemblage.

—Driscoll (2008)

There is another body of scholarship that has developed and grown around the figure of the young woman as 'girl', and this in turn, over the last thirty years, has given rise to a specific field of 'girlhood studies' (Mitchell and Reid-Walsh 2007). This traverses the humanities and the social sciences, from studies of girls as 'tweens', to research on girl fans of popular fiction such as *Twilight*, to accounts of sexualisation of girls by the media and in consumer culture, e.g. the marketing of items such as bras and bikinis to small prepubescent girls, and the encouragement of beauty rituals and 'pampering' to this same cohort. (The Pink Stinks campaigns of the early 2000s drew attention to this phenomenon within consumer culture.) The most significant development in girlhood studies has been the turn to race and ethnicity. Key here is the report Black Girls Matter by the African American Policy Forum and authored by Kimberlé Crenshaw, Priscilla Ocen and Jyoti Nanda (2015). This study shows the impact of negative stereotyping of young black women in two education districts in the U.S. and it also reveals the extent to which black girls have been marginalised – if not excluded – from youth research. The backdrop is the new stricter and more disciplinary regimes in the school system. The Crenshaw et al. report shows how the implementation of zero-tolerance policies in U.S. schools leads to early exits of black and Latino girls, who are already facing many challenges in day-to-day life and for whom coun-selling and other forms of support would have kept in the system. Judged more harshly than their white counterparts, these girls are also subject to processes of 'adultification' – that is, they are taken to be overburdened as teenagers by family and domestic obligations. Deemed to be mature for their years, these girls are often overlooked in the classroom, disregarded and subject to academic neglect.

Crenshaw and the other authors of the report indicate how society in general and the school system in particular remain reliant on images of family life based on the white nuclear-family model, which in turn results in the pathologisation of black families that deviate from this norm. This accounts for the harsh treatment of young 'teen' mothers, often excluded from further schooling or at least segregated and set apart from their friends, and so overall much less likely to gain the qualifications needed for jobs that would bring in more than minimal wages. Low retention rates of black girls in schools that adhere to zero-tolerance therefore contrib-utes directly to worsening outcomes, a future in the low-wage sector and high likelihood of poverty. The report describes how an atmosphere in the schools created by the excessive emphasis on discipline and the presence of security personnel and police officers becomes a disincentive for learn-ing and many girls become disengaged. The authors also point to the extent to which the experience of sexual assault and violence on the part of black girls gets much less attention than is the case for white young women, and this means that trauma goes unrecognised and hence unsupported.[7]

Where several of these themes were investigated in the past by UK feminists such as Ann Phoenix, this American work is useful not just for the contemporary light it casts on the impact of racism on young black women in the school system, but also because of its focus on the worsening of circumstances created by school programmes that are lauded for improving grades and for endorsing pathways to 'excellence'. The girls within this neoliberal teaching regime become even more disadvantaged than before. The report from 2015 therefore proposes radical changes that would give the young women more of a say in the day-to-day pedagogy. A more democratic 'right to learn' approach would allow them to feel safe without threat of punishments. A raft of more compassionate measures would also go some way in severing the increasing interconnections between the school system and the juvenile justice regime. This overlapping of punitive regimes corresponds with the shape of so many neoliberal policies over the last three decades that are aimed at disadvantaged people, including the criminalisation of welfare (Wacquant 2009). Under the smokescreen of advocating success and emphasising the potential of high-income careers thanks to the provision of meritocratic pathways, the 'top girls' projects are highly divisive regimes punishing those who cannot participate in the more fiercely competitive education apparatus. The 'at risk' girls are frequently abandoned as school failures, left to their own devices, or removed altogether from the school because teachers' careers and school budgets are reliant on the high bands of results they are expected to achieve. The economic logic of neoliberalism in the school system exacerbates the inequalities and social injustices of race.[8]

The persistence of stereotyping and the many battles young women of colour must fight to enjoy leisure and some degree of freedom in their teenage years has been documented by recent ethnographers of black girlhood (Bettie 2003; Cox 2015; Thomas 2011). These studies draw attention to the important role of black popular culture. Aria S. Halliday's account of the enjoyment for black girls in dancing together and twerking is a good example. Not only is there a 'pleasure in blackness', but the dance routines offer 'possibilities for self-expression and sexuality' (Halliday 2020). These are diasporic dance practices in a context where young black women are constantly demonised across so many sites of societal judgement for their bodies, their skin colour and their socioeconomic status. This idea of dance practices as creating and keeping alive different forms of diasporic culture is shown to be a site of struggle. It is endlessly appropriated by the white pop music and entertainment industry, contributing to the vast wealth of the stars and celebrities while at the same time, in the everyday context of urban black culture, girls and young women are subjected to the racial stereotypes of 'unruly' black womanhood. Many of these themes have, of course, been considered over a longer stretch of time by (among others) bell hooks, whose writing on black girlhood encompasses both the autobiographical and the theoretical (hooks 1997). She recalls her reaction to reading Toni Morrison: 'Not enough is known about the experience of black girls in our society. Indeed one of my favourite novels in the whole world is Toni Morrison's *The Bluest Eye* … she explained her focus on "the people who in all literature were always peripheral … little black girls who were props, background: those people who were never center stage and those people were me"' (hooks 1997:97).

hooks weaves into her account of black girlhood in the southern state of Kentucky, where she grew up, questions of poverty and of material hardship. She also provides the foundations for understanding how deeply entrenched the brutalities and everyday cruelties of racism are and have been and how they impact on women. hooks's methodology is important for the way in which she blends memoir and poetic writing with sociological analysis of the structures upon which white patriarchal supremacy has been build.[9] Interweaving her own personal experience with the range of cultural and literary activities that she takes part in, hooks provides a unique mode of conversational address to readerships well beyond the academic institutions. There is, for example, an analysis of the performances and persona of Tina Turner, alongside so many other reviews of films, books and television programmes. hooks also inserts into her writing things that have happened to her as a black woman academic in the course of her teaching and while attending events, and even while having dinner with colleagues. This self-reflexivity creates an atmosphere of conviviality and affection for her audiences and readers. It is also an overtly and unapologetically emotional pedagogic strategy for working with black young women, inviting them to draw on their own experience.

Saidiya Hartman's cultural history of young black women's lives in urban post-abolitionist America also marks a major achievement in black feminist scholarship in girlhood studies (Hartman 2021). Hartman discovers the chaotic way in which poor young 'wayward' black women in post-abolitionist America were abandoned by the state and barely accounted for in the public records and files of the time. Their names and details were often missing, as they were pushed through the state detention centres, foster homes and justice system. She found random photographs left lying around with no names, children and girls for whom there were no records of their lives, almost nothing in the public archives. These girls were only recognised on the basis of their troubled and unrespectable lives. But Hartman also turns this around and, developing a methodology of 'fabulation', she honours these lost girls, restoring to them an identity and a lively and even exuberant 'way of life'. Though they are invariably cast as immoral and even dangerous, she shows how the girls eked out a living in the nighttime entertainment economy of urban America. Interweaving fiction with social history and sociological analysis, Hartman re-scripts the girls' lives, she gives them a name and an identity and she shows them to be rebellious and queer as well as joyful, full of love and attachment. She describes their love of fashion and finery, their beauty rituals and the pleasure they sought in nightlife and in the black music cultures of early twentieth-century urban America. This is a kind of black social history that brings retrospective dignity and meaning to those girls whose lives had barely merited them being named and recognised as human beings. The lasting importance of Hartman's writing is that it provides a historical account of racialised capitalism from the viewpoint of gender and sexuality in a way that resonates directly with the punitive regime which neoliberal capitalism now inflicts on so-called 'at risk' black young women whose lives have been blighted through the limited chances they have had to gain the education and training needed to provide for themselves and for their families. From Crenshaw to hooks, from Halliday to Hartman, a radical pedagogy which fully took into account these historical factors of exclusion, stereotyping, of overt punishment and of trauma would seek first and foremost to create more equal conditions of listening to the voices of these young women and of giving them space to find collaborative ways of learning without being subjected to the hard metrics culture of the neoliberal classroom and its adjacent institutions.[10]

Empowerment as Moral Agency

New topics within girlhood studies have been appearing on a regular basis. Feminist art history has reflected on the trope of 'the girl' in the field of modern art (Grant and Waxman 2011). There have been studies and reports on girls and menstruation politics and the strategies needed for de-stigmatisation around period poverty. In the U.S. over the decades, Kearney's focus on girls' agency and on their cultural production and participation in social media content creation has challenged the dominant emphasis on social control and surveillance (Kearney 2006). Coleman has provided a reflexive and embodied account by considering girls' immersion in so many various media forms such that there is a seeming porosity between bodies, technologies, images and spaces like the bedroom or the classroom (Coleman 2009). Driscoll's historically framed account of the various social and institutional processes which have functioned over the decades to create the category of girl as a figuration which brought connotations of positivity and goodwill to ideals of modernity in a way that was not confined to Western modernity, marks an important and defining moment: the historic girl as a moral force for good, a kind of exculpation factor for the ills bound up with capitalist progress, exploitation and oppression (Driscoll 2002, 2008). Of course, this was predicated on earlier religious, missionary and moralising discourses and on the exemplary role white women were expected to play in nation and empire building as evident across the civilisationist discourses of the nineteenth century. Driscoll traces these ideas through the rise of the *Girl's Own Paper*, published by the Religious Tract Society from 1880 to 1956. Driscoll also considers the presence and presumptions about the 'girl' in key figures such as the literary critic F.R. Leavis, who saw the girl as a passive dupe, easily swayed and in effect the mindless face of the new consumerism. (De Beauvoir provides the important feminist correction to much of the typecasting by showing how if girlhood meant a time dominated by patriarchal demands, only womanhood could promise freedom.)

By focusing on the 'category' of girl, Driscoll's genealogy inevitably points also to the recent past and to Butler's querying of girlhood *per se* as a process of social construction, a reiterated crafting of gender onto and across the body of the child. Butler brought to the field a more substantial theorisation of gender and the body and in doing so she also destabilised further the embedded historical and cultural connotations and expectations – indeed, requirements – around ideas of girlhood (Butler 1990, 1993). Butler's work showed just how much was at stake in the securing of normative and widely accepted notions of girlhood. Butler argued that sanctions were imposed on those girls who could not abide by the requirements to acquire and demonstrate an attachment to the ideal of femininity upon which intelligibility as a young woman rested, thus suggesting that lesbian, queer or non-binary young women or trans boys might find that life itself, without political solidarity, was not survivable. The wider and now well-established field of girlhood studies has therefore recently embraced this questioning of the very idea of girlhood as a centuries-old cultural fiction which has been a powerful tool for the grip of the heterosexual matrix, as Butler called it, and for patriarchal capitalism to secure masculine domination across its institutions.

Those clusters of meanings, including goodness and cheerful positivity, which have been indelibly linked to girlhood have recently been shown by feminists working in development studies to be nowadays imposed on the bodies of girls and young women in countries of Southeast Asia, Africa and South America with the added gloss of Western feminist empowerment discourse. Feminism becomes a kind of moral duty. It is as if these meanings have been transposed from the bodies of girls from the global north to those populations of young women living in the poorest countries in the world. Campaigns undertaken by major corporations such as Nike that appear to champion 'the girl' draw attention to girls' capacity for hard work; they are deemed worthy of investment in the form of micro-credit. In campaigns like 'gender equality as smart economics', what we might call the 'development girl' will fulfil many of the requirements of the global neoliberal regime with 'hyper industriousness', including having an entrepreneurial outlook and an eagerness to be a kind of busy economic agent (Wilson 2015; Banet-Weiser 2018). Old colonialist stereotypes are reworked to encourage young women to 'make sacrifices' with long working hours while also continuing with duties at home. Overall they become cyphers for the contemporary intensification of labour based on the seeming liberation provided by paid work and employment (McRobbie 2020). The development girl is also a piece of 'human capital' who will control her fertility, become educated and be prepared to work hard in the long term as a breadwinner for the children she will have. The various programmes set up across African countries as well as in Asia and supported by the World Bank and other organisations and corporations (Because I'm A Girl, Girl Up, Plan International) rely on processes of 'girling' young women according to this logic and are invariably accompanied by attractive visual promotional material including films, videos and billboard advertisements. Being deemed worthy of investment confers on the 'development girl' ideas of agency and empowerment.

A new moral economy is established on both sides of this equation. The large corporations seek to gain credibility by these actions of corporate social responsibility, and the girls themselves are cast in a positive light for their assumed personal qualities, including their willingness to take part in the projects and their abiding sense of duty. It is set up as a win-win situation garnering approval at every point, though, as various feminist scholars have pointed out, little is known about the day-to-day workings of these programmes, the actual outcomes and how the girls themselves experience the projects. The only results that are mentioned are usually good-news stories about successful entrepreneurship. Detailed reports are generally not available to the public; there are only the glossy brochures and advertising material. The idea of empowerment is deployed as if to stretch to the limit the positivity of the girl as a deserving subject, while also attributing to a range of governmental and nongovernmental as well as corporate bodies a progressive function. As Banet-Weiser (2018:212) comments, there is also a 'market for empowerment. ... Girl power ... refers to girls as powerful consumers, who represent a primary market (where girls have their own income), a market of influencers (where girls influence their parents' consumer choices), and a future market (where girls' consumer loyalty is cultivated as future customers)'. This is a complex scenario where the potential female consumer markets play just one role in the wider set of initiatives. The global corporations are desperate to show social awareness, and energetic young women from the global south are their ideal subjects, especially when leading political figures like Michelle Obama have championed their needs. By plugging into these wider public health discourses, the companies reduce the accusation of this being modern-day imperialising activity. Empowerment for girls also breathes new life into tarnished or tired human rights agendas while addressing the young women performatively as moral agents.

Some Conclusions

In the above sections, I have attempted to summarise some of the key themes which have dominated the fields of research which back in the mid-1970s I was drawn to, albeit with some degree of trepidation. The rationale for this lengthy introduction is that when there is a sense of political urgency, in this case stemming from the need for feminist perspectives on key social issues of the day, cultural studies and sociology seem well suited to taking something of a long view. Hence, the impact of neoliberal values across the social field in the last decade in the UK is better understood when Stuart Hall's prescient analysis of the times of Thatcherism is taken into account, and likewise when we confront the prevalence of racist attacks on young black women in Britain today, Hall et al.'s seminal *Policing the Crisis* of 1978 helps us to understand media stereotypes and policing practices (Hall 1988; Hall et al. 1987). There is also the question of the seismic changes that have taken place over these decades, and in the above discussion I have sketched how so much emphasis was placed on self-improvement on the part of young women as a 'technology of the self' in the early 2000s. There was a nebulous idea that this would deliver so many positive outcomes, including the ethos of female competition and entrepreneurship. Alongside this, young women were directed away from more dangerous feminist ideas that would provide clearer political understanding of prevailing inequalities. When feminism eventually found a place again in everyday life, it was a watered down 'neoliberal leadership feminism' based on various matrices of success that were endorsed (Sandberg 2012). At the time of writing, in 2023, this whole juggernaut of seemingly popular 'neoliberal feminism' is, however, if not entirely stopped in its tracks, at least slowed down and coming almost to a halt during and after a series of major events. The election of Donald Trump and the unadulterated misogyny of that world leader acted as a wakening call for the need for new forms of feminist activism. The many different variations of feminism that have emerged since 2016 are a testimony to the scale of the support for change from women across the boundaries of race and class and age. Likewise the brutal racist killing of George Floyd in 2020 and the emergence of the Black Lives Matter movement has fuelled a wide and popular black feminist politics, which has swept across British society with so many new campaigns and support groups coming into being (for example, the Black Child Agenda). Alongside these changes, and in the light of the COVID-19 pandemic of 2020, the young women who had been the subjects of the female individualisation process I referred to above have grown up and entered the labour market. Many have found that, faced with years of wage stagnation, the ethos of 'personal choice' means very little, and that renewed forms of social solidarity and union organisation offer the best means to have their voices listened to. Alongside the forms of industrial action being currently undertaken (in 2023), it is the nurses, in the past a traditionally female sector, that have become the most vocal, while also of course drawing attention to their own ethos of care.

The Chapters That Follow

Part 1 (chapters 2, 3, 4 and 5) comprises a series of overview and topic-based accounts to accompany the work first published from the mid-1970s. They are all written with a view to enabling A-level and first-year BA students to undertake further reading and to formulate topics for research projects. (I have desisted from providing lengthy reading lists of contemporary scholarship for reasons of space.) In chapter 2, there is an updating of the magazine as a genre now displaced by digital and social media. There is also an attempt to put the magazine form into a historical context where its wider role in the formation of nation and citizenship is marked. Chapter 3 provides an overview and reconsideration of three topics: subcultures, the ideas underpinning girls work and the politics of feminist research. Here I argue that the recent writing that brings queerness to subcultural theory, important as it is, has tended to omit the sociological perspectives that the work of Stuart Hall and the CCCS colleagues had developed to account for questions of class and race and ethnicity in modern British society. In chapter 4, I provide an account of two themes in regard to the question of young women's involvement and investment in pop music. These are the gender inequalities that are still rampant in the music industry, and the question of young women and black music as diasporic expressive culture. Finally, in chapter 5, I turn my attention to young women's involvement in vintage clothing and in resale sites such as Depop. The recycling ethos that underpins vintage style marks a decisive shift in consumer culture, while the whole world of second-hand clothing needs to be seen from the viewpoint of its extensive and multi-sited labour markets.

The essays reprinted in part 2 begin with the analysis of *Jackie* magazine, which is then followed by three quite short chapters, one on girls and subcultures (co-authored with Jenny Garber), the next comprising a feminist critique of subcultural theory, notably the work of Dick Hebdige and Paul Willis, followed in turn by a more self-reflexive essay on the doing of feminist research (including a range of quite detailed references to what were then current concerns). The last three essays include some early thinking on 'women and rock' co-authored with Simon Frith, which is followed by the article I wrote in the post-punk moment on the way in which subcultures were generating their own small-scale economics of second-hand and vintage fashion, and finally there is the co-authored essay (with Sarah Thornton) from 1995 where we make the case for the revision of the concept of moral panic on the grounds not just of the proliferation of different multi-mediated forms of everyday panic from the early 1990s onwards, but also because the 'folk devils' or their representatives had found the ways and means of 'fighting back', thereby countering their own denigrated stereotypes.

Notes

1 The most often cited disagreement pitched the famous historian E.P. Thompson against Stuart Hall, who, Thompson argued, engaged with 'theory' in a way that underestimated and undermined the capacity of social groups and classes to organise and resist the forces of their oppression. Thompson also challenged the anti-humanism of the French philosopher Louis Althusser, whose theory of ideology was enormously influential on CCCS scholarship (Thompson 1978).

2 There was also a struggle to get feminism taken seriously in the febrile atmosphere of the Birmingham Centre at the time. A strong working-class perspective on women avoided the suspicion that feminism was a liberal middle-class phenomenon.

3 TV programmes such as BBC *Nationwide* were subjected to analysis by Brunsdon (1987) and Morley (1980); the equivalent programme today is BBC's *The One Show*. See also Dorothy Hobson on the soap opera *Crossroads* (Hobson 1982).

4 There are many definitions of neoliberalism, but key elements are the dominance of the free market and finance capitalism, the so-called small state and with it the undermining of all the social institutions associated with periods of social democracy, privatisation, the elevation of the ethos of competition and individualisation, the idea of 'self-entrepreneurialism' and 'self-responsibilisation' and, most importantly, significant reductions in welfare spending replaced by an emphasis on human capital and the spreadsheet mentality (see also Harvey 2005).

5 Hall's earlier writings focused on the shift to the right from the days of the Thatcher government onwards; see Hall 1988.

6 As Stuart Hall pointed out, some decades earlier the Thatcher revolution committed to break up the power of the trade unions as a key political goal (Hall 2011).

7 Racial violence against black girls in the educational environment has been exposed in the UK, with shocking scenes of a young girl being beaten up by five white assailants having first circulated on social media and then prompting protests by the local black community and eventually police action including arrests and charges being made (Taylor 2023). See also the recently formed campaign group called the Black Child Agenda (https://www.theblackchildagenda.org/).

8 Ann Phoenix in the UK was in fact one of the first feminist scholars to undertake research on how the neoliberal values in the school system impacted adversely on young black males. She drew attention to what amounted to public shaming rituals with teachers reading out loud and to the whole class the scores and grades awarded on the now almost weekly testing (Phoenix 2004).

9 Through the 1990s, hooks did not shy away from using terms like white supremacy, while in academia this was often avoided as too inflammatory, even within leftist sociology. Paul Gilroy in the UK also made extensive use of the term.

10 Performance, drama therapy and radical pedagogy have been explored and staged in, for example, Clare Barron's *Dance Nation* (2011).

2

The Girls' and Women's Magazine: A Disappearing Genre?

Introduction

Nearly fifty years ago when I first started working on the topic of the girls' magazine as genre, there was very little work out there in the world of scholarship. And the same was true for women's magazines. It must have been a topic that had no legitimacy among scholars in both the humanities and the social sciences. I have clear memories of days and weeks spent searching for material that could comprise a review of literature. In the British Library, I did come across a handful of books on the history of the 'ladies' journals' (White 1970; Adburgham 1972). At least in the Birmingham University Centre for Contemporary Cultural Studies (CCCS) at the time there was a lively interest in this kind of topic. I recall my colleagues there pointing me in the direction of Mattelart and Dorfmann and the comic genre– this work looked at how the Disney corporation used cartoons and comics to play an ideological role in maintaining American imperialism through its demeaning depictions of people from the global south (Mattelart and Dorfman 1975; Dorfman 1983). This was helpful for the reason that it recognised the political role and powerful influence that this seemingly innocent and highly popular form could have.

The magazine has been a long-standing feature of popular culture, and in the UK, part of the formation of national political culture.[1] Indeed it is the seemingly wide space between the two (girls' magazines have typically been seen as harmless fun, women's magazines as merely about the home) that has permitted this important role to be maintained, and even safeguarded. The ostensible purpose of providing for female leisure and entertainment, escapism and other delights, over the decades, consistently disguises the deeply ideological work being carried out. And the fact of this being a gender-specific genre (even though in the early days it was typically edited by men) made the magazine sector all the more significant as a site for the continuous formulation and reformulation of societal expectations for women and girls. But in the last two decades, the changes away from print to digital media have meant that the old format of the magazine genre has been transformed so that it is almost unrecognisable. Hard copies do still exist, and they still sit (if a little forlornly) on the newsagent's shelves and supermarket stands. But they have lost their sense of cultural identity. They are no longer so familiar. The front covers seem to command less presence. They may even have lost some of the 'hailing power' they once had. The genre has become fragmented, cut up into 'pieces', dispersed and scattered into all sorts of sub-genres with the exponential rise of social media in the last fifteen years. It is no longer a matter of avidly turning the pages. It is a matter of phone scrolling or tablet or laptop scrolling. We might even say that the old-fashioned magazine barely exists anymore. Only rarely does one see a young woman sitting on the London Underground reading a hard copy of a glossy magazine. The purchasing of the monthly magazine by millions of women is almost a thing of the past, and this suggests the loss of a set of national institutions. This is something that has been happening over time, as the uniqueness of the weekly or monthly gave way to the magazine supplement formats being adopted by so many newspapers, thus pulling away advertising revenue from the familiar women's titles. It has often been noted that the conversational mode of the magazines was transferred to the daytime TV formats (from the *Oprah Winfrey Show* in the U.S. to ITV's *Loose Women*). Readers have increasingly been replaced by communities or followers or subscribers. The advertising copy which provided the funding for the glossier magazines has been entirely reinvented for digital media. Given that this transformation is so seismic, what is urgently needed is an analysis of these processes for the sector overall. This would involve looking at the decline of magazine journalism, the job losses and the much more precarious lives of those who still work in this form of media (Duffy 2017; Rocamora 2017). There is little way of knowing what alternative employment has been sought by those whose jobs have disappeared. Another unanswered question is how this all plays out for the older employees across the sector: Have they been shunted out earlier than they would have expected?

New Methodologies

For scholars of the magazine, whether sociologists or cultural studies researchers, these changes also require new, more agile methodologies. How to develop rigorous tools to analyse the constellation of technologies and devices and specifically the many kinds of screen formats which are now host to what remains of the magazine genre? And then to find a systematic mode of analysis of the fast-changing content which is nowadays accompanied by readers' comments and various other forms of participation?[2] Nor is there a range of at-hand methodologies for investigating a phenomenon that is no longer a genre with the kind of fixity it once had. Most hard-copy magazines adhered to a standard way of ordering the content, from *Vogue* to the more mid-market titles. The reader would know how to read the magazine accordingly: what typically came first and what was to be found in the end pages. The range of generic content could be understood in terms of codings (in the old semiological sense), e.g. the code of 'romance' or the code of 'fashion and beauty'. Now there is an endless proliferation of new magazine formats scattered across social media, with seemingly unpredictable running orders and page layouts. The idea of an editorial narrative, in effect a way of introducing and framing the issue, has also lost its prominent place. And with the decline of the genre as a whole, it is even possible for ambitious editors, writers, bloggers and influencers who were once employees to establish their own personal online magazine with the aim of monetising the title and using it as a springboard for other freelance activities.

It is as though everything in the old world of the magazine is now dispersed so that the format of the genre has become increasingly unrecognisable. In the past it was the well- honed practice of textual analysis which held the key to unlocking the ideological world of the magazine and how this form of media relied on a variety of techniques of naturalisation, so that what were 'social constructions of reality' appeared as always already in place and so more or less unquestionable. On the basis of this kind of analysis it was possible to develop arguments about social class, gender and sexuality, race and ethnicity, nation and citizenship as being factors inherent to the rationale of the magazine genre. But this methodology makes almost no sense when the appearance of the single image is subject to such rapid change and articles are posted for such brief periods and then disappear or become part of an archive which means being separated from the overall 'issue'. Semiology was predicated on the still image as having a longer lifespan and being reproducible (even if just for the purposes of reprinting in an academic journal article). The impact of algorithms also means that individual readers are having material served to them in a more personal manner, so there is further fragmentation and a more private process of media consumption according to 'taste' or to past searches. This must mean that from the magazine point of view the idea of their readers being part of an identifiable community is a rapidly shrinking horizon.

Birmingham Perspectives

The work on the popular girls' magazine *Jackie*[3] that I undertook at the CCCS in the mid-1970s (reprinted in this volume, chapter 6) borrowed widely from the concepts that had come into play specifically for the analysis of popular forms, mostly through the writing of Roland Barthes, Louis Althusser and the Italian Marxist Antonio Gramsci. Both Althusser and Gramsci had demonstrated the role played by ideological forms for the organisation of consent in late capitalist society (Althusser 1971; Gramsci 1974/2021). The emphasis in Gramsci was on how non-authoritarian forms of power operated through the mobilisation of pleasure and enjoyment, to win active approval for the status quo, for or on behalf of the forces of domination. Gramsci's concept of hegemony rested on the securing of non-coercive consent and agreement with the prevailing social order. This hegemony was, however, always fragile, always somehow threatened, which accounted for the need, on the part of those in power, to constantly reassert and to repeat the various themes and narratives. Althusser's theory of ideology was based on the idea that specific sets of values were built into the material organisation of the large social institutions. These seem taken for granted, for example, the organisation of the school and its classrooms, or in our case, the layout, shape and organisation of the magazine form. Ideology operated by making what were in fact socially constructed 'realities' appear as if they were common sense. This analysis therefore drew attention to the power relations embedded in small, taken-for-granted aspects of social institutions. These were also understood by Althusser as distinct and seemingly autonomous apparatuses organised according to their own established traditions and structures. Magazines were part of the 'media apparatus'. The genre had its own distinctive styles and formats, especially the almost standard front cover, a young woman's (almost always) white, smiling face, looking outwards as if to 'hail' and thus capture the interest of the similarly aged young woman who might be passing by. This device facilitated an identification with the image, with the address in the form of the title of the magazines, and so prompting an inter-est, a desire to purchase a copy, though this process was at the same time harshly excluding to black and Asian readers. Black feminist writers have often described this adolescent experience of being unseen and unheard.[4]

Given the absence of feminist scholarship on the magazine genre, it also proved necessary to look more widely across media and cultural theory. Semiology, or the science of signs, as outlined in the writing of Barthes, provided a valuable methodology (Barthes 1957/1972). Stuart Hall had already drawn on Barthes for his analysis of the news photograph (Hall 1973). The technical terms such as the idea of the visual codes, the elimination of polysemy and the 'preferred meaning' that is achieved through the 'anchorage' function of the 'linguistic message' provided a set of identifiable markers that gave to the magazine a regular and distinctive format; the code of romance (the picture love stories), the code of fashion and beauty (the fashion and makeup tips), the code of personal life (the problem page) and the code of pop music (the teen idols and pop stars). These familiar and unchanging qualities of the weekly magazine made it reliable and reassuring, like a trusted best friend. The distinctive ensemble of codes created an intimate kindly voice, such that the magazine seemed to be designed to be read alone at home, in the bedroom, and then per-haps given to a younger sister, or handed on to a friend. And so what was established as a hailing and attention-grabbing mechanism on the front cover was then developed and sustained across the pages in a systematic way. The friendly words and the choice of a 'teen' language style were standard, popular writerly modes. With this focus on the teen girl as the ideal reader, it was the ideologies of (heterosexual) romance and, with this, of (normative and binarised) adolescent femininity that emerged as dominant meaning systems. Romance was the cultural coding which both managed and defined sexuality, giving shape to female desire. So much work was put into securing this culture of heterosexual romance. The girl was instructed on how to make herself desirable through a style of demure femininity that did not challenge, contest or threaten male dominance. Being appealing to 'boys' remained the highest priority.

The ethos of upholding the most limited and strict values of conventional femininity, with girls seen only as future housewives, at a time when more widely the students' movement and women's liberation were insistently challenging to the core these ideas, reflected the deeply conservative values of the publisher of *Jackie*, D.C. Thompson, based in Dundee in Scotland. This was an anti-union firm, staffed by a predominantly male workforce. Yet, even with this old-fashioned setup, it still created a magazine with extraordinary reach and popularity.[5] It somehow became more than its contents, as the magic of pop culture gnawed away at the pious moralism of the editors. Arguably the formula that produced this success, such that its colourful A3 format eventually made the magazine something of a cult object, was the vibrant coding of pop music, fashion and romance, laced with a sprinkling of personal problem issues which prised open a window into the world of sexuality, at a time when sex education was often nonexistent in schools and at home. There was a fleeting moment of freedom through these pages, a glimpse of excitement, in the form of teenage girl friendships along with the pop revolution which had started with the Beatles in the 1960s and that was still going on in the mid-1970s, laced with the promise of sexuality, which then had to be constrained and pulled back from the brink.

Psychoanalysis and Feminism

My own work on the magazine *Jackie* was not carried out entirely in a vacuum. A handful of graduate students were pursuing similar lines of enquiry, with Janice Winship (also at Birmingham CCCS) producing various articles on the domestic world of women's magazines and Joke

Hermes in Holland moving more towards an incorporation of readers and the ways in which they responded to, or decoded, the magazines, often in less predictable ways than my own analysis had inferred (Winship 1985; Hermes 1995). Then a few years later, discussions widened out to incorporate the concepts from feminist theory, especially those from psychoanalytical accounts which had focused on the acquiring of femininity (Rose 1986). This is where the Freudian idea came in that heterosexual femininity is always only partially stabilised for the girl who was never sufficiently separated from her mother, a same-sex love object. Because, unlike her brothers, she has no Oedipal complex to go through, the transition to the 'proper' love object has to be repeated, as if to drum it into her that she is expected to love a boy, and later a man. There has to be constant repetition to ensure that she somehow fixes onto the right kind of object.

Jacqueline Rose's important psychoanalytical writing contributed to our understanding of repetition and familiarity in these women's genres, their unchanging formats. Two further contributions widened this field of feminist scholarship. Judith Williamson's classic study of women and advertising, taking as her objects of research the kind of images (often perfume adverts) typically found on the pages of the magazines, drew on Lacanian psychoanalysis and semiology to dissect the production of meaning (Williamson 1978). (It would be an interesting teaching project to go back to this classic study for the reason of its detailed image-by-image or shot-by-shot analysis of the still widely familiar and often unchanging genre of the perfume advert on both the printed page and the TV and cinema screens). With a focus on Hollywood film, Laura Mulvey's path-breaking theory of the male gaze in the setting of narrative cinema likewise created a much fuller theoretical lens through which the patriarchal power relations that underscored visual culture could be more fully understood, again psychoanalytically (Mulvey 1975/1999). Mulvey showed how the camera gaze towards the woman in Hollywood was conflated with an assumed male viewer both behind the camera and sitting there in the audience.

Multi-Mediated Technologies of the Self

From the mid-1980s, magazine scholarship came to be largely absorbed into feminist media and cultural studies rather than sociology. And this continues to be the case today. As magazines abandoned the format of having stories or romantic narratives inside their pages, similar stories proliferate in and across all the other media sites such as TV, film, 'chick lit' genres of popular fiction and so on. My own scholarship repeated this movement, with magazines splintered and now part of the larger media world (McRobbie 2008). For example, the analysis of the 'post-feminist masquerade' is envisaged as a formulaic device, a 'technology of the self' created as if specifically for post-feminist neoliberal times. This entailed a cross-genre focus on the newspaper columns, from the book version and then the massively successful film of *Bridget Jones's Diary*, to the U.S. TV series *Sex and the City*, to the image of the typical 'fashionista' whose immersion in consumer culture is endlessly described back on the pages of magazines like *Grazia*, *Red* and of course *Vogue*. This multi-mediated approach has also characterised the work of feminist media scholars including Rosalind Gill (2007), Akane Kanai (2018), Rebecca Coleman (2009) and Sarah Banet-Weiser (2018). It is a mode of inquiry which reflects the new media ecology defined broadly by 'users', communities and followers, rather than by readers and consumers of single texts. The idea of representation, which was a major reference point for cultural studies analysis, has over the decades been replaced by vocabularies of affect, emotion, atmosphere, user participation and of 'public feeling'. Lauren Berlant's writing on public feeling and especially on the idea of 'cruel optimism' provides a powerful new vocabulary for understanding women's and girls' magazines as expressions of 'national sentiment' (Berlant 2011).[6]

Nowadays, social media are omnipresent alongside conventional media; the iPhone delivers what was once magazine 'content' and it exists in a much more personalised, always-on and intimate connection with its owner than could have been imaginable two decades ago. In effect, intimate technologies have supplanted the magazine as genre, and this calls for so many new modes of feminist inquiry (Evans 2017). But the magazine, even if it is a dying form, continues to play an important role in creating national feminine imaginaries taking the form of figurations, or composite devices which relay or telescope dynamics of change, possibility and gender stabilisation in a time of flux. The professional work undertaken by magazines' editorial staff and journalists requires that they absorb and respond to wider changes in the culture and find the most appropriate way of giving the magazine an identity which continues to attract readers and brings in advertising revenue. In the UK, the number of titles that undertake this kind of work has shrunken, but some are still visible on the shelves, such as *Grazia, Elle* and *Red*. The magazine plays a prefigurative and a performative role inventing new 'technologies of the self' that enunciate and enact possible and timely ways of 'being womanly'. The intense work of cultural production that goes on behind the scenes in the magazine offices comprises the commercial and institutional investment in the making and shaping of subjectivity. The reader is presented with positions, stances, bodily norms, ways of acting, ideas about selfhood.

Most of the critical writing on magazines in the last decades has adopted this looser multimedia-inflected mode of Foucauldian scholarship. His writings were not widely available in English until the mid-1980s, the most significant for feminist scholars being the later *History of Sexuality* (Foucault 1987). This vocabulary offers a different understanding of culture and power from that of Althusser and Gramsci (as discussed above). Figurations, like technologies of the self, are the product of intense category-formation activity. Institutional practices, forms of writing, expert opinions, statements, reports, documents, features, profiles and so on, along with different forms of visual material, are brought together to produce an assemblage of information, administration and reportage, which, in this case, is then moulded into the form of defining recognisable social and bodily types. In other words, this is about the production of norms. Foucault developed his theory of the power of discourse through a focus on the role of statements in the formation of public life and social institutions. New forms of governing populations were made possible through this kind of accumulation of knowledge. Foucault drew on so many historical sources to show how specific categories of persons that previously had no formal existence came into being through language and through so many descriptions, including drawings and images. There is a kind of rush to pin new phenomena and new behaviours down, such as the 'homosexual' who emerged through the course of the nineteenth century (Foucault 1987). The point of this activity on the part of agents and administrators of the modern state was to render certain human activities and practices 'knowable' so that they could be better managed and controlled. Historical research on the Victorian period might therefore draw on the women's magazine genre to understand the emergence of the 'housewife', the middle-class 'mother' who, as we do know from the earliest housekeeping manuals, was encouraged to be an 'angel in the house'. Foucault's colleague Jacques Donzelot began this work on nineteenth-century France in his classic study of the policing of the family (Donzelot 1979). But he stopped short at the point at which a full-blown study of the magazine genre as the conduit for this figuration of maternal femininity might demonstrate the sociopolitical importance of the genre, one that was key to the inculcation of middle-class values, with the idea of maternal citizenship as moral duty (Riley 1992).

For Foucault scholars, the body is always at the forefront, and power circulates and flows, it is more diffuse and also invitational. Pleasure is a vital ingredient. And the kind of figurations of femininity which emerge out of these proliferations of reflections, deliberations, policies and reports – indeed, the whole panoply of 'discourse' – encourage the appropriate forms of womanly activity. Nowadays, the female subject is expected to be active rather than passive, she is to be self-governing and capable of discovering her own agency. Women are now widely understood to be empowered with a specific agency, even by an avowed 'feminist' agency. This activity-generating element is what has been historically distinctive about the figurations that have emerged from within the pages of the magazines. The two recent figurations (or social types) which I have argued perform a specific kind of work on behalf of the dominant culture are first the 'high-achieving working mother' and second the 'resilient girl' (McRobbie 2020). The former inverts past feminist complaints about the drudgery of housework and motherhood to reimagine these instead as joyful and wonderfully fulfilling activities, now entered into through the (neoliberal trope) of personal choice and enhanced by the presence of a feminist-friendly husband who will share in the daily tasks, allowing his wife or partner to maintain a successful professional identity. In this repertoire, the 'alpha' mother who does 'batch cooking' for the family late into the evening is also slim, fit and a household manager whose family can be understood as a small business enterprise with everyone's needs being catered for. It does not take a stretch of the imagination to see how this composite of feminine figurative activity correlates with the wider neoliberal economy where the family is now its own welfare state, as public services have been diminished and shrunken (Brown 2015; Cooper 2017). The family is required to become a domestic space for asset building so that children as human capital are to be nurtured and educated on the basis of a 'return on investment' (Brown 2015). These figurations (for example, the glamourous thirty-something mother out in the park running with her jogging buggy) mark out the parameters of the new moral economy of the family today: able to attend fully to its own needs and to take care of itself without help from the state (McRobbie 2020). Similar articulations can be traced with the emergence of the 'resilient young woman' who, again in gym kit, exudes strength and stamina in a figuration which also draws on the new popular feminism translating its meaning to bring it into line with the requirements of consumer culture and the current styles of governmentality, which also rely on ideas of self-responsibilisation (an awkward but apt term, as Wendy Brown argues). Resilience is a term marking tension and ambivalence. It acknowledges that women and girls still experience various forms of sexual inequality, but the challenge is that they must learn how to deal with or manage the disadvantages of gender, and this is where the magazines have got a role to play. The idea of resilience comes into being across the pages of the magazines (online and digital and scattered across so many blogs and websites) and, in Gill and Orgad's account, it demands that young women (their example is from *Marie-Claire* magazine) develop the capacity to 'bounce back' and to be able to deal with life's adversities (Gill and Orgad 2018). Resilience also marks a kind of rollback away from the tough neoliberal requirements to be highly competitive 'alpha girls'. Resilience discourse does not rest on the fantasy of perfection. Life's painful experiences, including those arising from gender inequality and discrimination, can be alleviated with resilience training. Wholly compatible with the new 'popular feminism', without jeopardising the profit margins of the feminine consumer culture, this is an adaptive technology of the self, an aid to 'empowerment'.

Radical Magazines and Conclusions

The question of the dominant whiteness of the magazine genre has been challenged over the years by different generations of black feminists. Not surprisingly, one outcome of endemic racism in the media industries has been the setting up of independent black publications, edited by black women and directed to black readers. The entire women's and girls' magazine media apparatus is in urgent need of a full-scale critique from the viewpoint of race and ethnicity (Young 2000). For example, when we consider the familiar front cover images, the very idea of Althusser's interpellation as, in this case, a kind of production of the young female subject by means of a hailing process which then seeks to secure her as a specific kind of feminine subject is and was underpinned by assumptions about her whiteness. She, the black or Asian girl or woman of colour, is rendered invisible, she is denied the same mode of recognition, and even though that entails subjection and compliance, it also brings with it a sense of belonging and national identity. How then is the black girl subjectivised through being unaddressed, overlooked, not granted the status of being a young female citizen and subject, not afforded the task of being a moral agent, a 'good girl'? Butler has used the word 'arrest' in her discussion of the concept of interpellation in order to emphasise the disciplinary force of this process; in her account, it entails the requirement – indeed, assumption – of heterosexuality (Butler 1997). So interpellation imposes itself upon the subject, requiring of her submission with the threat of punishment. Butler draws on a psychoanalytic vocabulary to understand this subject-formation process. The question is, how does this work for young black women, who are violently excluded from this invitational repertoire which is also a coercion and a constraint? She is doubly arrested. There is a question mark over her rights, her 'Britishness'. She is captured psychically through the violent force of exclusion. She may even, as a child reader of girls' genres, feel she must imagine herself as white. She has to search out available black girl images, black girl characters.[7] An 'economy of visibility' is offered to her only through so many negations (Banet-Weiser 2018). The new, and still very recent, visibilities of black models on the covers of magazines require a much fuller analysis. What does black feminist psychoanalysis offer in this regard? What are the socio-psychic forces brought into play in the commercial world of black representation across the fashion and beauty industries? How do predominantly black fashion spreads alter the genre of fashion photography, especially if the creative direction team behind the camera is also black? Then there is also the issue of readership, nowadays displaced, as remarked upon above, by the formation of new categories of users, followers, subscribers or communities (Sobande 2020).

There have been overtly feminist and LGBTQ magazines in circulation for many years, even though over time many have folded, and, more recently, existing titles have moved online. The best known in the UK was *Spare Rib*, in the U.S. the legendary *MS* and more recently *Bitch*, in Germany *Courage, Emma* and *Missy*. The new wave of feminism from 2008 has produced a range of publications where all the topics which the mainstream pushes to the side can be and are fully engaged with. Racism. Poverty. Sexual abuse and harassment. Here it is possible to hear the voices and see the bodies of the body-positive movement, and of trans activists. Here also the very category of the girl is contested. Sadly the black feminist magazine *gal-dem* was forced to close due to loss of funding in March 2023, but there the reader did find in-depth articles that interrogated the contemporary practices of seeming racial inclusion, but only so as to put into circulation further racialising stereotypes.[8] Publications like *Bitch*, *Missy* and *gal-dem* have created a genre, but these have always struggled to survive without the advertising revenue of the big brands and they have also often relied on unpaid labour on the part of editors and writers. And yet the cultural form of the magazine, even in its online format, remains a popular genre. Young women, older women, LGBTQ, trans and non-binary people constitute enthusiastic readerships. And this enthusiasm begs a whole set of further questions about the radical circumvention of 'interpellation' in favour of forms of community building and the creation of various platforms for discussion. Alongside this is the question of the money and finance required to launch and maintain alternatives to the mainstream, all online nowadays. In the past, there were feminist collectives, social enterprises and not-for-profit ventures which also were able to leverage support in the form of grants from local authorities and even from central government. An ethnography of the full landscape including the internal structure and organisation of radical feminist magazines is long overdue. Where do the writers, editors, designers, etc., move on to when a 'zine folds? To draw this chapter to a conclusion, we could say that there is an urgent need for more sustained research on the issues surrounding both the death of the hard-copy magazine and its various digital replacements.[9] We need to interrogate also the space in-between, the bridges linking one form to the other. Not only has the form itself splintered into so many offshoots and forms of social media but so have the modes of analysis developed a more multimedia perspective. While new methodologies for the digital age are clearly an urgent matter, we should not forget that more traditional sociological questions are also of importance: for example, the fate of women's magazine journalism as an occupational sector which for decades has provided women in the field with a foothold in an otherwise male-dominated world. Little is known about how these careers have changed in the last decade. An intergenerational study of the changes to career patterns between old and new media would be illuminating in so many respects.[10]

Notes

1 Women's magazines have held a unique and important place in British society. They have been a regular point of reference, their titles well-known and the editors seen as establishment figures.

2 For an extensive bibliography on digital methodologies including ethnography, see the LSE Digital Ethnography Collective website (https://zoeglatt.com); see also Markham and Baym 2009.

3 First published as a CCCS Stencilled Paper in 1977 under the title 'Jackie: An Ideology of Adolescent Femininity', then reprinted McRobbie (1982).

4 See e.g. hooks (1997) and Sobande (2020).

5 The magazine was Britain's best-selling teen magazine, reaching sales of over 600,000 in 1976. (In reality, this means at least three times the figure, on the basis of multiple readers per copy). In later years, women editors and journalists talked on TV programmes about how until then young teenage girls were not catered for at all, as previous magazine formats were out of date, or too childlike in format.

6 'Cruel optimism' refers to the way in which women's historic immersion in so many of these genres as a kind of popular education in gender learning promises pleasures and rewards that are always frustrated, and the dreams that underpin the ideas of femininity are also the very obstacles that hinder their realisation (Berlant 2011).

7 Black mothers concerned about these exclusions have taken steps to create new online magazines. See, for example, *Cocoa Girl* magazine, founded in 2020. From their website: 'Inspired by her daughter, founder Serlina launched the UK's first magazine to celebrate Black girls, *Cocoa Girl*. Giving Black children a voice whilst educating the community about the Black culture:

Cocoa magazine is filled with inspiring and empowering content for children aged 7–11 years old. Many have said it was 'the most exciting launch in the Children's sector with a real USP' *Cocoa* is the UK's first magazine representing Black children and gives them a voice. As seen from extensive media coverage *Cocoa Girl* issue 1 has sold over 11,000 copies just from online orders, at one point it was selling over 1,000 copies a day.

Cocoa is an educational tool that teaches children about Black culture whilst profiling Black role models. The magazines help to build a strong community for young Black girls and boys who are often misrepresented by mainstream media. ...

Cocoa WON the 'Newcomer Award' at The Independent Awards 2020 and 'Launch of the Year' at The BSME Awards 2020' (www.cocoagirl.com).

8 See, among others, the review article on 'Nappily Ever After' by Miranda Thomas, *gal-dem*, October 2018. The magazine's goodbye letter can be found at https://gal-dem.com/gal-dem-goodbye-letter/.

9 Mumsnet in many respects now occupies the (online) media space formerly held by magazines like *Women's Own* (Winch 2014).

10 An additional area for further research falls within the field of audience or reception studies. How can we assess the way in which 'readership' has changed in light of the switch to digital and online material, which in the past would have been contained within the regular magazine format? Rebecca Coleman have undertaken work which interrupts and redefines the ways in which readership practices were previously perceived (Coleman 2009). Her account follows a pathway associated with the writing of Deleuze. It sees an experiential plane of interaction of bodies and objects, and a kind of constant intermingling which means looking, sending texts and images, circulating pictures from devices and smartphone cameras, and of course creating one's own personal social media profile with posted content – all part of a kind of incessant flow.

3

Youth Cultures: From Street Corner Society
to Studentification?

Introduction

This chapter encompasses topics addressed across three of my early articles (written between 1975 and 1981). I have chosen to update and comment on them together because they are linked in their concerns. I was
engaging back then with new research on subcultures by my male counterparts at Birmingham CCCS that was focused almost entirely on boys
and young men. In the first article (titled 'Girls and Subcultures' and
co-authored with Jenny Garber), there was a lot of manoeuvring in order to
find a fit with the neo-Marxist paradigms already in place. With the ideas
of 'teenybopper culture' and 'bedroom culture', we wanted to call attention to the power of the commercial pop music industry that was directed
at a young female audience creating specific kinds of relationships. In the
second article ('Settling Accounts with Subculture'), I was challenging the
inattention to girls and young women and considering how a feminist perspective might disrupt some of the claims made in relation to the question
of subcultures and the politics of resistance. The third article ('The Politics
of Feminist Research') marked a move into a more autonomous space of
research about young women, largely working-class girls, who had, by the
early 1980s, become valid subjects for sociological research. This coin-
cided with and was part of the feminist-led project of 'girls work', a youth
centre and leisure-based initiative.

While the word 'subculture' is nowadays used loosely across the
mainstream media (radio and TV) to refer to youth phenomena such as
the rise of the misogynist criminal Andrew Tate as an internet figurehead

for boys and young men who follow his every move,[1] the best way to think sociologically about 'subculture' is to abandon that word and replace it with the words 'youth cultures', understood to be non-cohesive, much more dispersed, loosely linked communities of taste, style and interest.[2] By retaining the word 'youth', we hold on to the idea of 'generational consciousness' with the teen years as a time of transition and experimentation. From Glastonbury to the Brixton Academy, musical tastes give shape to young people's identities, from clothes to hairstyles to other leisure activities. Music sits supreme as the driver and the director of youth cultures. Meanwhile, a halo has been put round the old idea of subculture; it has been 'museumised'.[3] The history of British subcultures has been memorialised in so many films and TV documentaries and elevated into a kind of national hall of fame. The use value of subculture for the world of brands and consumer culture has been acknowledged now for many years (Klein 2000). There is no longer anything clandestine about gatherings of youth – almost everything now takes place under the glare of social media. Images of young people, as they create selfies, and make their own videos for posting and thereby displaying their current attachments and identifications in real time, become part of a vast and sprawling commodified screen culture. Youth are inseparable from their devices, the instant channel for expressions, opinions, events and activities. The swirl of short-life social media youth cultures have replaced the older clusters of alienated youth hanging about on the streets. There is no longer a 'street corner society' (Whyte 1943/1993).

Hipsterisation Effect

Hall and Jefferson's paradigm for understanding subcultures was based on their analysis of the socioeconomic position of postwar working-class male youth (Hall and Jefferson 1975). Drawing on Gramsci's idea of the conjuncture, the authors incorporated a social history of postwar Britain from the viewpoint of class relations and class conflict as these were played out against the backdrop of the move to a post-industrial society. Half a century after the publication of *Resistance through Rituals,* there have been further changes that have resulted in new alignments of class, race and gender. For young people, one of the most significant factors is

the expansion of post-sixteen higher and further education and concomi-
tantly much lower rates of youth unemployment, although with high con-
centration amongst black British youths. It was the Blair government of
1997 which pledged to increase the rate of young people getting into university to study for a degree, and for the last twenty years we have seen,
especially for young women, the idea of gaining a degree qualification as
becoming mark of status and identity, as well as a virtual requirement for
the job market. The introduction of student fees has also meant graduating
with a high level of debt, which in turn pushes young people onto more
professional tracks than was the case in the past, even if (ironically) some
of these occupations are low-paid internships in the fashion, music and
media creative industries.

Subcultures have, especially since the mid-1990s, generated their own
'subcultural capital' which led to leverage of this core of special knowledge by the big brands in search of new ideas (Thornton 1995). 'Deviant'
subcultures were glamourised and achieved a new visibility through
novels and then film adaptations such as *Trainspotting* (Welsh 2001). The
rave scenes of the 1990s celebrated hedonism, and despite appealing to
working-class youth *en masse*, there was a clear shift away from the ideas
of social critique that had informed and run through the song lyrics and
the style choices of the bands and musicians from the previous decade.
Instead there was an ecstasy-led idea of unity and of bodily pleasures
across the boundaries of gender and class, and to a lesser extent race and
ethnicity. The commercial value of the 'underground' became apparent
to the insiders (DJs, club owners, promoters, etc.) whose deep knowledge
of new sounds, styles and venues became an asset that could be realised
across so many of the new culture industries (Thornton 1995). And, as
Thornton also pointed out, the creation of hierarchies of taste and distinction within subcultures put paid to what she argued was ultimately a
woolly idea of resistance in the Birmingham CCCS writing. Thornton was
certainly right in that what started with 'subcultural capital' and with the
'cool hunters' then developed a momentum, attracting the attention of
government. The moment of Cool Britannia in the early 2000s marked the
point at which the idea of subculture came to be something that could be
capitalised on and professionalised as the creative economy. New degree
courses brought modes of accreditation in areas such as music production,

sound engineering, fashion and style journalism. The various models, pop stars and record label owners invited to Number 10 Downing Street by PM Tony Blair had mostly (including Kate Moss) emerged through the hedonistic rave scenes that were associated with independent record companies, and magazines such as *i-D* and *The Face*. Whether it was so-called grunge or 'heroin chic', this was about creating a new field of (sub) cultural production, precisely as a format that had been bubbling under, but which had the potential to create sizable incomes for the key figures in the various scenes (Thornton 1995). This was the pathway followed by young people like Edward Enninful, now editor of British *Vogue*. Back in the late 1990s, he was a stylish young black teenager, spotted on the train from Croydon as a possible model for *i-D* magazine, and this led to a rapid career as a writer, fashion stylist, editor and by now a leading black spokesperson against racism in the creative sector as well as in everyday life in contemporary Britain (Enninful 2022). But prior to this, and years before the re-radicalisation of youth in Britain following the explosions of energy around Black Lives Matter and the #metoo movements, the figure of the urban hipster, in effect a subcultural entrepreneur, came to stand for a whole range of activities that disregarded issues such as gentrification as well as the poverty and deprivation found in many of the neighbourhoods in which these young people set up home. This decade from 1999 to 2009 was a time when the ideas of subcultures were capitalised and monetised, creating career pathways and new forms of urban lifestyle.

Queer Subcultures

There is a body of work, mostly from the U.S., that has recently revived subculture and brought it back into circulation mostly through the optic of queer theory and connecting it to new art worlds, to fiction and visual media. Post-punk (body modification, gender fluidity) has been excavated for its subterranean queer and trans elements. The (late) U.S. author Kathy Acker vividly represented this sexual underground both in her personal style and in her writing. This has given rise to new studies of queer subcultures in cinema genres, in the field of media arts and in theatre and performance studies (Gürbüz 2021). Jack Halberstam had already established this approach as a critique of the assumed heteronormativity which underpinned the original work from the CCCS (Halberstam 2005). Halberstam argued that the original subcultural theory was predicated on a certain linear model of life- stages, such that adolescence and its various activities of freedom would eventually give way to a return to family life and settling down. The wild styles, music productions and the clubbing would be surrendered to coincide with the start of adult life. In contrast, queer clubbing subverts the life-cycle norms of heterosexual culture. Halberstam was contesting the stages-of-life narratives which were part of the cultural scripts for adolescent transitions. He argued that queer subcultures do not adhere to this kind of chronology, that there is an alternative temporality which can mean that leisure culture is not punctuated by the heterosexual norms of lifestyle and 'age appropriate' activities leading to family and children (Halberstam 2005). In fact, in the period since that essay by Halberstam was first published, so much has changed across the whole landscape of LGBTQ politics. Many queer couples have indeed opted to inhabit conventional lifestyles comprising engagement, extravagant weddings and planned parenthood. Others have found extended family life a much more welcoming environment than would have been the case in the past. It may even be that the idea of queer subcultures is also a disappearing phenomenon. Munoz, for example, brings together ethnic minority queer lives with that of subculture as a mode of convivial solidarity (Munoz 1999; Bey 2022). What began as a move to retrieve and landmark 'subculture' as having a particular resonance in queer lives is nowadays also a field of fluidity, of evolving and mutating self-expressive activities.

These perspectives (dating back to the early 2000s) have some omissions. The historical materialist analysis of the CCCS work is overlooked and instead there is a focus on cultural artefacts such as films, music, media and theatre and performance arts. I note this not out of hubris, but because the leading articles in the *Resistance through Rituals* book of 1975 rooted the concept of subculture in a neo-Marxism that was also a radical intervention in the sociology of youth, crime and deviancy. This whole dimension seems to have been forgotten, and instead it is subculture as a wide visual repertoire, as a subversive aesthetic (notably punk and all the variation of post-punk) that has appealed to a different constituency of mostly visual arts and media arts as well as humanities students and scholars, especially in queer studies. This does make sense if one reflects back to Hebdige's classic text (Hebdige 1978). But there was always a wider field of research. Hebdige did acknowledge the theoretical work of Stuart Hall and others in the *Resistance through Rituals* collection, but his springboard came from literary theory as it was developing at the time, including semiology, structuralism and post-structuralism, all of which were also informing film studies from the late 1970s. Hebdige's book effected a transition away from the sociological underpinnings of the Hall approach. The emphasis was almost wholly on the images, the styles, the spectacles of street theatre, the punk lyrics, the bondage trousers and the mohawk hairstyles. Hebdige made of subcultures a new kind of avant-garde. And there was always a sense that the young people had taken flight from not just the parent culture, but from the entire institutional underpinnings of everyday life, from family, from school and further education, from paid work.

In the article titled 'Settling Accounts with Subculture', reprinted in this volume, I asked the question what did these boys do when they went home at night, who cooked and cleaned for them, who washed their clothes and did their ironing? True, the model of kinship that underpinned my feminist questions was the nuclear heterosexual family. But the queer and trans young people of today also rely on the social reproduction that is undertaken at home. And contemporary sociological work on queer post-punk subcultures tends to omit attention to everyday life and social reproduction. It is only in a few anecdotes that family relations emerge as a point for discussion, such as in the recent autobiography by Edward Enninful, who described the period when, growing up as a British Ghanaian in South London, he was more of less forced to leave home and did not have contact with his father for more than fifteen years because he had chosen to work in fashion and style, but more realistically because he was gay (Enninful 2022). (And, thinking back to that post-punk period, someone like Boy George has often referred to his own working-class Irish family and then to the various London squats he lived in during the period before he became so famous that he could afford a huge Gothic mansion in Hampstead.)

The Hall and Jefferson work in effect politicised a terrain of youth research which, despite a humanist gloss, had underplayed questions of poverty, inequality and racism as impacting on the mostly migrant youth who gathered on the street corners or who were subsequently labelled as delinquents (for a selection of reprints from the Chicago School of Sociology, see Gelder and Thornton 1997). The absence of Hall's vocabulary in more recent discussions of queer subcultures means that even the most insightful analyses of, for example, the queer culture of voguing back in the late 1980s in New York overlooked the desperate economic marginality of these mostly trans, poor, unqualified Afro-American and Latino dancers who, as someone noted some years after the debate about the film *Paris Is Burning* (1990, directed by Jennie Livingston 1990), were not able to survive the harshness of the conditions in which they were living as marginalised disenfranchised youngsters. In the film, Angie Xtravaganza suggests that the younger transwoman Venus, who had been earning money as a sex worker, was strangled by one of her clients. Others pointed out that there were few dancers still alive a decade or so later (see Martin 2003). For sure this also brings us into the zone of black necropolitics and queer and trans seemingly unviable lives. Addressing questions of policing, of the criminalisation of sex work, of housing and homelessness could have been immensely valuable for a fuller analysis of voguing.

Black Critique of Subculture

The dearth of black scholars in the universities of the affluent west, for reasons of systemic racism and material disadvantages limiting access to higher education, accounts for the lack of young researchers who were able to really extend, for example, the paradigms laid out by Paul Gilroy in his many articles on issues pertaining to the criminalisation of black youth and the institutional racism of the UK police force (among others, see Centre for Contemporary Cultural Studies 1982; Gilroy 1987). Despite the prominent place in the public sphere in the UK given to the murder of Stephen Lawrence in South London in 1992 and the attention drawn to both the violent activities of white supremacy youth groups in the UK and to the deep-rooted racism amongst the London Metropolitan police force, this still did not lead, until many years later, to the setting up of scholarships and bursaries needed to recruit young ethnic minority sociologists into the fields of sociology and cultural studies. These issues were indeed being addressed head on but by the art school–trained black filmmakers like John Akomfrah and Isaac Julien, both influenced by Stuart Hall and Paul Gilroy, and who, from the 1980s, began to make films such as *Who Killed Colin Roach?* (Julien 1983) and *Handsworth Songs* (Akomfrah 1986), each concerned with the racist policing of black youth. At the time, the audiences for these works were relatively limited and they were not shown in mainstream cinemas or art galleries. This attention by artists rather than by sociologists was prescient, and arguably any return to the topic of youth cultures would surely need to look again closely at this work, including Isaac Julien's 1991 *Young Soul Rebels* (his first feature film), which charted the black 'soul boy' subculture and the pirate radio stations broadcasting from the tower blocks of London's working-class council estates at the time. Likewise, it would be important to go back to John Akomfrah's documentary film about the drum n' bass musician and former graffiti artist Goldie titled *Goldie: When Saturn Returnz*, which he made in 1998 for the BBC. All of these films doubled as documentary records of events that the mainstream of society avoided engaging with. Issues were raised that were of vital sociopolitical importance. This small and underfunded corner of black cultural production was arguably where sociology was being done at that time.[4]

At the same time as the subcultures work was being undertaken, Stuart Hall was also writing what became his famous study *Policing the Crisis* (Hall et al. 1978). This book charted the demonisation and criminalisation of black youth by the local media and by the police, which provided the government in office at the time with a popular mandate for a 'law and order society' (as against the decade of '60s liberalisation). The authors of *Policing The Crisis* argued that this ramping up of media coverage and the intensification of policing led to an undermining of solidarity across class and race divides and ultimately created a more polarised society in which black people and migrant communities were subjected to pervasive everyday racism while also being deemed to exist outside the frames of national belonging and citizenship. A few years later, in 1987, in his *There Ain't No Black in the Union Jack,* Paul Gilroy interrogated and disputed the concept of subculture from a black perspective, arguing that the generational cleavages referred to, i.e. the parent culture and the youth culture, which in the CCCS account had found a kind of semi-autonomous existence from which it could wage its own symbolic class struggles through style, music, ritual, etc., did not pertain in circumstances where the black community *per se* understood itself to be subjected to so many forms of institutionalised and everyday racisms where children and young boys and girls[5] were particularly vulnerable, such that the idea of a generational break made little sense. Family and intergenerational relations were highly valued features of what Gilroy called the urban 'counter cultures of modernity', where memories and experiences were mediated primarily through the aesthetic of black music, a binding intergenerational force rather than a divisive one.[6] This was not to say that black young people did not have their own parental battles on the home front, but culturally and politically it was to suggest that the concept of 'subculture' needed closer inspection from the optic of race.[7] The CCCS writers had drawn on American sociology and psychology of the '50s and '60s. 'Youth culture' was part of that mainstream U.S. discussion based on fears of (implicitly white) family breakdown as a result of 'affluence' and of postwar youth being in effect the spoilt generation, with time on their hands and expressing an inexplicable alienation from the wonders of the new consumer culture (the 'rebel without a cause' scenario). Hall et al. reworked this kind of perspective dominant in U.S. social science to bring to bear on it a critical class analysis. But this concept of subculture, when viewed from a critical race perspective, gave rise to a number of questions.

The norms of nuclear family life and of mass consumerism, which the white working-class population was invited to embrace, were never extended to black and Asian British people, and indeed the idea of the 'age of affluence' from the '50s to the '70s, which envisaged a society of families (in this context, aspirational white working-class families) gathered round their newly acquired TV sets, was predicated on policies which permitted some degree of white working-class upward mobility by means of upskilling, but at the expense of the new migrant populations who were expected to take the low-paid unskilled jobs which did not come with the benefits of the social wage, i.e. pensions and other provisions (Lewis 2000; Shilliam 2018; McRobbie 2020). This too destabilised the concept of subculture since the rewards of the age of affluence did not make their way into black households. The original argument in *Resistance through Rituals* was that subcultures were at least partly formed out of the alienation effect that some degree of affluence brought. The parent culture still experienced class inequality and political powerlessness, but they had acquiesced, such that it was the youth culture that took up their latent class struggles, while at the same time making a break with the lifestyles of their mothers and fathers.

In *Policing the Crisis*, Hall et al. do see something of a rupture on the part of sectors of the black youth of the 1970s who experienced the hard edge of youth unemployment at the time and for whom the bitter realities of everyday racism compounded their sense of marginalisation. The youths who were drawn to the ideas of Rastafari often did break with family life, refusing to submit themselves to the endless humiliations of the dole and preferring instead small-scale 'hustling' and immersion in the musical cultures of reggae and the imported sounds from Jamaica. But here Gilroy saw continuity, such that theirs was in effect an important historical and a community voice, one that spoke directly back to the parents and sisters and cousins and uncles, reminding them of past and present suffering, rather than being simply a mark of a generational schism.

Feminism and Girls' Projects

I arrived in Birmingham University and the Centre for Contemporary Cultural Studies in 1974 with the idea of a feminist thesis on young women and the immense power of the pop culture industry that was addressed to them, such as girls' magazines. I was immediately brought in as the only female student (later joined by Jenny Garber) to the 'subcultures' research group, which was preparing an issue of the *Working Papers in Cultural Studies* journal. This was aiming to develop a Marxist analysis of working-class youth culture which would challenge some of the existing sociological accounts by foregrounding questions of class and contemporary capitalism. My own role was to find a vocabulary to understand the role of young women within this overarching analysis of class and subculture. In 'Settling Accounts with Subculture', I reflected on Paul Willis's ethnography of white working-class boys in the education system. I challenged the somewhat heroic stature that he accorded to the 'lads' who disrupted school schedules. They did so in highly sexist and racist language. This was part of the vernacular 'at hand' that they drew on to express their anger and alienation from the school system (Willis 1978). Dick Hebdige was attentive to the male camaraderie, even homosociality of the subcultures, but the overtly subordinate place of girls and young women did not seem problematic. It was some years later that the feminist and lesbian sexual politics of women in punk was more widely acknowledged, inside and outside academia. The fact that punk women openly challenged so many elements of the double standard by rehabilitating words like 'sluts' and 'whores' and that they self-consciously dressed to look 'tarty' or 'cheap' and called their bands names like The Slits eventually confirmed the idea that punk femininity suggested a departure from and critique of middle-class heterosexual ideals. There was also the empirical question of who these young women actually were. What prompted the appeal of punk? Did they leave school and pursue a job or a career? Did they try to get jobs in the music or fashion industries at the time, or did they live that life as a leisure and nighttime activity, and take more mundane jobs in the meantime?

Only now are these questions being answered in journalism and across the liberal press and in the various exhibitions[8] and in the autobiographies that have been written (Albertine 2014). The articles and obituaries in April 2022 for Jordan (Pamela Rooke), who was the archetypal punk girl and shop assistant for the early Vivienne Westwood and Malcolm McLaren store, described how she had retrained as a veterinary assistant. We might also ask the same questions of the famous black British punk 'n' reggae women who were also drawn into this world of music and gigs and the wider field of pop culture. There have been several exhibitions and radio and TV programmes and public appearances featuring Pauline Black of the Selecter, whose music performances showed the multicultural 'cut 'n' mix' intersectional constellation which the idea of subculture at that time could generate (Black 2011). But little is known in more sociological detail about black girl youth cultures of that time. It is only recently that black feminist historians as well as popular writers have begun to fill this gap (Carey 2021).

It was a struggle for feminist studies of youth culture from the late 1970s to find any place in academia. The only space that was open to this kind of topic was criminology. In sociology, youth meant male, and it was relatively easy to win grants to study football hooligans, or topics like youth unemployment and crime. Partly to avoid being trapped into seeing young women as a problem and aware that inside the subcultures there was as much sexism and male dominance as outside, feminist research about young women came to focus instead on mainstream everyday culture, on the material issues of class inequality which locked them into career trajectories of low-paid, low-status traditional women's work. There were few young black feminist scholars undertaking research on black girlhood (see Mirza 1992). Ann Phoenix wrote about how young black mothers found themselves constantly pathologised within a racialising discourse about dysfunctional non-nuclear black families, and her important work showed how young mothers were in fact competent, well-organised and able to return to education and training (Phoenix 1991). And bell hooks in the U.S. was indeed writing about girlhood, as a literary and film scholar (hooks 1992, 1997). In the UK, these debates began, from the late 1980s onwards, to be more widely discussed on the pages of academic journals, especially *Feminist Review*. From the viewpoint of black and Asian feminist scholars, the emphasis tended to be family and the community, the state, policing, citizenship and diasporic spaces (Brah 1996).

Questions of sexuality and the experiences of young lesbians also came to the attention of feminist scholars in sociology and cultural studies (Savier and Wildt 1978; Cowie and Lees 1981; Nava 1982). These studies mostly took the form of action research, often based in youth clubs or youth centres. Many of the organisers of the various projects moved into social work and community work, setting up autonomous spaces and working with local authorities and the education departments to secure support for girls and training projects. This field gradually became established as 'girls work', and in the UK it had a base in Bradford University's Social Work and Social Policy department. The 'action research' dynamic involved projects for getting girls into nontraditional jobs, careers and training programmes. And it was around issues of doing research at the same time as others were more fully involved in organising projects that gave rise to tensions about the role of academic feminist research, its obligation to the subjects of the research, and the ethics of its methodologies. Questions such as the right to represent others, which are now central to feminist ethics of research, were aired early on in this field of girls work (Nava 1982). Girls work was an important part of '70s and '80s feminist grassroots activity, and it also connected with prevailing debates in feminist theory through the attention to domestic labour and what girls back then were expected to do at home. It also provided insight on gender-segregated labour markets and on the experiences of girls who entered nontraditional fields such as apprenticeships in building work, plumbing and other manual trades. With a focus on working-class lives and girls' expectations at the time, this kind of feminist activity was intergenerational and informal, which meant that the organisers were not figures of authority. Records of these projects nowadays lie mostly untouched and rarely accessed in various archives and libraries, and there could be some value for feminism today in bringing these activities and the debates back to life.

The Issues Still at Stake

Music becomes a force that defines place, and for black youth in Newham it is enhanced by Black Atlantic flows that fuse together the local, the national and the global. Black musical creative expression offers a form of flourishing and provides a way to hold out against a rendering and representation of black lives that implies they have no value.

—Joy White in conversation with Paul Gilroy[9]

In the last two decades, there have been socioeconomic shifts as well as decisive pathways adopted by government which have given rise to two interconnected processes. First, there is the professionalisation of what were subcultural interests as occupational pathways for the fashion, media and creative industries. This has also resulted in new degree courses and various forms of training. The second and related shift has been the process of 'studentification', set in motion as noted above by the then New Labour Prime Minister Tony Blair and his advisors, who in 2000 announced the expansion of higher education with the aim of recruiting more than 50% of young people into degree courses. Suddenly, going to university became a mass social and cultural experience. Since then, the renewed wave of radical politics (from LGBTQ activism to environmental campaigns to Black Lives Matter and the decolonisation of the curriculum and the toppling of statues) has gestated in the student unions as well as in the seminars, classrooms and lecture theatres. This points to a shift of locations: the universities are now the meeting points for young people. Writing essays (and helping to fund the cost of a degree by working shifts in a local cafe or bar) has therefore eroded the expanses of time needed to undertake what were in the past core subcultural activities. Few young people can afford to spend their time creating a band, rehearsing, deciding on an image, shopping the vintage stores or charity shops for the right look, attending gigs and concerts so many nights of each week, or simply hanging about with each other, if not on street corners than at least in the local pub, unless it is part of a professional career plan. And with university as a widely held goal, there is now a much greater emphasis on exams and on doing well at school. Disadvantaged young people are urged to work hard, do well at school and succeed in life, and this ethos pervades the 'academy' system of schools which instil these habits with a much more intense disciplinary regime of strict uniforms, punctual timekeeping with sanctions for any unruly behaviour and the possible reward of places at Oxford or Cambridge for those who abide by the rules. Across the board, the UK education system has become focused on grades and on ideas of excellence, with parents also more involved in monitoring homework and in the university application process.

After-school time for early teens is more home-based (even bedroom-based) than before, with computer games, iPhones, TikTok and constant communications with friends by electronic means. The time-space relations of school homework have reduced the totally unsupervised activities of working-class young people in previous decades.[10] Gender relations and gender issues are most clearly played out inside the school nowadays and at a later stage on university campuses through these processes of stu-dentification and extended education (Ringrose 2015). Subcultures have therefore almost been squeezed out of existence. But this does not mean there is simply affluence, the end of class, poverty and hardship. Even the idea of being more 'bedroom based' than before requires unpacking in terms of socioeconomic status and family life. Access for young people to the paraphernalia of social media, the tablets and smartphones and laptops, relies on high levels of family income. Those young people who fall through the net, whose family lives are defined by poverty and hardship, whose mothers are holding down several jobs at the same time, and whose fathers are working in the low-paid or casualised sectors, are inevitably even more marginalised than before. These are the factors which contribute to gang-based activity, knife crime and high levels of incarceration for young black men.

The global grime star Stormzy regularly points out in interviews that his choices growing up poor in Croydon were limited and pushed him towards gang culture, from which his music talent alone rescued him. We need to remember that a large swathe of the youth population does not go to university and are now locked into the low-paid labour market. Many further training opportunities or job release schemes are now unavailable or are fee-based. This factor feeds directly into the widening of social polarisation among young people, itself the outcome of the massive reductions in youth centres and public provisions for young people. 'Street corner society' may no longer exist as it once did, but there are many communities of vulnerable and traumatised young people living in areas of high deprivation. Often they are excluded from school and find themselves on the street and preyed upon by older drug dealers and professional criminals who can offer them some of the signs of wealth and status (smart clothes, designer labels and expensive trainers) in return for selling drugs and doing the 'county lines'. While some glamour, excitement and even success in the music business might also emerge from within these activities, the more mundane and tragic foreshortening of lives through violence and incarceration is the real outcome of years of racial injustice in education, in the labour market, in health and welfare services, in housing and in the criminal justice system. Some of the most astonishingly original and important music genres of our times such as drum 'n' bass, jungle and grime, alongside rap and hip-hop, have come into existence through the interstices of the everyday lives of marginalised, outcast and 'wayward' youths. As Joy White argues, these black Atlantic aesthetics create for black youths maps of belonging where they are otherwise and routinely dispossessed (White 2020). They express sorrows but they also speak back to others like them and more widely. The music conveys the joyful energy that has gone into the processes of production, and the words and lyrics are, as White also points out, ethnographic narratives about 'enduring inequality'.[11] Alongside the glamourisation of violence, these musics are about more than just dispossession: they chronicle the huge disparities that have characterised British society over the last four decades. Without these loud and angry channels of expression, the mainstream of society would happily have these voices go unheard, and under such circumstances, the various genres hail their listeners and audiences as powerful counter-interpellations.

To sum up, this chapter has drawn attention to the value of the kind of materialist and historical analysis of what were subcultures provided by the Birmingham CCCS, even if at the time there was little attention given to women as sisters or as mothers of 'the boys'. Thus, despite my feminist critique at that time, there is nowadays, I would argue, much to be retrieved from that mode of analysis. Likewise, Gilroy's cultural history of black Atlantic music and diasporic culture positions young people as the bearers of these traditions in conditions of continuing adversity. And so, while the idea of subculture has become synonymous with youth roles in brand innovation, cultural difference and racialisation processes remain critical concepts for understanding the vulnerabilities of young people in Britain today.

Notes

1 *Today Programme*, BBC Radio, 13 February 2023.
2 There are still many style leaders or young people usually working in the fashion or media and tech industries who on their Instagram accounts and with obsessive attention to detail describe and at the same time create new trends, often based on retro sneakers, trainers and other items more often considered unappealing but now given a new lease of life (Cochrane 2022).
3 See the Museum of Youth Culture, https://museumofyouthculture.com/.
4 In the film John Akomfrah made about Goldie, there are many painful moments when he describes how his mother, a white Scottish working-class woman, put him into 'residential care' as a mixed-race child. Goldie says that he did in fact, some years later, forgive her for this act of abandonment.
5 A young black schoolgirl was subjected to strip searching at school when officers were called in because teachers wrongly thought she had been smoking cannabis. see Quinn (2022).
6 This point is borne out in the countless references by young black people to the treasure trove of their parents' and extended families' record collections. See for example DJ Lynnée Denise (2019).
7 There has been some discussion about how young black women, i.e. teenagers and children, are frequently subjected to 'adultification' by the main social institutions, a racialisation process which robs black children of the white privileges of childhood.
8 For example, photographer Anita Corbin's 2016 *Visible Girls* exhibition, which displayed her work from the 1970s and early '80s.
9 White and Gilroy (2020). The series of talks is called Short Takes and is hosted at UCL London.
10 The black British prize-winning artist Sonia Boyce in a recent documentary about her work described how, as a child growing up in a working-class housing estate, she and her friends would be playing outside and even wandering about the streets, until late in

the evening, with her mother calling out the window when it was time to come home. 'Sonya Boyce: Finding Her Voice', *Imagine...*, BBC One, 7 November 2022, https://www.bbc.co.uk/programmes/m001f0q7.

11 See the film *Feltham Sings* (2002, directed by Brian Hill). I wrote briefly about rap and hip-hop in my chapter on Paul Gilroy in McRobbie (2005). Joy White's book about the Borough of Newham in East London, the birthplace of grime, provides an insightful analysis of the decades-long impact of neoliberalism and the 'mask of the meritocracy' on young black people in the neighbourhood of Forest Gate. This too is an intergenerational narrative of deprivation and economic exclusion from all but the most low-paid jobs in this now post-industrial area, overlooked, however, by the wealthy City and also a neighbourhood that is now designated a site for regeneration. But changes and improvements do not reach down to the lives of these young people, and the grime scene expresses with precision their limited horizons. See White and Gilroy (2020).

4

Young Women and Popular Music

Introduction

One argument made in this chapter is that the patriarchal popular music industry has typically required of young women that they must fit the box of being 'feisty' and therefore, in my own parlance, 'phallic girls' (Bennett 2018; McRobbie 2008). Across the genres, including even the typically softer and more jangly chorded 'indie' music scenes, girls generally display a kind of feistiness as a refusal to subscribe to conventional sexualised images, opting instead for a range of typically 'quirky' or pre-adolescent or even childlike images. For black women in popular music, feisty or phallic styles are translated into indicators of 'strength', and this corresponds with those racialising and subjectivising practices which have historically bifurcated the music industry along the lines of colour, even though, as Stuart Hall points out, there are always traces of the black in the white mainstream of the music industry (Hall 1992/1996). These forms of feminine typecasting are managerial strategies, not so much enforced as encouraged, expected, predictable, as a kind of 'habitus' or permitted space of action, within the field of popular music (Bourdieu 1984). The figurations of normative femininity in pop music take different inflections across race and ethnicity boundaries. For black women, there are much more punitive sanctions when the permitted parameters are breached.[1] Feisty phallicism, re-coded for black women as 'strength', provides girls and women performers with an acceptable degree of agency and 'empowerment' without rocking the boat of the male-dominated industry.

There is also an implicit anti-feminism inscribed within these managed styles of self-presentation. Many stars, from Patti Smith and Debbie Harry to former Spice Girl Geri Horner, have actually distanced themselves from feminism. So tough are the women of rock that it is as if feminism denotes some sort of weakness or victim status. And then, in light of the return of feminism during and after the various #metoo protests and alongside the Black Lives Matter movement, there is frequently expressed a hasty comment 'of course I'm a feminist!' (or its equivalent), as if nothing more needs to be said.[2] The celebration of strong, powerful, phallic girls has been a convenient and uncomplicated way of handling women's participation in a sphere that has long been a male domain. The feisty image of young women has worked as a managerial tool, across the departments of the major record companies. It has also become part of the working culture of the popular music sector, a way of matching the transgressive and charismatic image of the male rock star. As a professional identity, this idea of feisty young womanhood shapes the everyday culture of the sector. It functions as a *dispositif* in the Foucauldian sense, i.e. a set of discourses and devices that combine to form a coherent directive for the management of specific groups of people, in this case female musicians. Much of this work takes place in the marketing departments, whose job it is to 'work on the image'. There are misleadingly progressive connotations attached to the idea of the feisty and 'empowered' young women, and nowhere is this more marked than in the music business (Banet-Weiser 2018). They are independent, determined and outspoken, with a strong personality. The packaging of the female performer is a key element in the reproduction of the value system which has underpinned the music industry and the gender inequalities that have for so many decades characterised the sector.

This chapter focuses on just two different areas of attention in the 'circuit of culture' for women's involvement in popular music culture (Du Gay and Hall 1997). The first of these is the industry itself, and the second is the new black and queer feminist critiques. The chapter is divided into three sections. First there are some general points, then there are comments on two recent industry studies, then finally a section on black and queer feminist scholars and musicologists. Some of these writers have suggested that engaging with industry perspectives on questions of gender and inequality will merely reproduce the dominant neoliberal 'diversity and inclusion' model, and thereby contributes to the ever more sophisticated modes of exclusion which corporate social responsibility programmes foster (Goh and Thompson 2019; James 2021). They look instead at those spaces that lie outside the provenance of the music-industry complex to the (over-looked) everyday practices of music-making, where within a context of subaltern lives music plays a primary role as a popular, dominant and life-affirming aesthetic (Gilroy 1987).

Nonetheless, from my perspective, it is important to retain a focus on the music industry, and this forms the second prong of the argument in this chapter. It generates billions of pounds of revenue annually and is an integral part of British cultural life. In many ways, it is the strangeness of the culture of the record labels that makes the music industry so reliant on a dream factory ethos. If everything hinges on being 'signed' or then, some years later, possibly being 'dropped', the artist on signing becomes a kind of immediate star and employee at the same time. This is so different from other career pathways in the creative industries. How it works in terms of pay and actual salary is rarely considered in academic research. And if there has been massive underrepresentation of black, Asian and ethnic minority people and women right across the industry, then this has to be addressed. Without an inflow of feminist cultural policymakers, issues such as the need for disadvantaged and racially excluded people to get jobs in the record companies will not be aired.

The music industry was overwhelmingly male when I began to dip my toes into writing a few music gig reviews as a graduate student back in the mid-1970s,[3] and while I was comfortable in the left-feminist punk scene in Birmingham, the wider world of pop music felt unwelcoming to women, even though of course the '60s had seen a flowering of so much female talent. Indeed, I recall that on many occasions back then, having both a deep interest in popular music and a stock of knowledge about key musicians and bands such as Can or Lee 'Scratch' Perry was deemed peculiar or unfeminine, especially if one was not either a trained musician oneself or a 'feisty' journalist. Sociological research was sparse, emerging out of youth cultural studies with a focus on leisure as a contrast to all the work on crime and deviance. The leading figure was Simon Frith, who also had a widely recognised profile as a music writer for many of the leading newspapers and magazines in the U.S. as well as the UK (Frith 1978). He alone in academia occupied this kind of space.[4] As a sociologist, my focus was on consumers, listeners, audiences, crowds and fans. Male pop stars functioned as figures for sexual fantasy for adolescent girls whose bedroom walls would be decorated with the pull-out posters of mainstream and sanitised stars like David Essex or David Cassidy who were manufactured, like boy bands are today, to appeal to this teen and preteen demographic. Pop music was a major part of the 'bedroom culture' of teen girls. Inside the home, along with fashion, it was a symbolic marker for generational separation and identity. Young people would listen to different music from their parents or older siblings. Girls would listen to different music from their brothers. Music culture helped to perpetuate these gender divides. So there was indeed much work to be done on the meaning pop music had for young girls, the way it organised certain kinds of emotional response and confirmed their status as fans. Romance and sexuality were scripted through these male performances. They made their way into private listening at home, so that passivity and receptivity came to characterise the available subject positions for girls. There was so much psychosocial feminist work that could have been done, for example, on the entire Beatles phenomenon, in particular the 'screaming' girls (Feldman-Barret 2021). Feminist scholarship ought also to have reflected on how racialising processes were in place across the industry to the extent that it was bifurcated, with substantial media effort put into ensuring that white girls would be following white boy bands and an assumption that their black counterparts were immersed in an entirely different black music culture. There is now a thriving field of black feminist music scholars and a radical epistemology that charts how black music narrates the 'racialising assemblage of subjection' as well as the 'lines of flight and freedom dreams' (Yates-Richard 2021).

The academics contributing to journals such as the *International Journal for the Study of Popular Music* (*IJSPM*) and *Popular Music* have been predominantly men with ethnomusicological backgrounds. More recently, this has changed, and there are women, several of whom have previously worked for the big labels, or who are trained musicians and have now moved into academia to teach on the range of undergraduate and post-graduate courses on popular music studies and on the more practical and technical courses on music production. These women (including Vick Bain, whose reports are referred to below) are forming a bridge between the universities, industry and the field of policy-making with an agenda for redressing gender inequalities. Prior to this cohort, feminist pedagogy and research on popular music had developed primarily with a focus on fandom studies, on media representation and the sexual politics of music videos, on the star system and on individual women recording artists. There have also been cultural histories of specific formats such as 'girl groups' as well as studies of stars such as Dusty Springfield, Madonna, Nico and others.[5] What has been missing, however, is the fuller industry perspective, the detailed insider ethnographies that would chart how signings take place, how decisions are reached, how new female 'talent' is packaged to fit with a specific kind of feminine image, with the marketing departments drafted in right from the start to work on the personal styling of the female stars, from head to toe.

But inevitably there have been barriers to undertaking the kind of research on the routine workings of the music industry from the viewpoint of gender bias, race and racism as well as other factors responsible for the reproduction of dominant white masculinity in the field. Few record companies or big labels will open their doors to doctoral researchers or, for that matter, to senior academics.[6] There is a sense in which the world of popular music culture has been a male domain which is also closely guarded by those inside; a kind of proprietorial attitude prevails around the entire paraphernalia like 'vinyl collections' or 'rare records' or the 'music press', as if access to knowledge has been ring-fenced. The music press has operated with a kind of custodianship granting access to young women journalists only if they show the right kind of attitude.[7] Music writing has often been dominated by a desire to emulate in print the wild or transgressive lifestyles of the rock guitar heroes, and this has created further hurdles of credibility for women, who often, over time, move from covering pop music to becoming lifestyle journalists.[8]

The Music Industry

Toby Bennett points to the male-dominated professional and occupational spectrum, from the label heads to the leading A&R executives, the managers, the DJs, the pluggers, the lawyers, the rights managers, as well as the engineers and technical support workers (Bennett 2018). The day-to-day working culture of the sector has, he argues, relied on 'clubbable homosociality and juvenile laddish banter (or female feistiness)'. Bennett presents an analysis of the everyday functioning of the industry and the mythologies that typically eulogise excess and transgressive behaviour as a corollary of (male) genius. There is a sense in which the industry is not keen on listening to female voices. Bennett refers to the 'touchy' response on issues of gender by male executives. There is possibly now real concern about disclosures or accusations.[9] Quoting Rosalind Gill, Bennett notes how corporate culture adopts its own managerial ways of attending to diversity issues; these involve bolstering the confidence of individual female employees to come forward, while avoiding the question of full-scale organisational change. For so long, the music industry could thrive on its own reputation for being an exceptional place of work, a space that blurs the lines between night and day, as well as between work and play. The self-image is that of a sector that relies on a workforce who are passionately attached to what they do and to the music world as a whole, and this seems to mean submitting uncritically to its internal working culture. Not only does this ethos militate against collective action for change, but it also reduces the likelihood of employees stepping back and looking coldly at questions of racism, sexism and inequality. It is the public image of the sector as well as its day-to-day working practices that together act as barriers for the kind of thorough self-examination and transformation that is required. As Bennett puts it, there are 'optimistic "progress narratives" that imply "equality is somehow inevitable and requires no active intervention"' (Conor, Gill and Taylor 2015: 7, quoted in Bennett 2018). 'They conceal, even reinforce, other dynamics through which young women are filtered out while (white, able-bodied, relatively affluent) men tend to endure' (Bennett 2018).

Some of the most probing engagement with questions of sexism and gender inequality can be found in commissioned reports and in articles by feminist campaigners, and, as Vick Bain points out, there are now many activist initiatives and campaigns led by women to confront the endemic sexism and discrimination in music. Vick Bain has also produced the most comprehensive and up-to-date analysis of the sector as a whole, titled 'Counting the Music Industry' (Bain 2019). Its most striking feature is the statistical breakdown. For example, the fact that 82% of CEOs are male, and that despite the ethos of diversity being embraced, only 14% of artists signed by106 music publishers are female. As she comments,

There are 68 UK labels which have no solo female artists, compared to 15 which have no male artists. There are 59 UK labels which have no female musicians in groups compared to 22 which have no men in groups. 29 UK labels have no females at all on their rosters (12.60% of the data group); neither solo artists nor musicians compared to one label which has only female musicians. (Bain 2019)

Since being signed by a label is the way of building a career, these figures tell us a great deal about the inability of popular music – as part of the creative industries and therefore a sector that has been a focus for government attention in the last two decades – to generate and support change from within. There is a sense of only minimal steps being taken. Bain offers an overview of the state of play across the various activities which have characterised the sector. Some of these have already been the focus of criticism, such as festival lineups and their organisation and management. But if the entire professional and occupational structure of the industry has been so disproportionately male-dominated, then it is not surprising that underrepresentation of female acts is the norm. There are male gatekeepers at every point in the process of entering and developing a career in the sector. It starts with the (in)famous role of A&R (almost always referred to as 'A&R men'), whose job it is to scout out at gigs and prepare acts for signing. This has long been a prestigious position in the labels, with successes bringing huge financial rewards to the person who discovers the band and oversees the signing. But it is an occupation where women are few and far between.[10] There are then considerable 'barriers to entrance', and Bain enumerates the different ways in which these operate. The long-hours culture of pop music, the need to be spending evenings at concerts and gigs and just hanging about in so many venues or indeed in the studio is not an attractive option for women who want to enjoy a family life. And only the stars at the top can afford the support needed in terms of nannies and housekeepers, etc. The mystique of the studio and the sound systems for live music continue to be male preserves, which means that women going into the industry as studio engineers will be hugely outnumbered, and these environments have been like this for so long that the working culture is wholly tilted to everything from late-night beers to the usual 'banter'. (One need only watch music documentaries that involve studio sessions to see the close camaraderie in action.)

Even when women do make it into the industry as signed talent, the evidence shows that they are more likely to be marketed on the basis of their bodies and physical appearance than their male counterparts, and this costly activity, the so-called glam tax, confirms a process of standardisation and inevitably conformity with existing feminine ideals. So, on the one hand, the pop music industry exists as a kind of dreamworld for aspiring musicians, as demonstrated by programmes like *Britain's Got Talent*, with a never-ending flow of young women hopefuls, and as consumers of pop, young women are again voluble and engaged. And on the other hand, when it comes to participation in the sector as a career pathway, there is a way in which girls and young women shrink back, as if there is some prior sense as to what it is like and that it is 'not for me' despite the fact that at both school level and as undergraduates the gender ratio in music education is more or less equal (Bain 2019).

In this scenario, young women are both isolated and individualised when they try to get into the music business. There is little of the support culture that would be found in many other professional fields, for example, even the police force, or in the law or other sectors of the creative industries such as fashion, journalism or TV. There are organisations like Women in Journalism, but this tends to favour the news media. This isolation factor is particularly the case for young black women, who find it much more difficult to navigate the world of internships for the big record labels in London.[11] In pop music journalism in the UK, it's possible to count the number of women staff writers on one hand. In this context, the word 'feisty' has the ring of approval, as if it is a job requirement. While seemingly marking dynamic female agency, as noted above, it is in fact problematic, suggesting a punchy and gregarious femininity.[12] The term 'phallic girl' refers to the way in which in the early 2000s a post-feminist iteration of female agency permitted young women, under certain conditions, to take up features of dominant and youthful masculinity (McRobbie 2008, drawing on Butler 1990, 1993). This came to be linked with young women in the media industries and especially those in popular music who took on the trappings of 'laddish' masculine behaviour. The idea was that girls were now free to act like young men, with impunity, as if a new moment of gender equality had arrived. There were two obvious caveats: first, the feisty (phallic) girl would not confront sexism or harassment in the music industry. The second caveat was that these young women were to remain within the realm of heterosexual desirability upon which male approval rested. The phallic girl was expected to embody all the high standards of the mainstream beauty industry.

However, the marketing, management and packaging of black women performers has consistently operated with a different lexicon. Strength is almost assumed as a mark of cultural difference. This is combined with a 'being in control' element, as if to suggest that black female superstars like Beyoncé and Rihanna have struggled to succeed and have reached a position where they are able to dictate their own terms in regard to the music industry, as entrepreneurs, as global superstars, as powerful women whose sexuality also belongs to and is controlled by them alone. They can 'call out the guys' who may treat them badly. Their bodies are 'toned' rather than conventionally slim. Following Stuart Hall and Homi Bhabha, this shows that women performers like Beyoncé and Rihanna are required, according to the racial logic of the overwhelmingly white music industry, to be extraordinary. They are 'spectacularised' (Hall 1997/2013). They are lifted out and pushed upwards by the regime of representation, as if to stretch the racial stereotype of sexualised feminine difference as far as it can go. The sphere of their celebrity is somehow exaggerated beyond the clichés of being 'superstars'. And the performance formats reflect these qualities. bell hooks laid the foundations for studies of black women superstars in her essay on Tina Turner (hooks 1992) and likewise Stuart Hall examined the publicity and promotional devices that surrounds black sports stars, his point being that there is an attributing of spectacular char-acteristics as a kind of mechanism that pinholes the star as exceptional, and so seemingly cut off from the norm of everyday racialising processes (Hall 1997/2013). They are somehow 'beyond race', but the point is that this very process makes the star 'intelligible' without disturbing the exist-ing racial hierarchies.[13] They are therefore still very much 'inside race'. Following Bhabha's analysis of the racial stereotype, this is a way of making the extravagantly beautiful black female singer 'more than' in order to be, after all, reassuringly 'less than' (Bhabha 1986; McRobbie 2005).

With the #metoo movement, the idea of laddish, heavy-drinking young women as embodying a kind of sexual equality quickly fell apart.

And with Black Lives Matter, a new generation of young black feminist writers and scholars have challenged the whole range of racialising processes. The myth of post-feminist equality has been exposed as a
sham, with the new feminist activists drawing attention to violence against
women and endemic racism and sexism in work and in everyday life. The
media and entertainment industries have as a result been forced to subject
themselves to scrutiny and introduce new policies for recruitment, diversity and inclusion, as well as for anti-harassment strategies. The music
industry has been seemingly resistant to self-scrutiny and evasive about
addressing the steps that would need to be taken to begin to make the pop
music industry a rewarding place of work for women. And alongside this,
the individualising process which has been the undergirding of the production of the star phenomenon in popular music has meant that there
have been few collective initiatives to tackle inequality on the part of the
best-known women stars and performers. There have been no organisations set up involving female musicians to challenge the male dominance
across the industry. Individual stars will voice their support for many different campaigns, such as Black Lives Matter or against domestic violence
or against the laws restricting women's access to abortion, but there have
been no concerted moves to bring gender equality to the sector. If women
in the film sector have founded support groups, and likewise in TV and
broadcasting as well as in journalism, it is markedly not the case in pop
music. And those changes that do take place tend to occur around the
edges of the industry, for example in the trade organisations, the unions,
the public sector organisations with large music facilities, provision and
obligations, such as the BBC, or in music journalism in liberal newspapers like the *Guardian*, which will run pieces about campaigns to get more
women into the industry. These outlets will also carry longer features on
official reports on gender and race inequality.

There is a paradox however, because when it comes to performance,
stage presence, image and attitude, young women in popular music have
often been shining lights for embodying feminist principles, speaking
out for freedom and equality and penning lyrics that are in all respects
compellingly feminist. In their own music performances, there is often a
strong feminist voice. And this has been the case for decades, from Aretha
Franklin and Nina Simone to Poly Styrene, Beyoncé, Lady Gaga and even

in the last few months bands like Wet Leg, whose lyrics, we might imagine, send shivers of discomfort amongst male listeners for their dissection of male masturbatory fantasises. Some years previously, Courtney Love (with her band Hole) pulled a bloody tampon out of her vagina, tossing it into the audience. There have been many lesbian and non-binary musicians, and these acts have made popular music an exciting terrain for performance and participation, also one that speaks directly to young people across the boundaries of class, sexuality and ethnicity and without the requirements of high cultural capital which the mainstream arts inevitably expect of audiences, readers, viewers or listeners. Sexual politics has a powerful, even thrilling presence front of stage, but somehow this does not necessarily filter through to the backstage and with what goes on behind the scenes in the day-to-day workings of the industry.

Black Feminist Musicology

In African-American life and in black British culture, music is omnipresent and so deeply ingrained as to be inseparable from everyday life. As Stuart Hall wrote, 'In its expressivity, its musicality, its orality ... in its rich production of counter-narratives, and above all, in its metaphorical use of the musical vocabulary, black popular culture has enabled the surfacing of ... other forms of life, other traditions of representation' (Hall 1992/ 1996). Music is a constant companion to daily life, from cleaning the home to rifling through the parents' record collections, to singing and playing music in church.

By the time I met Aretha, she was already two generations deep into my family's weekly cleaning practices. In my mother's home, and in her mother's home, Aretha Franklin set the stage for high soul domestic order. For the rest of my life I would associate 'Chain of Fools' with scrubbing the tiles and 'Dr. Feelgood' with cleaning the kitchen. While mama bounced to the demand of 'R.E.S.P.E.C.T.'— barely lit cigarette held with confidence between thick lips—we held imaginary microphones and bumped hips. We sang into the brooms we used to sweep the floor with. (Denise 2019)

The historical presence of the music of the black Atlantic that Paul Gilroy has written about so powerfully brings with it a language of politics, a source of identity and self-realisation, also an antiphonic aesthetic form that is unbifurcated by ideas of high art and low culture; it 'protests as it affirms' (Gilroy 1987). Music is then a transnational 'way of life' and, to repeat the Raymond Williams definition of culture, it is also 'ordinary' (Williams 1957). This kind of perspective puts the music in the hands of ordinary people, as a kind of commons, a shared possession, it foregrounds the dense social relations and the world-making capacities that prevail around the forms and genres. And a focus on women musicians considers their specific contribution to this vernacular black music culture (Rose 1994). Much has been written about the distinctive voices of women performers across the jazz tradition to the current day, engaging, en route, with the girl group phenomenon of the '60s and of course the women of Tamla Motown, onwards to today and figures like Missy Eliot and Lizzo.

Goh and Thompson (2019), along with Robin James (2021), provide a fresh perspective on the terrain of study previously occupied by Tricia Rose, Greg Tate, bell hooks, Stuart Hall, Paul Gilroy and others whose work on black music and popular culture was published mostly through the 1990s. In this new work, there is a noticeable change in vocabulary away from difference and from diaspora aesthetics. The knowledge base which has informed sociological accounts of popular music has been too fixated, it is claimed, on the 'Western ear'. The question is asked, how can feminist accounts of popular music not end up 'centring the experiences of white women'? James refers to the writing of McKittrick and Weheliye to begin to answer this question. Their quest is for a way of working with music as habit, feeling and muscle memory, but, as James indicates, 'they do not translate them into terms that the academy can then appropriate and co-opt; these knowledges remain coded as sonic aesthetics. In this way, they retune the poetics of theory/philosophy to perceive what philosophy's traditional poetics perceptually code out of circulation, such as "the unacknowledged care work demanded from the Black female voice in popular music"' (McKittrick and Weheliye 2017: 24, quoted in James 2021). This then points to a set of musical practices that have allowed 'people to relate to one another in terms other than those dictated by patriarchal racial capital' (James 2021). In an argument that echoes the flow of Gilroy's writing on the music of the black Atlantic, James argues for approaches to music that understand it as a sublimely popular aesthetic form that has also been a form of communal social care, a force of love, and system of welfare for black people, so that they can 'access ways of life above and beyond (or under and below) the kinds of lives that patriarchal racial capitalism demands' (James 2021). She continues, 'music, music making, music sharing, music dancing, music jumping, music singing—the act of loving music deeply, the act of feeling and loving music intensely—is one way black communities physiologically and neurobiologically navigate racist worlds.' James takes one specific example:

As a beloved song connecting generations of participants in a black queer and trans subculture/subgenre, the remix of 'The Ha Dance' also exemplifies McKittrick and Weheliye's (2017) claim that loving music intensely can be a way that otherwise problematic material can rewire the threads that connect people to form communities that are less oppressive than the relations expressed in the original 'Ha' sample. In changing how that 'Ha' sample sounds, Masters at Work also changed what is heard in it: not just the racism (and cisheteromasculinity) of the original, but the black queer and trans aesthetics.' (James 2021)

This perspective offers a radical optic on black expressive culture from the viewpoint of gender, sexuality and technology. Black and queer feminist music writing finds new points of departure. It is predicated on music as a shared aesthetic that wraps itself round the bodies of the teenage girls at home dancing to the music of Aretha Franklin while doing the house-work rota such that the boundaries between body and sound system are constantly dissolved (Denise 2019). Goh and Thompson, Yates-Richard, James and Denise extend the work of writers like Hortense Spillers and bell hooks into the terrain of music (Spillers 1987, hooks 1992). The value of this more fluid and rhythmic research practice is multifaceted. It provides openings for young scholars to bring their own experience to bear on the subject matter of their research, and it helps them get their bearings and grapple with exclusionary forces of the academic canon with its hierarchies of cultural capital. Black music culture and women's participation therein might better be understood then from a newly revised cultural studies tradition of everyday life, involving oral history as well as attention being paid to otherwise overlooked phenomena such as informal music-making practices and sound systems (Henriques et al. 2021). This brings us back to the home, the family, the bedroom, the church, the school, as well as the performance space.

But an additional and perhaps more problematic feature of this new black feminist and queer scholarship is that there is less attention paid to mixing and to hybridity, to intercultural and syncretic forms and to the politics of urban multiculture which Hall, Gilroy and other sociologists, including Les Back, take as a kind of sociological and historical starting point (Back 1996). Goh and Thompson and James look instead to fields of knowledge production which are 'coded out' by the mainstream. But is 'subaltern knowledge', as Foucault put it, so fully 'coded out', so self-encapsulated, so carefully bounded? And how do we define where it starts and where it finishes? In previous feminist postcolonial studies, there was a focus on mix and mingling, on impurity and on 'diasporic space' (Brah 1996). Music culture was full of hybrids of black and white elements and styles, and this was seen as a potent symbol of a future where 'race' did not matter, indeed where it no longer existed. The new black epistemology elevates knowledge systems, but do they stand apart from what in the past were understood as dense ways of life, as 'culture' or as counter-cultures of modernity (Gilroy 2000)? Do knowledge and epistemology here replace 'culture'? Is there a danger that claiming these coded-out spaces as authentically black could lead to a new kind of 'ethnic absolutism' (Gilroy 2000)? To suggest that a set of aesthetic forms is somehow wholly located within subaltern lives is to draw some lines of demarcation even though people themselves mingle and mix. Multicultural Britain is a place of mixing and mingling, especially in its classrooms, and Paul Gilroy has written extensively about black and white crossovers in music (Smiley Culture, The Streets). So although the coded-out spaces of culture referred to by Goh and Thompson and by James may play a key role as 'situated knowledge' in nurturing and caring for the communities, they are never entirely apart from the rest of the society. And this is important because intercultural dialogue is also a space for building new solidarities and for alliances. A new antiracist gender politics of music solidarity could after all include the role white women in positions of authority in the music industry might play in drafting and implementing the kinds of policies which would be beneficial to black girls and women in the field of popular music. Alliances and solidarities would also extend to critiquing and overturning the representational framing and the politics of meaning which still revolve around the reworking and updating of racial stereotypes about black women's sexuality.

How then can we draw some conclusions from the discussion so far? I have argued that inside the music industry, in the marketing departments and in the talent management, there is a requirement of the young (white) female musicians that they have to be feisty phallic girls. Attributing to women an idea of empowerment and independence as a pre-emptive move means that there can be a disavowal of feminism, such that the industry is (hopefully) absolved from the gender critique that is long overdue, and even exonerated from the 'bad behaviour' associated with the sector. These are women or girls who can 'look after themselves.' This deployment of feistiness as a subjectivising discourse, one that creates a kind of habitus, or space of experience, for women in music is very much the work of the marketing departments. It is here that the idea of empowerment finds so many different expressions. The marketing *dispositif* is a key site of power for the production of gender in the music industry. This chapter has also reflected on gender, genre and the racial divides in popular music. We have considered how black women are 'spectacularised.' They are more-than-feisty and more-than-phallic. This point is reflected in, for example, bell hooks's memorable essay on Tina Turner (1992). As she writes, 'Tina Turner's singing career has been based on the construction of an image of black female sexuality that is made synonymous with wild animalistic lust.' hooks then makes the point that when she eventually freed herself from the violent partnership with Ike Turner, Tina Turner emerged 'as the autonomous black woman whose sexuality is solely a way to exert power ... Appropriating the wild woman pornographic myth of black female sexuality created by men in white supremacist patriarchy, Turner exploits it for her own ends to achieve economic self-sufficiency ... The new Turner image conveys the message that happiness and power come to women who learn to beat men at their own game' (hooks 1992: 67–69). This chapter has proposed a far-reaching critique of the music industry as a priority for feminist sociological research, and also as a topic within the expansive field of creative industry research. Of particular importance is the role played by the management of female acts and the packaging of women musicians and performers that comes within the edict of the marketing departments. Let me end then with a call for a feminist analysis of music industry marketing practices as a key *dispositif* for gender and pop culture.

Notes

Thanks to Toby Bennett for his initial pinpointing of the idea of 'feistiness.'

1 See the recent case of Megan Thee Stallion, a female rap star known for her sexually explicit songs and videos. A full analysis would show how the violence of racialisation was focused with revealing intensity when the star was shot in the foot by a boyfriend, the Canadian rapper Tory Lanez, after an altercation at a party. Knowing the likelihood of police aggression, Megan did not immediately reveal she was shot by Lanez. Later, when charges were made and she took the stand in the courtroom, she was asked by the judge if the relationship between her and Lanez was 'exclusive,' as if to imply she was complicit by answering 'no' and that her moral status was also questionable. Further reports mentioned that the industry had stood behind Lanez, while her career as a musician was effectively over. Megan commented in court: 'I wish he woulda shot and killed me if I knew I would go through this torture' (Clayton 2022).

2 See Louis Theroux's interview with British Kosovar pop star Rita Ora (*Louis Theroux Interviews...*, BBC Two, 17 December 2022, https://www.bbc.co.uk/programmes/m001fr4r), which was scattered with quasi-feminist statements. One included a description of her female manager as a 'ball-breaking woman,' and the other, in response to her supposed conflict with Beyoncé, was what sounded like a PR-devised close-down: 'they [the press] always try to pitch women against each other.'

3 The Au Pairs were a left-wing feminist punk band based in Birmingham. I wrote a review of one of their first gigs and sent it to the *Melody Maker*, which at the time was looking for women writers. It was published, but I only did a handful of other subsequent reviews.

4 He was followed of course by Paul Gilroy, who has written about the music of the black Atlantic in a cultural historical frame since the mid-1980s.

5 See Vick Bain's website for a full bibliography: https://www.vbain.co.uk.

6 Those who have managed have had some prior professional connection with the labels, e.g. Parsons (1988); Negus (1992); Bennett (2018).

7 Moran (2011).

8 There are some who stick the course, such as Kitty Empire at the *Observer*.

9 The *Daily Mail* in November 2022 reported a case against the head of Atlantic Records in NY fourteen years after the alleged abuser's death. Paul Farrell, 'Music Manager Sues Estate of Late Atlantic Records Co-founder Who "Sexually Assaulted Her for Decades", under NY's New Adult Survivors Act, *Daily Mail*, 29 November 2022, https://www.dailymail.co.uk/news/article-11481387/Ahmet-Erteguns-estate-sued-music-manager-claims-sexually-assaulted-decades.html.

10 It would be important to investigate career pathways of successful A R women; see Parsons (1988).

11 In 2011, the Department of Media and Communications at Goldsmiths hosted an afternoon event with Universal Music as part of a links-with-industry initiative. By far the most vocal participants in the Q and A that followed the presentations came from young black women students, who said that they did not have the kind of insider contacts with people in the record labels which have always functioned as a way to gain internships or work experience. They said that the underrepresentation of black and ethnic minority music industry professionals meant that this pathway reproduced intergenerational whiteness across the sector. Following the event, and presumably under pressure from

other sources, Universal did adjust their policies regarding internships, so that information is more publicly available and there was a shift to introducing industry-wide guidelines regarding pay.

12 Caitlin Moran, the writer and columnist and in recent years very much an outspoken feminist, was, at least when younger, very much a phallic girl in the music industry (Moran 2011, 2020).

13 It would be interesting to undertake an analysis along these lines of the idea of 'black musical genius', a term Gilroy uses in regard to a range of musicians, in particular Jimi Hendrix.

5

Vintage: Fashion's New Frontier

Introduction: The Vintage Surge

What we see when we revisit the terrain of second-hand and vintage clothing as it has moved to occupy this suddenly prominent place in contemporary culture is a series of four countervailing flows. Urged on by the new wave of environmentalists, compounded by fears about drops in sales, the major fashion companies, from high-end international fashion labels to high-street supermarkets, are developing systems to take back for (refurbished) resale, 'own label' items which are no longer wanted by their owners. Just how this will play out in the longer term is difficult to envisage. Then there is a shift which has seen second-hand and charity shops as part of the wider consumer culture of today, becoming almost wholly destigmatised. They are no longer places that people feel worried about being seen in, though how and why this has happened would require more investigation than we have space for here.[1] In the UK, charity shops such as Shelter, Cancer Research, Help the Aged and the British Heart Foundation, with their crammed rails, all sit on so many high streets alongside the sports outlets, smartphone stores and coffee shops, often filling the spaces left behind by no-longer-viable businesses.[2] The third wind of change is that the workforce of these outlets, from volunteers to paid retail workers to senior managers of the leading charities, is now being recognised by sociologists and cultural studies scholars as part of a significant labour market, one that stretches from the creative economy (fashion graduates as well-trained curators of vintage) to the higher echelons of NGO and charity managers, down to low-paid shop-floor staff and volunteers (Kneese and Palm 2020; Ayres 2021). But there are also pressures on this workforce since the presence of the big brands with all the extra capital they have at their disposal throws into jeopardy the future of the smaller vintage independent stores, while also threatening the charity sector (and their workforces). The fourth permutation that has occurred in this sector has been brought about by the rise of fashion-tech, i.e. the processes by which platform capitalism has been able to grab hold of so many aspects of the fashion cycle, particularly online sales and distribution ('click and collect'). This has introduced a whole new political economy of second-hand and vintage with profound repercussions across the whole sector, from the charity shops now selling online to the hovering of venture capitalists and private equity firms currently willing to invest billions of dollars and pounds in companies like Vinted and Depop to high-end Vestiaire Collective (with its HQ in Paris). Simultaneously and building on the successful model of Etsy.com, there are now people across the world selling their unwanted fashion items, from teenage girls using the proceeds for pocket money to sophisticated vintage fashion-tech entrepreneurs. Second-hand dress has therefore become a much more energetic and participative activity, a space for generating micro incomes as well as for large-scale earnings.

The purpose of this chapter is fourfold. First, there are some self-reflexive commentaries and vignettes of auto-ethnography which convey something of the wider picture that lay beyond the writing of the original article reprinted in this book. This is followed by a brief overview of the recent research which extends those reflections by focusing more directly on the workforce. Thirdly, there is a section which attempts to map out the terrain of vintage that has been seized upon by the various forces of fashion-tech in conjunction with finance capital. Finally the chapter ends by (albeit briefly) addressing the question of the global south as a location not just for polluting the ground and the atmosphere with toxic materials from the large fashion production factories but compounded by the off-loading of second-hand clothes from the affluent West to poor countries in the developing world. This has consequences now being investigated in various fields, including African fashion studies (Bobie 2022; Darkwah 2022). While the mainstay of vintage has remained part of the unfolding logic of the urban creative economy, reflected in the idea of the small local shop or boutique, it nowadays also signals the scale of fashion's own internal crisis. Despite all the powers of algorithms and the whole machine of fashion 'big data', it is hard to predict just how far the vintage surge can go. If teen girls reduce their buying habits to help save the planet and if they turn to buying second-hand items and eventually reject fast fashion, the future of global chains like H&M looks uncertain. Meanwhile the fashion-tech giants race to invest in the resale sites enjoyed by these same teen girls. The fashion industry as a whole hangs on a precipice, forced to consider each and every part of its operations as a global sector. Within this repertoire, the idea of upcycling and reselling the 'pre-owned' items functions as an environmentally aware innovation for the sector, while at a deeper level perhaps haunting the private thoughts of the chief financial officers for the reason that a mandate to 'buy less' goes against the grain of more than a century's logic of capitalism and its consumer culture. The rapid ascent of second-hand could prove to be a liminal nightmare for the drivers of global capitalism, a site of renewed and sustained class, gender and race struggle.

Vintage Autoethnography

It is hard to find an account of the various cycles of second-hand fashion, over the decades from when I first drafted my own tentative analysis back in the mid-1980s, that does not begin with some autoethnographic notes. There is a recognition of the affective dimension prompted by items of clothing that belong in the past and that can be reclaimed for the present. When I worked on the essay that is reprinted here, it was still academically unseemly to talk about selfhood (in any guise) and to suggest that clothes had an emotional power.[3] Fashion as social memory was only by the mid- to late 1980s achieving some academic respectability within the frame of feminist studies (Wilson 1985). Four decades later, a rich terrain of study has emerged. And outside academia and across the media and popular culture, there is a good deal of recalling on the part of writers, and various others, that this aspect of one's own sartorial history is a key element in questions of self-identity, of who I am and where I am coming from. The stories of second-hand and vintage fashion accelerate the wider interest in popular memory and in 'history from below'.

My own recall of 'hippie Glasgow' in 1969 is vivid. It was also my first year at university, and the precise location of the cavernous vintage shop on Queen Margaret Drive quickly springs to mind. This is where my friends and I found the velvet skirts, fur coats, silk blouses, 'tea dresses', wide-brimmed hats, long cotton summer skirts and delicate smocked shirts that at the time caused something of a stir in the streets of the city for reasons of their being both old and outlandish, not what might be found in the city-centre boutiques and department stores.[4] These were finds that matched with our limited budgets of student grants. I was still living at home, and very few young persons in the quiet genteel streets of Kelvindale as it tipped into Kelvinside departed from the more conservative styles of dress that might be worn by law or accountancy students. My younger sister was even more drawn to the second-hand hippy looks that were coming up from London, Jimi Hendrix's ruffled shirt and plummy wine velvet jackets, and Marianne Faithfull's floaty dreamy wardrobe. Our parents were scandalised by this hippy turn and took to locking up the clothes in the garden shed, with my father taking the key with him to work as he slipped out of the house before 7 am.[5]

The second-hand clothes shops were an integral part of the local arts community. They provided wardrobes for the poets, artists, 'heads', musicians and others. The mostly female labours that went on behind the counter did not count for much in the male-dominated Glasgow hippy underground. It was simply a matter of providing a service and being able to claim to be part of this scene, since these shops also advertised events and accepted flyers for upcoming poetry readings, music gigs and various other performances. These vintage styles that brightened the streets of Glasgow in the '70s were 'vernacular urban spaces', in this case running along the stretch of Byres Road and taking a left turn up by the university to where it meets Gibson Street, and likewise along the Great Western Road to Kelvinbridge and just beyond (Zukin 2012). These streets loop round the university and touch on the coat-tails of the Glasgow School of Art in Garnethill. As rents and business rates have risen over the years, there are nowadays fewer vintage boutiques, their place being taken by so many charity shops. Arguably this marks a loss, as the vintage shops were specialist suppliers and carefully curated. The idea was to provide an alternative to the mainstream of the fashion industry. In Glasgow's Byres Road, the historical presence of so many pubs is only accompanied nowadays by coffee and cake shops, alongside the many charity outlets. A case could be made that vintage boutiques provide a more active form of 'post-Fordist place making' for the reason that they connect with local music, arts and poetry scenes and they can also be spaces for self-employment, especially for young women, and this brings a more youthful presence to streets and to a neighbourhood without folding into the logic of gentrification (Colomb 2012). In Glasgow, this point appears to be lost to the local council and planning department.

The second city which formed the backdrop to my own immersive experiences of second-hand fashion was Birmingham. An enthusiasm for vintage shopping then overlapped with my academic focus on gender, music and youth culture. This took me into the heart of the Birmingham punk and post-punk scenes from 1976 onwards. The ragmarket in the Digbeth underbelly of the famous Bullring Shopping Centre provided the first port of call for, among other things, late 1940s crepe knee-length dresses and their summer equivalents in lighter crepes, printed cottons and silks, men's baggy shirts, light wool knitted and crocheted short cardigans and sleeveless jumpers, possibly from the early 1950s. Stallholders by this time were also beginning to modify some of the original stock, making new items from old fabrics. Two friends at the time were fashion students at Birmingham Polytechnic and they were collecting and gathering from so many outlets across the city and then putting together looks for local punk bands and their friends. These two young women curated pieces, they picked up ladies' light wool two-piece suits from the late 1950s and early 1960s, they also found herringbone coats and tweed jackets, and the kind of men's suits that could be adapted for women with the help of leather belts so that they bunched at the waist. They collected padded shouldered silk blouses of the type seen in Hollywood movies from the late 1940s which again were to be worn with baggy men's trousers, creating a 'film noir' silhouette which also matched with the strong sexual politics of bands like the Au Pairs. A classic vintage shop opened on Broad Street and it quickly became a gathering place for band members from across the West Midlands. The men in and around the two-tone music scene were on the lookout for pork pie hats for winter, and rakish straw hats for summer. They also bought pin-striped winter suits, and in summer Hawaiian shirts, worn with trousers with a pleated waistband. This became the basic wardrobe for DJs/band managers/music producers and as a vintage look it has lasted through the decades.

My research pathway from the late 1980s began to gravitate away from youth culture towards the experience of young fashion design graduates as they embarked on their own studio practice. How did the so-called enterprise culture, a lynchpin of the Thatcher government, work out in practice? By that point in time, in the mid-1980s, it was possible to trace a movement from the youth cultures with their exuberant fashion and style imaginaries, in through the doors of the arts schools, where the ideas were turned into a professional practice, emerging uniquely as British fashion design.[6] As discussed in more detail in chapter 3, this pathway also led to the rapid commercialisation of subculture, as, bit by bit, it surrendered its 'subcultural capital' to the club scenes, fashion and lifestyle industry as a whole (Thornton 1995). Or alternately it produced and then expanded its own labour market, creating new ways of making a living in the cultural sector for the precarious post-industrial society. Magazines such as *The Face* and *i-D* and then later *Dazed and Confused* were the key channels for the fuller commercialisation of style, and at the same time the creation of a new cadre of stylists and fashion experts who were designated by the end of the century as part of the 'talent-led economy'. Kate Moss recounted her love of vintage pieces. Very quickly fast-fashion teen-oriented high-street stores like Topshop began to feature their own in-house vintage rails.

Migrant Histories and Working Conditions

Questions of class and history underpin the wider meaning of vintage shopping. An older generation who at least witnessed, if not themselves experienced, high levels of poverty in a city like Glasgow might shudder at the thought of having to rely on 'castoffs'. This would be acutely felt by those whose families had a few generations back migrated from Ireland. In Glasgow, Paddy's Market in the poor working-class area near to the Barrowlands Ballroom and the River Clyde was well-known as the ragmarket organised by and for penniless people arriving off the boats. Recently social historians have looked in depth at the connections between migrant culture and the urban ragmarkets. Le Zotte shows how in the U.S. the philanthropic arm of American capitalism with so many bases in the churches muscled in to take control of the more informally organised street markets, thereby removing the traces of the more lively and multicultural migration histories (Le Zotte 2017). A moralising discourse is then imposed on the whole field of activity, and the ties with religion and the various urban missions become dominant. Thrift comes to be associated with the deserving church-attending poor, leaving the popular economies that had sprung up in slum neighbourhoods such as pawn shops and junk shops to become more heavily stigmatised and associated with disease and infestation. The politics of the urban poor has therefore to be factored into discussions about second-hand dressing and the shame felt by so many who had no alternative but to rely on things thrown away or no longer wanted by their social superiors. This applies to the slave labourers in pre-abolition America for whom clothing was by definition castoffs from the masters and mistresses. Dress historians of colonialism and the plantations emphasise the important role played by local tailors and dressmakers within the slave and post-slave communities for the reason that bright new clothes gave a sense of dignity to those who wore them.[7]

There is also the point that vintage dress is part of the fashion system which means it is designed and styled as well as curated. Within the dominant field of fashion where second-hand items now have a recognised place, there are various exclusions of taste and boundary-marking activities which ensure class hierarchies remain intact. In the glossy magazines such as *Vogue* or on Instagram, older female fashion influencers, bloggers or well-known figures who are shown wearing vintage do so in a way that mixes new and recognisably expensive or luxury items with their 'found' pieces, so as to compound their belonging to a social hierarchy of style and taste and not be mistaken for being poor, older women, or even just on a tight budget.

The second body of recent research which investigates the landscape of second-hand dressing has a specific focus on work and employment. Jennifer Ayres makes a strong argument that working conditions in thrift stores, charity shops and vintage outlets need to be improved with unionisation and a raft of rights and entitlements (Ayres 2021). The ethical and philanthropic underpinning does not in fact suggest an alternative, non-capitalistic model; instead it is part of the wider workings of the fashion industry and the urban creative economy. (In this regard, vintage shops have also been seen as part of the hipster scene of the early 2000s and of the 'neo-bohemia' neighbourhoods of cities, from Montreal to Chicago, from Portland, Oregon, to London's Shoreditch [Lloyd 2006].) Then, as the hipster economy came under fire for pushing out the poor from run-down neighbourhoods ripe for regeneration and for bringing in wealthier consumers, vintage shops were also tainted on the basis of their catering for white, middle-class consumers, often visitors or tourists to the now interestingly 'gritty' neighbourhoods.

Ayres carried out ethnographic research across different sites of second-hand outlets in Philadelphia and New York, as well as visiting and observing in a range of other towns and cities. At the bottom end of the chain, the Goodwill consignment centres, the micro-entrepreneurial practices are predominantly part of the informal economy, bestowing a degree of dignity and control on the part of the sorters as they sift through bins of goods. Their role is to find things of some notional value from bins which are full of household debris. Hierarchies of extractive value also characterise the different settings that Ayres observes in the more upmarket vintage stores donating to HIV charities and then finally in the exclusive appointment-only vintage studio in New York which caters to clients from the high-end fashion sector. There are abusive managerial practices as well as routine bag checks against theft at the end of the working day. The second-hand clothes sector is no different from mainstream retail, but its workers and volunteers are subjected to more heightened expectations of emotional labour because of the philanthropic or charity dimension. They are expected to bring a moral purpose to what they do. This marks a full integration of charity, as well as the more style-oriented vintage, into the world of precarious post-Fordist service-sector jobs.

This expansion of work in the charity milieu has been extended further with the move to online selling (Oxfam has been doing this for many years). Ayres draws attention to the often overlooked or even unpaid labour that thrift shops and second-hand boutiques rely on from sales staff as they double as e-merchandisers. They are expected to write pithy and succinct copy describing items, to cut down on returns. They also must take countless photographs as well as selecting those for official posting and manage the business of payment and navigating PayPal or equivalent systems. Kneese and Palm refer to this work as 'listing labour' (Kneese and Palm 2020). They offer the most up-to-date account of the vintage online economy, drawing attention to so many tasks which are now required of these platform labourers, from the precise descriptions encompassing exact measurements, fabric type, quality of condition, buttons, zips, and other such details, to ensuring 'delicate packing'. Alongside repairs and other garment modifications which might be required, they must also take care of inventory, which means cataloguing, inspecting, photographing, as well as issuing friendly requests to purchasers for good online reviews. This is predominantly minimum-wage work, a further extension of the digital labour landscape as it unfolds. The digital economy has been instrumental in encouraging people to sell directly their own no-longer-wanted items and make money in the process.[8] eBay and Etsy have created trickles of income for so many people as a kind of hobby activity. This enjoyment factor, alongside the spirit of entrepreneurship of start-up culture, militate against the idea of rights and entitlements. Vintage labour blends in with the new landscape of bloggers and fashion influencers and with the idea of making (some) money from what people 'love doing' (Duffy 2017).

Fashion-Tech and Vintage-Washing

We have charted a move from subcultural vintage stalls to the spread of charity shops, now ubiquitous on every high street across the length and breadth of the UK, to second-hand fashion online sites which are fully part of the e-commerce engines of Instagram and Facebook. Platforms worth billions of dollars such as Vinted and Depop (recently purchased for $1.6bn by Etsy.com) and the upmarket exclusive Vestiaire Collective (recently invested in by the Gucci parent company Kering) are now amongst the biggest online fashion-tech companies. At the same time, fast fashion e-companies such as ASOS (based in London) and Zalando (HQ in Berlin) both now include extensive second-hand websites (employing hundreds of people to service them). ASOS states on its website that second-hand purchases offer a 'great way to be unique' as well as helping to reduce the carbon footprint. Zalando hosts an extensive second-hand site. Under the filter for women's tops, blouses and dresses, the page shows 50 items for a collection of 428 items.[9] And while this all takes place online, there is unsurprisingly a huge decline of the vernacular urban spaces due to high rent thresholds charged by both private landlords and by city councils. The brand value for ASOS was £1.1bn in 2022, up from £.8bn in 2020.[10] According to Forbes, in 2021 Zalando was worth $28.4bn, with a workforce of 14,194. It is no exaggeration to say that these companies are giants, but often employing people on low to minimum wages, especially at the packing level. In line with other platform companies, such as Depop in London, the workforces also remain small in comparison to the scale of the activity. Much of the labour force will be outsourced to delivery companies such as DPD, Uber, Hermes, etc.

The dominance of this kind of finance capital in so many cities in the UK and the impact that it has on shopping areas means that the enjoyment of lingering and browsing is gone. There are new shopping areas such as Coal Drops Yards at King's Cross, which has allocated spaces for a recycled denim workshop run by Blackhorse Ateliers and for fashion independents Wolf & Badger, where there is an integrated second-hand stock. But more widely the pleasure referred to at the start of this chapter loses much of its appeal when there are only charity shops which generally do not highlight vintage pieces and instead they jostle alongside recently discarded fast-fashion items. The more specialist vintage market has moved almost wholly online, and the digital economy is the preferred launch pad for both old and new independent fashion designer collections. Some young graduate designers now specialise in reworking old clothes or vintage pieces, or salvaged stretches of fabric (deadstock), transforming them either into something completely new, or else simply revamped or altered in some way.[11] This is a virtual business model, without the trappings of social interaction in a real-life shop environment. The idea of vintage dissolves then into the new rhythms of circular and sustainable fashion cycles. Innovators in this arena can find themselves adopted by and invested in by much larger companies looking to fulfil their ethical responsibility remit. This kind of circuit also marks out the parameters of a massively devolved and disaggregated fashion sector, with many of the big companies in crisis as young consumers threaten to abandon fast fashion, leaving these producers flailing about in all directions to find ways of doing vintage themselves.

Vintage sourcing and selling is integrated into the wider fashion ecology, and it becomes hard to extrapolate vintage out as a separate entity. Instead, second-hand fashion is embedded within multiple interest groups, including the global fashion companies such as H&M and their offshoots COS and ARKET, as well as with the luxury brands, all of whom find themselves not just under scrutiny from their previously more loyal customers, but also increasingly being held to account by their share-holders in the light of falling profits. Disaggregated and in turmoil (also in light of the global pandemic of 2020), the companies are having to come up with strategies that were previously unthinkable. These recent activities also mean employing a new workforce who will inspect used and now returned goods, arrange them for cleaning and repairing and then have them ready to go back on the rails or prepare them for online posting. We might assume that this now comprises the new retail job description. The global brands are learning to be adept at managing and reselling their own used or 'pre-loved' stock (Dior handbags, Gucci silk shirts, etc.). If COS does this and if Chanel follows suit, the activities of the small independents are under threat. We see much higher levels of competition and extractive labour deployed across the pre-loved fashion landscape, conducted in the name of sustainability and environmental responsibility.

The key issue in this second-hand fashion landscape is the corporate phenomenon of vintage-washing and how this plays a role in fashion's new political economy. How sure can we be that the buyback of old purchases and the reselling of pre-loved items really functions to reduce the damage to the environment? How can we ascertain that the various stages and the labour processes that are entailed in these new cycles of production and consumption adhere to the new ethical principles that the brands announce as part of their corporate social responsibility pledges? Most often the detailed information from behind the scenes is subject to corporate confidentiality, and few journalists – never mind academic researchers – can access this kind of insider data. What we can be sure of are the large budgets devoted to publicising the various commitments and pledges. A further focus for analysis here has been the role of the charity shops on the UK high streets and the new regime of retail labour which historically depended on voluntary work and now stretches to the low-pay or minimum-wage economy. A case could be made for these shops to be more fully recognised and even aim for trade union representation as they become stable features of the UK high street while also playing a leading part of the green agenda and hence the green economy. Also important for a fuller understanding is the global picture. As authors from African countries have noted, unsold second-hand stock from the UK tends not to be disposed of in the UK but is sent in huge crates to African countries such as Ghana (Bobie 2022; Darkwah 2022). It is not only unwanted, pushing local second-hand suppliers out of work, but it contributes directly to the further harm being done to the environment, with huge landfill mountains polluting ecosystems and destroying coastlines. These second-hand clothes from the UK and elsewhere in Europe undercut the already fragile local economies in used clothes (Norris 2012). Without a more fully global perspective that foregrounds fashion culture in the developing world, and the labour forces and working conditions, the account of second-hand clothing and vintage markets remains partial. Second-hand and vintage clothing has become almost fully integrated into the global capitalist fashion industry. There is an opportunity now to recast the field of consumer culture studies and fashion pedagogy to reflect this terrain from multiple vantage points, including vintage as a site for women's work and employment in the new economic geography of global labour, and at the same time prioritising for critical analysis its place in the logic of fashion offshoring, to the detriment of jobs, local popular economies and the environment in the world's poorest countries.

Notes

1 Thanks to Alida Payson for the Second-Hand Cultures Conference she co-hosted in June 2021. She referred to the austerity politics which the UK government imposed on the population in light of the financial crash of 2008 which resulted in media popularising the idea of thrift, often cast in housewifely 'retro' terms. Since then, the rise of so many food banks across the UK in the last decade has undercut the cheerfulness and upbeat note of the 'make do and mend' TV programmes. Payson also referred to the TV presenter and shopping expert Mary Portas, whose chain of new style charity shops bear her name. Portas had complained about the smell and aimed for her shops to the get rid of the muskiness (Payson 2021).

2 Local councils offer reduced rent and rates to charity shop but not to commercial vintage shops. This means that very few can afford high-street retail spaces (e.g. Retro in Argyll Street, Oxford Circus). See also many reports about shop closures in the UK, one report suggesting that up to fifty stores closed for good every day in 2022 (Kollewe 2023).

3 Fashion itself had been the subject of serious sociological attention as part of the rise of urban modernity by Georg Simmel and also by Walter Benjamin; however, this was only intermittently followed up, mostly in the field of art history and visual culture (Wollen 2003; Rocamora and Smelik 2016). Benjamin is especially relevant because his focus was indeed on items that were no longer in fashion, and that stood forlornly as out-of-date objects in the windows of the Parisian shopping arcades.

4 Sited just a few minutes' walk from the old BBC Scotland building, shops like this would also have been suppliers for the costume departments for film, TV and theatre.

5 A friend at university grew his straight blonde hair so long that it draped down his head and shoulders, swishing like a curtain when he walked, and, having acquired a sewing machine and large quantities of old velvet curtains found at jumble sales, he began to make bright-coloured 'loon pants', taking orders for both sexes. He moved to sourcing sheets of leather and taught himself how to make 'unisex' shoulder bags and jackets. Wearing his own wardrobe of tight velvet trousers, floral fabric second-hand jacket, with a floppy, felt, wide-brimmed hat, he attracted a good deal of homophobic abuse from passing van drivers and others. He later became a leading theatre and opera costume designer.

6 At the degree show of Stella McCartney in 1983, her runway collection's most memorable pieces were silky slip dresses that could have been from the 1940s- and early '50s-sourced lingerie rails in a vintage boutique, over which were worn men's-style pin-striped jackets, again easily sourced from the curated stalls in Portobello Road.

7 See Square (2020).

8 'Currently, Haroutounian spends about three to four hours a day shopping online for clothes, and hours upon hours shopping for pieces on the weekend with her mother. When Haroutounian is ready to list, she photographs herself for four hours at a time, three times a week. "I have a tripod, but the remote broke, so I use a self-timer," she says. "And I have a painter's tarp that catches the flash." With each post on Depop, Haroutounian adds a snippet of history about the item she is selling. Under a burgundy puffer by Japanese designer Keita Maruyama, she explains, "Most of the pieces from this collection were car-themed with Maruyama's initials in the style of the STP [Standard Temperature and Pressure] logo." For a plaid Chantal Thomass for Ter et Bantine dress she writes, "Chantal Thomass started designing around age 18. Thomass would design clothes, her mother would sew them together, and her boyfriend would paint designs onto them with turpentine paint." Although the research takes a bit of time, she enjoys it. "I feel like people are far more interested in seeing something by somebody they've never heard of before, and learning something," she says' (Satenstein 2020).

9 www.Zalando.com.

10 'Brand Value of ASOS worldwide from 2020 to 2022', https://www.statista.com/statistics/1246129/asos-brand-value/.

11 See, for example, https://www.greatergoods.online/.

PART 2

Birmingham Centre for Contemporary Cultural Studies: Research and Writing

6

Jackie: An Ideology of Adolescent Femininity (1977)

Jackie: Cultural Product and Signifying System

Another useful expression though, is the pathetic appealing look, which brings out a boy's protective instinct and has him desperate to get you another drink/ help you on with your coat/give you a lift home. It's best done by opening your eyes wide and dropping the mouth open a little looking (hanging your head slightly) directly into the eyes of the boy you're talking to. Practice this (*Jackie*, 15 February 1975).

One of the major reasons for choosing *Jackie* for analysis is its astounding success. Since its first appearance in 1964 its sales have risen from an initial weekly average of 350,000 (with a drop in 1965 to 250,000) to 451,000 in 1968 and 605,947 in 1976. This means that it has been Britain's longest selling 'teen' magazine for over ten years. *Boyfriend*, first published in 1959, started off with sales figures averaging around 418,000 but had fallen to 199,000 in 1965 when publication ceased. *Mirabelle*, launched in 1956, sold over 540,000 copies each week, a reflection of the 'teenage boom' of the mid 50s, but by 1968 its sales had declined to 175,000.[1]

However my aim here is not to grapple with those factors upon which this success appears to be predicated, instead it will be to mount a rigorous and systematic critique of *Jackie* as a system of messages, a signifying system and a bearer of a certain ideology; an ideology which deals with the construction of teenage 'femininity'.

Jackie is one of a large range of magazines, newspapers and comics published by D.C. Thomson of Dundee. [...] With a history of vigorous anti-unionism, D.C. Thomson is not unlike other-large mass communication groups. Like Walt Disney, for example, it produces predominantly for a young market and operates a strict code of censorship on content. But its conservatism is most overtly evident in its newspapers which take a consistently anti-union and 'law and order' line. The *Sunday Post*, with a reputed readership of around 3m (i.e. 79% of the entire population of Scotland over 15) is comforting, reassuring and parochial in tone. Comprised, in the main, of anecdotal incidents drawn to the attention of the reader in 'couthie' language, it serves as a 'Sunday entertainer' reminding its readers of the pleasure of belonging to a particular national culture.[2]

One visible result of this success has been, at a time of inflation and of crisis, in the publishing world, 'enviably' high profit margins of 20% or more. More than this, D.C. Thomson has expanded into other associated fields, with investments for example in the Clyde Paper Co. (27.15%) and Southern TV (24.8%).

Two points should be made in this context. First, without necessarily adhering to the 'traditional' conspiracy plot thesis, it would be naive to envisage the 'interests' of such a company as being purely the pursuit of increased profits. D.C. Thomson is not, in *Jackie*, merely 'giving the girls what they want'. Each magazine, newspaper or comic has its own conventions and its own style. But within these conventions and through them a concerted effort is nevertheless made to win and shape the consent of the readers to a set of particular values.

The work of this branch of the media involves 'framing' the world for its readers, and through a variety of techniques endowing with importance those topics chosen for inclusion. The reader is invited to share this world with *Jackie*. It is no coincidence that the title is also a girl's name. This is an unambiguous sign that its concern is with 'the category of the subject,'[3] in particular the individual girl, and the feminine 'persona'. *Jackie* is both the magazine and the ideal girl. The short, snappy name itself carries a string of connotations: British, fashionable (particularly in the 60s); modern; and cute; with the pet-form 'ie' ending, it sums up all those desired qualities which the reader is supposedly seeking.

Second, we must see this ideological work as being grounded upon certain so-called natural, even 'biological' categories. Thus *Jackie* expresses the 'natural' features of adolescence in much the same way as, say, Disney comics are said to capture the natural essence of childhood. Each has, as

Dorfman and Mattelart writing on Disney point out, a 'virtually biologically captive, predetermined audience.'⁴ *Jackie* introduces the girl into adolescence outlining its landmarks and characteristics in detail and stressing importantly the problematic features as well as the fun. Of course *Jackie* is not solely responsible for nurturing this ideology of femininity. Nor would such an ideology cease to exist should *Jackie* stop publication.

Unlike other fields of mass culture, the magazines of teenage girls have not as yet been subject to rigorous critical analysis. Yet from the most cursory of readings it is clear that they, too, like those more immediately associated with the sociology of the media – press, TV, film, radio, etc. – are powerful ideological forces.

In fact women's and girls' weeklies occupy a privileged position. Addressing themselves solely to a female market, their concern is with promoting a feminine culture for their readers. They define and shape the woman's world, spanning every stage from childhood to old age. From *Mandy*, *Bunty* and *Judy*, to *House and Home*, the exact nature of the woman's role is spelt out in detail, according to her age.

She progresses from adolescent romance where there are no explicitly sexual encounters, to the more sexual world of *19*, *Honey* or *Over 21*, which in turn give way to marriage, childbirth, home-making, child care and the *Woman's Own*. There are no 'male' equivalents to these products. 'Male' magazines tend to be based on particular leisure pursuits or hobbies, motor-cycling, fishing, cars or even pornography. There is no consistent attempt to link 'interests' with age (though readership of many magazines will obviously be higher among younger age groups) nor is there a sense of a natural inevitable progression or evolution attached to their readers' expected 'careers'. There is instead a variety of possibilities with regard to leisure [...], many of which involve active participation inside or outside the home.

It will be argued here that the way Jackie addresses 'girls' as a monolithic grouping, as do all other women's magazines, serves to obscure differences, of class for example, between women. Instead it asserts a sameness, a kind of false sisterhood, which assumes a common definition of womanhood or girlhood. Moreover by isolating out a particular 'phase' or age as the focus of interest, one which coincides roughly with that of its readers, the magazine is in fact creating this 'age-ness' as an ideological construction. 'Adolescence' and here, female adolescence, is itself an ideological 'moment' whose *connotations* are immediately identifiable with those 'topics' included in *Jackie*. And so, by at once defining its readership *vis-à-vis* age, and by describing what is of relevance, to this age group, *Jackie* and women's magazines in general create a 'false totality'. Thus we *all* want to know how to catch a man, lose weight, look our best, or cook well! Having mapped out the feminine 'career' in such all-embracing terms, there is little or no space allowed for alternatives. Should the present stage be unsatisfactory the reader is merely encouraged to look forward to the next. Two things are happening here. 1) The girls are being invited to join a close, intimate sorority where secrets can be exchanged and advice given; and 2) they are also being presented with an ideological bloc of mammoth proportions, one which *imprisons* them in a claustrophobic world of jealousy and competitiveness, the most unsisterly of emotions, to say the least.

Jackie and Popular Culture

There are several ways in which we can think through *Jackie* magazine as part of the media and of mass culture in general.

The first of these is the traditionalist thesis. In this, magazines are seen as belonging to popular or mass culture, something which is inherently inferior to 'high' culture, or 'the arts'. Cheap, superficial, exploitative and debasing, it reduces its audience to a mass of mindless morons,

the open sagging mouths and glazed eyes, the hands mindlessly drumming in time to the music, the broken stiletto heels, the shoddy, stereotyped 'with it' clothes: here apparently, is a collective portrait of a generation enslaved by a commercial machine.[5]

Alderson, writing explicitly on girls' weeklies, takes a similar position. Claiming, correctly, that what they offer their readers is a narrow and restricted view of life, she proposed as an alternative, 'better' literature, citing *Jane Eyre* as an example.[6]

The problems with such an approach are manifest. 'High' culture becomes a cure for all ills. It is, to quote Willis, 'a repository of quintessential human values',[7] playing a humanising role by elevating the emotions and purifying the spirit. What this argument omits to mention are the material requirements necessary to purchase such 'culture'. And underpinning it is an image of the deprived, working class youngster (what Alderson calls the 'Newsom girl') somehow lacking in those qualities which contact with the arts engenders. Mass culture is seen as a manipulative, vulgar, profit-seeking industry offering cheap and inferior versions of the arts to the more impressionable and vulnerable sectors of the population. This concept of culture is inadequate because it is ahistorical, and is based on unquestioned qualitative judgements. It offers no explanations as to how these forms develop and are distributed. Nor does it explain why one form has a particular resonance for one class in society rather than another.

The second interpretation has much in common with this approach, although it is generally associated with more radical critics. This is the conspiracy thesis and it, too, sees mass culture as 'fodder' for the masses; the result of a ruling class plot whose objective it is to keep the working classes docile and subordinate and to divert them into entertainment. [...] By this logic, *Jackie* is merely a mouthpiece for ruling class ideology, focused on young adolescent girls. Again, mass culture is seen as worthless and manipulative. Not only is this argument also ahistorical, but it fails to locate the operations of different apparatuses in the social formation (politics, the media, the law, education, the family, to name but some) each of which is relatively autonomous, has its own *level* and its own specific material practices. While private sectors of the economy do *ultimately* work together with the State, there is a necessary separation between them. Each apparatus has its own *uneven* development and one cannot be collapsed with another.

The third argument reverses both of the first two arguments, to the extent that it points to pop music and pop culture as meaningful activities: 'for most young people today ... pop music and pop culture is their only expressive outlet'.[8]

Such a position does have some relevance to our study of *Jackie*. It hinges on the assumption that this culture expresses and offers, in albeit consumerist terms, those values and ideas held by both working class youth and by sections of middle class youth. Youth, that is, is defined in terms of values held, which are often in opposition to those held by the establishment, by their parents, the school, work, etc. Such a definition does not consider youth's relation to production, but to consumption, and it is this approach which has characterised that huge body of work, the sociology of culture and of youth, subcultural theory, and which includes, too, delinquency theory.

To summarise a familiar argument which finds expression in most of these fields: working class youth, denied access to other 'higher' forms of culture, and in any case associating these with 'authority' and with the middle class, turns to those forms available on the market. Here they can at least exert some power in their choice of commodities. These commodities often come to be a hallmark of the subcultural group in question but not exactly in their original forms. The group *subverts* the original meaning by bestowing additional implied connotations to the object(s) thereby extending the range of its signifying power. These new meanings undermine and can even negate the previous or established meaning(s) so that the object comes to represent an oppositional ideology linked to the subculture or youth grouping in question. It then summarises for the outside observer the group's disaffection from the wider society. This process of re-appropriation can be seen in, for example, the 'style' of the skinheads, the 'mod' suit, the 'rocker' motor bike, or even the 'punk' safety-pin![9]

But this approach, which hinges on explaining the choice of cultural artefacts – clothes, records or motor bikes etc., – is of limited usefulness when applied to teenage girls and their magazines. They play little, if any, role in shaping their own pop culture and their choice in consumption is materially extremely narrow. And indeed the forms made available to them make re-appropriation difficult. *Jackie* offers its readers no active 'presence' in which girls are invited to participate. The uses are, in short, prescribed by the 'map'. Yet [...] this does not mean that *Jackie* cannot be used in subversive ways. Clearly girls *do* use it as a means of signalling their boredom and disaffection, in the school, for example. The point *here* is that despite these possible uses, the magazine itself has a powerful ideological presence as a *form*, and as such demands analysis carried out *apart from* these uses or 'readings'. [...]

While the argument made here will include strands from the positions outlined above, its central thrust will represent a substantial shift away from them. What I want to suggest is that *Jackie* occupies the sphere of the personal or private, what Gramsci calls 'Civil Society' ('the ensemble of organisms that are commonly called Private').[10] Hegemony is sought uncoercively on this terrain, which is relatively free of direct State interference. Consequently it is seen as an arena of 'freedom', of 'free choice' and of 'free time'. This sphere includes:

not only associations and organisations like political parties and the press, but also the family, which combines ideological and economic functions.[11]

[...] *Jackie* exists within a large, powerful, privately owned publishing apparatus which produces a vast range of newspapers, magazines and comics. It is on this level of the magazine that teenage girls are subjected to an explicit attempt to win consent to the dominant order – in terms of femininity, leisure and consumption, i.e. at the level of culture. It is worth noting at this point that only three girls in a sample of 56 claimed to read any newspapers regularly. They rarely watched the news on television and their only prolonged contact with the written word was at school and through their own and their mothers' magazines. Occasionally a 'risqué' novel like Richard Allen's *Skingirl* would be passed round at school, but otherwise the girls did not read any literature apart from 'love' comics.

The 'teen' magazine is, therefore, a highly privileged 'site'. Here the girl's consent is sought uncoercively and in her leisure time. [...] While there is a strongly coercive element to those other terrains which teenage girls inhabit, the school and the family, in her leisure time the girl is officially 'free' to do as she pleases. And as we have seen, teenage girls show a marked lack of interest in organised leisure activities, showing instead a preference for dancing or merely 'sitting about'. Otherwise the girls in the sample defined their leisure interests in terms of consumer goods – clothes, make-up, magazines, records and cigarettes. It is on the open market then that girls are least constrained by the display of social control. The only qualification here is the ability to buy a ticket, magazine or Bay City Roller T-shirt. Here they remain relatively uninterfered with. [...]

Commercial leisure enterprises with their illusion of freedom have, then, an attraction for youth. And this 'freedom' is pursued, metaphorically, inside the covers of *Jackie*. With an average readership age of 10 to 14, Jackie pre-figures girls' entry into the labour market as 'free labourers' and its pages are crammed full of the 'goodies' which this later freedom promises. Jackie girls are never at school, they are enjoying the fruits of their labour on the open market. They live in large cities, frequently in flats shared with other young wage-earners like themselves.

This image of freedom has a particular resonance for girls when it is located within and intersects with the longer and again ideologically constructed 'phase' they inhabit in the present. Leisure has a special importance in this period of 'brief flowering,'[12] that is, in those years prior to marriage and settling down, after which they become dual labourers in the home and in production. Leisure in their 'single' years is especially important because it is here that their future is secured. It is in *this* sphere that they go about finding a husband and thereby sealing their fate. [...]

The World of *Jackie*

What then are the key features which characterise *Jackie*? First there is a 'lightness' of tone, a non-urgency, which holds true right through the magazine, particularly in the use of colour, graphics and advertisements. It asks to be read at a leisurely pace, indicating that its subject matter is not wholly serious, is certainly not 'news'. Since entertainment and leisure goods are designed to arouse feelings of pleasure as well as interest, the appearance of the magazine is inviting, its front cover shows a 'pretty' girl smiling happily. The dominance of the visual level, which is maintained throughout the magazine, reinforces this notion of leisure. It is to be glanced through, looked at and only finally read. Published at weekly intervals, the reader has time to peruse each item at her own speed. She also has time to pass it round her friends or swap it for another magazine.

Rigid adherence to a certain style of lay-out and patterning of features ensures a familiarity with its structure(s). The girl can rely on *Jackie* to *cheer her up, entertain her, or solve her problems each week.* The 'style' of the magazine, once established, facilitates and encourages partial and uneven reading, in much the same way as newspapers also do. The girl can quickly turn to the centre page for the pin-up, glance at the fashion page and leave the problems and picture stories which are the 'meat' of the magazine, till she has more time.

Articles and features are carefully arranged to avoid one 'heavy' feature following another. The black and white picture stories taking up between 2½ and 3 full pages are always broken up by a coloured advert, or beauty feature, and the magazine opens and closes by inviting the reader to participate directly through the letters or the problem pages.

This sense of solidness and resistance to change (*Jackie*'s style has not been substantially altered since it began publication) is reflected and paralleled in its thematic content. Each feature (as will be seen later) comprises workings and re-workings of a relatively small repertoire of specific themes or concerns which sum up the girls' world. These topics saturate the magazine. Entering the world of *Jackie* means suspending interest in the 'real' world of school, family or work, and participating in a sphere which is devoid of history and resistant to change.

Jackie deals primarily with the terrain of the personal and it makes a 'turning inwards' to the sphere of the 'soul', the 'heart', or less metaphorically, the emotions. On the one hand, of course, certain features do change – fashion is itself predicated upon change and upon being 'up to date'. But the degree of change even here is qualified – certain features remain the same, e.g. the models' 'looks', poses, the style of drawing and its positioning within the magazine and so on. All that does change is the length of the hem, shade of make-up, style of shoe, etc.

Above all, *Jackie*, like the girl she symbolises, is intended to be 'looked at'. This overriding concern with visuals affects every feature. But its visual appearance and style also reflect the spending power of its readers. There is little of the extravagant or exotic in *Jackie*. The paper on which it is printed is thin without being wafer-thin. The fashion and beauty pages show clothes priced within the girls' range and the adverts are similarly focused at a low budget market featuring, principally, personal toiletries, tampons, shampoos and lipsticks rather than larger consumer goods. [...]

The Code of Romance: The Moment of Bliss

The hero of romance knows how to treat women. Flowers, little gifts, love letters, maybe poems to her eyes and hair, candlelit meals on moon-lit terraces and muted strings. Nothing hasty, physical. Some heavy breathing ... Mystery, magic, champagne, ceremony ... women never have enough of it.[13]

Jackie picture stories are similar *in form* to those comic strips, and tales of adventure, time travel, rivalry and intrigue which regularly fill the pages of children's weeklies. Yet there is something distinctive about these stories which indicates immediately their concern with romance. First the titles clearly announce a concern with 'you', 'me', 'love' and 'happiness'. Romantic connotations are conveyed through the relationship between titles and the names of 'pop' songs and ballads. (*Jackie* does not however use the older *Boyfriend* technique of using a well-known pop song and its singer to both inspire the story and give it moral weight!)

The title, then, anchors the story it introduces. In our sample these include:

'The Happiest Xmas Ever', 'Meet Me On The Corner', 'As Long As I've Got You', 'Come Fly With Me', and 'Where Have All The Flowers Gone?'

This concern with romance pervades every story and is built into them through the continued use of certain formal techniques and styles.

For a start, the way the characters look indicates clearly that this is serious, not 'kids' stuff'. They are all older and physically more mature than the intended reader. Each character conforms to a well-established and recognisable standard of beauty or handsomeness and they are all smart, fairly sophisticated young adults, rather than adolescents or 'teenagers'.

The most characteristic feature of 'romance' in *Jackie* is the concern with the narrow and restricted world of the emotions. No attempt is made to fill out social events or backgrounds. The picture story is the realm, *par excellence*, of the individual. Each story revolves round one figure and the tiny web of social relationships surrounding him or, usually, her. Rarely are there more than two or three characters in each plot and where they do exist it is merely as part of the background or scenery – in the cafe, at the disco or in the street.

Unlike comic strips, where the subject is fun, excitement or adventure, these stories purport to deal with the more serious side of life – hence the semi-naturalistic style of the drawings and the use of black and white. This, along with the boldness of the drawings, the starkness of stroke and angularity of the figures, conspires to create an impression of 'realism' and seriousness. The form of the stories alone tells us that romance is important, serious and relevant. Yet simultaneously in the content, we are told that it is fun; the essence and meaning of life; the key to happiness, etc. It is this blend which gives the *Jackie* romance its characteristic flavour. In general terms this is nothing new, these stories owe a great deal to popular cinema romances, and to novelettes. For a start the characters closely resemble the anonymous but distinctive type of the 'film star' – dewy-eyed women and granite-jawed heroes. Their poses are equally soaked in the language of film – the clinch, the rejected lover alone by herself as the sun sets – the moon comes up – to name but a few. But this cinematic resemblance is based on more than just *association*. The very form of the comic strip has close links with the film. Strung together, in a series of *clips,* set out across and down the page, the stories 'rise' to a climax and resolution, graphically illustrated in larger images erupting across the page.

From these clips we can see clearly that the emotional life is defined and lived in terms of *romance* which in turn is equated with *great moments* rather than long-term processes. Hence the centrality and visual impact of the clinch, the proposal, the wedding day. Together these *moments* constitute a kind of orchestration of *time*; through them the feminine career is constructed. The picture stories comprise a set of visual images composed and set within a series of frames laid out across the page to be 'read' like a text. But these frames communicate *visually*, resemble film-clips and tell the story by 'freezing' the action into sets of 'stills'. Unlike other comics (*Bunty* or *Judy*), *Jackie* stories do not conform to the convention of neatly mounted images set uniformly across the page. Instead a whole range of loose frames indicating different kinds of situations or emotions is used. This produces a greater continuity between 'form' and 'content', so that as the pace of the story accelerates, the visuals erupt *with* the breathless emotional feelings, spilling out over the page.

Each separate image which makes up the story is 'anchored' with sets of verbal messages illuminating the action and eliminating ambiguity. [...] Thus the moment of reading and looking are collapsed into one, and the reader is spared the boredom of having to read more lengthy descriptions; she merely 'takes it in' and hurries on to the next image. The techniques through which this relay operates are well known; – dialogue is indicated by the use of balloons issuing from the mouths of the speakers and filled with words; – and thoughts are conveyed through a series of small bubbles which drift upwards away from the character's mouth – thinking being associated with a 'higher' level of discourse, an 'intellectual' pursuit.

The central and most dramatic incident in each story is specified by the spilling out of one visual image over the page. This image sums up graphically the fraught nature of the moment; the moment when the timid shy heroine catches sight of her handsome boyfriend fascinated by her irresistible best friend at a party which she stupidly invited her to; or when the girl, let down by her boy, rushes out of the coffee bar across the street to be hit by a passing car ... and so on.

Each frame represents a selection from the development of the plot, and is credited with an importance which those intervening moments are not. Thus the train, supermarket, and office have meaning, to the extent that they represent potential meeting-places where the girl *could well* bump into the prospective boyfriend, who lurks round every corner. It is this which determines their inclusion in the plot; the possibility that every-day life could be transformed into *social life*.

Within these frames themselves the way the figures look, act, and pose contributes also to the ideology of romance. For a start there is very little variation in types of physical appearance. This homogeneity hinges on a blend of modernity and conservatism which typifies the *Jackie* 'look'. The girls are 'mod' but neat and conventional, rarely are they 'way-out'. Boys may look acceptably scruffy and dishevelled by displaying a kind of man-aged untidiness.

This appearance is matched by language. Deriving seemingly from the days of the teenage commercial boom it has a particularly 50s ring about it. Bereft of accent, dialect, slang or vulgarity it remains the invention of the media – the language of pop, and of Radio 1 disc jockeys. Distinctly modern it is also quite unthreatening, peppered with phrases like:

'rave', 'yacked', 'zacked', 'scrummy hunk', 'dishy', 'fave', 'come on, let's blow this place', 'I'm the best mover in town',

all of which convey an image of youth 'on the move', of 'a whole scene going' and of 'wowee dig the slick chick in the corner', 'a nice piece of talent', teen-agers 'doing their own thing'. But these teenagers are a strangely anony-mous and unrecognisable grouping, similar only, perhaps, to the 'Young Generation' seen on TV variety shows or the young people in Coca Cola or Levi Jeans adverts. It is a language of action, of 'good times', of enjoyment and of consumerism. The characters in *Jackie* stories and in Coca Cola TV adverts at least seem to be getting things done. They are constantly seen 'raving it up' at discos, going for trips in boyfriends' cars, or else going on holiday. And yet as we shall see, the female and male characters in *Jackie* are simultaneously doing nothing but pursuing each other, and far from being a pleasure-seeking *group*, in fact these stories consist of isolated individuals, distrusting even their best friends and in search of fulfilment only through a partner. The anonymity of the language then parallels the strangely amorphous *Jackie* girls. Marked by a rootlessness, lack of ties or sense of region, the reader is unable to 'locate' them in any social context. They are devoid of history. Bound together by an invisible 'generational consciousness' they inhabit a world where no disruptive values exist. At the 'heart' of this world is the individual girl looking for romance. But romance is not itself an unproblematic category and what I will be arguing here is that its central contradiction is glaringly clear and unavoidable even to the girl herself who is so devoted to its cause. This contradiction is based round the fact that the *romantic moment,* its central 'core', cannot be reconciled with its promise for *eternity.* To put it another way, the code of romance realises, but cannot accept, that the man can adore, love, 'cherish' and be sexually attracted to his girlfriend and simultaneously be 'aroused' by other girls (in the present or the 'future'). It is the recognition of this fact that sets all girls against each other, and forms the central theme in the picture stories. Hence the girl's constant worries, as she is passionately embraced; 'can it last?' or 'how can I be sure his love is for ever?'

Earlier we asserted that *Jackie* was concerned with 'the category of the subject', with the constitution of the feminine personality. Indeed 'personality' itself forms an important organising category in the magazine. Each week there is some concern with 'your' personality, how to know it, change it or understand those of your friends, boyfriends, families. In the picture stories 'personality' takes on an important role alongside 'looks'. The characters depend for their meaning on well-known stereotypes. That is, to be 'read' correctly the reader must possess previous cultural knowledge of the 'types' of subjects which inhabit his or her social world.

Jackie boys fall into four categories. First, there is the fun-loving, grinning, flirtatious boy who is irresistible to all girls; second, the 'tousled' scatterbrained 'zany' youth who inspires 'maternal' feelings in girls; third, the emotional, shy, sensitive and even 'arty' type; and fourth, the juvenile delinquent usually portrayed on his motor bike looking wild, aggressive but 'sexy' and whom the girl must 'tame'.

In every case the male figure is idealised and romanticised so that there is a real discrepancy between *Jackie* boys and those boys who are discussed on the Cathy and Claire page. The central point here is that *Jackie* boys are as interested in romance as the girls.

'Mm! I wish Santa would bring me that for Christmas ... so how do we get together?'

and this, as countless sociological studies, novels and studies of sexual behaviour indicate, simply does not ring true. Boys in contemporary capitalist society are socialised to be interested in *sex,* although this does not mean they don't want to find the 'ideal' girl or wife. [...]

Female characters, significantly, show even less variation in personality. In fact they can be summarised as three opposite or contrasting types. The 'blonde', quiet, timid, loving and trusting girl who either gets her boy in the end or is tragically abandoned; and the wild, fun-loving 'brunette' (often the blonde's best friend) who will resort to plotting and conniving to get the man she wants. This 'bitch' character is charming and irresistible to men although all women can immediately 'see through' her. Finally, there is the non-character, the friendly, open, fun-loving 'ordinary' girl (who may perhaps be slightly 'scatty' or absentminded). She is remarkable in being normal and things tend to happen *to* her rather than at her instigation. Frequently she figures in stories focusing round the supernatural.

Most of these characters have changed little since the magazine first appeared in 1964. Their 'style' is still rooted in the 'Swinging London' of the mid-60s. The girls have large, heavily made-up eyes, pale lips and tousled hair, turned up noses and tiny 'party' mouths (*à la* Jean Shrimpton). They wear clothes at least partly reminiscent of the 60s, hipster skirts with large belts, polo neck sweaters and, occasionally, 'flared' trousers. Despite the fact that several of these girls introduce themselves as 'plain', their claims are contradicted by the accompanying image indicating that they are without exception 'beautiful'. Likewise the men (or boys) are ruggedly handsome, young versions of James Bond (to the extent that some even wear 'shorty' raincoats with 'turned-up' collars). They have thick eyebrows, smiling eyes, and 'granite' jaws.

While some of the stories seem to be set in London, the majority give no indication of 'locale'. The characters speak without an accent and are usually without family or community ties. They have all left school, but 'work' hovers invisibly in the background as a necessary time filler between one evening and the next or can sometimes be a pathway to glamour, fame or romance. Recognisable 'social' backgrounds are rare. The small town, equated with boredom, is signified through the use of strangely anachronistic symbols – the coffee bar, and the motor-bike and the narrow street. The country, on the other hand, is where the girl escapes *to*, following a broken romance or an unhappy love affair. But when her problems are resolved, she invariably returns to *the city* where things 'really happen'. But it is a city strangely lacking a population that these teenagers inhabit. There are no foreigners, black teenagers, old people or children. No married couples and rarely any families or siblings. It is a world occupied almost solely by young adults on the brink of pairing-up as couples.

The messages which these images and stories together produce are limited and unambiguous, and are repeated endlessly over the years. These are (1) the girl has to fight to *get* and *keep* her man, (2) she can *never* trust another woman unless she is old and 'hideous' in which case she doesn't appear in the stories anyway and (3) despite this, romance, and being a girl, are 'fun'.

No story ever ends with *two* girls alone together and enjoying each other's company. Occasionally the flat-mate or best friend appears in a role as 'confidante' but these appearances are rare and by implication unimportant. A happy ending means a happy couple, a sad one – a single girl. Having eliminated the possibility of strong supportive relationships between girls themselves, and between people of different ages, *Jackie* stories must elevate to dizzy heights the supremacy of the heterosexual romantic partnership.

This is, it may be argued, unsurprising and predictable. But these stories do more than this. They cancel out completely the possibility of any relationship other than the romantic one between girl and boy. They make it impossible for any girl to talk to, or think about, a boy in terms other than those of romance. (A favourite story in both picture form and as a short story, is the 'platonic' relationship which the girl enjoys. She likes him as a friend – but when she is made jealous by his showing an interest in another girl, she realises that it is *really* love that she feels for him and their romance blossoms.)

Boys and men are, then, not sex objects but romantic objects. The code of romance neatly displaces that of sexuality which hovers somewhere in the background appearing fleetingly in the guise of passion, or the 'clinch'. Romance is about the public and *social* effects of and implications of 'love' relationships. That is, it is concerned with impressing one's friends with a new handsome boyfriend, with being flattered by the attention and compliments lavished by admirers. It is about playing games which 'skirt about' sexuality, and which include sexual innuendo, but which are somehow 'nicer', 'cleaner' and less 'sordid'. Romance is the girls' reply to male sexuality. It stands in opposition to their 'just being after the one thing'; and consequently it *makes* sex seem *dirty, sordid,* and *unattractive.* The girl's sexuality is understood and experienced not in terms of a physical need of her own body, but in terms of the romantic attachment. In depicting romantic partnerships, *Jackie* is also therefore constructing male and female roles ensuring that they are separate and as distinct as possible. They are as different as they 'look' different and any interchange between the sexes invariably exudes *romantic* possibilities. What *Jackie* does is to map out all those *differences* which exist between the sexes but to assert that what they do *share* is a common interest, indeed devotion to, 'romance'.

So far, I have outlined in some detail the organising principles around which this discourse (the picture story) is structured. Now, while I would not hold the separation of form and content as being either possible, or necessary for analysis, there are a number of recurring themes which can be identified through a process of extrapolation from both the image and the accompanying text. Thus, temporarily holding constant the formal features of the picture story – the 'balloon' form of dialogue; the action through 'relay'; and the style of illustration – we can go on to deal with the patterns, combinations and permutations of those stock situations which give *Jackie* its characteristic thematic unity.

The stories themselves can be categorised as follows:

(1) the traditional 'love' story;
(2) the romantic/adventure serial;
(3) the 'pop' special (where the story revolves around a famous pop star);
(4) the 'zany' tale; and
(5) the historical romance.

But those story-types are worked through and expounded by the use of certain conventions or devices and it is through these that the thematic structure can be seen most clearly.

The first of these is the convention of '*time*' or of '*the temporal*'. Under this heading four different modes can be categorised, including the *flashback*. Here the opening clips signify 'aloneness' conveyed through images of isolation; a single figure against, say, a rugged, beautiful threatening landscape. Along this same chain of signifieds and following 'aloneness' comes the explanation – that is – 'alone-andrejected-by-a-loved-one', or 'separated-from-a-loved-one'. Next comes the elucidation; what has caused such a state of unhappiness or misery, and this is classified and expounded upon through the use of the *flashback*. 'I remember only a year ago and it was all so ...' 'But Dave was different from the others even then'. The reader is transported into the narrator's past and confronted with scenes of love, tenderness, excitement etc. The difference between the past and present state is emphasised by changes of *season*, and particularly by changes of *expression*. Warm weather, for example, goes with smiling, happy faces gazing in mutual pleasure at one another.

From this point onwards different conventions intervene to carry the story along, and it is neatly concluded with a return to the present, and a 'magical' or intentionally un-magical resolution. (The boy reappears, or doesn't, or a new one takes his place –.)

Through this device the reader is invited to interpret her life, past and present, in terms of romantic attachments – her life has meaning through *him*.

The second temporal device is the diary. Again this allows the reader access to the innermost secrets of its writer, sometimes mediated through a plotting, and a guilty best friend reading her friend's outpourings. But it is the third convention, '*History*', which is without doubt the most popular.

By locating the characters in a specific 'period' the scriptwriter and artist are provided immediately with a whole string of easy, and ideologically constructed, concepts with which they can fill out the plot. History *means* particular *styles of clothing*, '*quaint*' *language, strange customs and rituals*. Thus we have the Victorian heroine connoted through her dress and background dissatisfied with her life and bored by her persistent suitor. When she is transported, magically, into the present she is, however, so horrified by 'liberated' women (policewomen and girls in bikinis) that she is glad to return to her safe and secure environment. Thus, culturally defined notions of the Victorian period are used to glamourise the past and criticise the present which is, by implication, bereft of romance. (Bikinis and uniforms don't connote frailty, passivity and fragility.) *At the same time*, this story is incorporating popularised notions of present phenomena which threaten the established order, and in doing so it is thereby diluting and ridiculing them. [...]

Likewise the Edwardian period, again recognisable through costume and this time carrying connotations of more active women, is used to relate a simple story of love, jealousy and reconciliation, with its participants (literally) carrying out their romances on bicycle saddles.

But history is not just novelty, it is also used to demonstrate the intransigence of much-hallowed social values, and 'natural resistance' to change. When a patrician (in the setting of Ancient Rome) falls for a slave girl he can only die for her thereby allowing her to escape with her slave boyfriend; he cannot escape or be paired off with her. Similarly, when a flower girl is attracted by a gentleman her thoughts only become romantic when she discovers that he is not *really* a gentleman but rather a bohemian artist. A nineteenth-century woman and her child arrive at the doorstep one Christmas but are turned away. Two guests help them and it emerges that the woman is the disinherited daughter of a wealthy man ... The messages are clear; love conquers and simultaneously renders unimportant poverty – which at any rate only 'exists' in the past (and is thus contained and manageable). People marry into their own class and their own race. (When a nurse falls for a wounded German prisoner in wartime Britain she knows her love cannot be fulfilled ... and the prisoner returns to Germany.) Similarly, social class, too 'controversial' an issue to appear in stories set in the present, can be acknowledged as *having* existed in the past.

History then provides the *Jackie* team with a whole set of issues which are more safely dealt with in the past; social problems, social class, foreigners and war. But history also means unchanging *eras* characterised primarily by splendid costumes (the code of fashion), exoticism (language and customs) and adventure. And yet despite this the reader can derive reassurance which lingers on a recognition of the *sameness* which links past and present. Underpinning all the adventures and historical tableaux is *romance*, the young girl in pursuit of it, or being pursued by it. Love, it is claimed, transcends time and is all-important, and history is, again, denied.

The fourth and final temporal device is that of the '*seasons*'. The importance of weather in reflecting 'moods' and creating atmosphere is a feature throughout the stories. 'Love' takes different forms at different times of the year, and holiday romances give way to autumnal 'blues'.

The second set of conventions we will be looking at are those which relate to the exigencies of plot. Thus we have (1) the 'zany' tale where romance is blended with comedy. Here the drawings are less dramatic and are characterised by softer lines. The plots revolve around unusual, unlikely events and coincidences resulting in romantic meetings. At their centre is the 'zany' boy whose bizarre hobbies lead him through a number of disasters until eventually he finds a steady girl who 'tames' him. ('Now they're crazy about each other.')

'Zany' girls of this type are rare. Girls are not really interested in anything outside the confines of femininity, besides which, no girl would willingly make a public spectacle of herself in this way. Often, perhaps instead, animals, always the subject of sentiment, figure strongly in these stories. A camel escapes from the zoo, is caught by a young girl in the city centre who has to await the arrival of the handsome, young, zookeeper. Another favourite centres around the ritual of walking the dog and taking an evening stroll in the local park where numerous handsome young men are doing the same thing or are willing to be pestered by *her* dog – and so on. 'Hmm, funny names you call your cats.'

Again the message is clear – a 'zany' absent-minded boyfriend is a good bet! He is unlikely to spend his time chasing other girls and is indeed incapable of doing so, he is the lovable 'twit', who needs mothering as well as loving. (Some Mothers Do 'Ave 'Em!)

Second, there is the plot which depends on a recognisable social locale. The hospital appears frequently here and carries rich connotations of romance and drama. A girl, for example, is recovering from a throat operation and discovers her boy is going out with someone else, but she overcomes her disappointment by meeting someone new in the hospital.

In another story a dashing young man catches sight of a pretty girl and follows her to her place of work, a bloodbank. Terrified to sign up to give blood he thinks of ways of getting to know her ...

But hospitals are not the only places where romance can happen; at the bus-stop, on the bus, in the park, in the flat downstairs, depending on luck, coincidence or 'stars'. 'He must be on day release ... he's on the train Mondays and Wednesdays but not the rest of the week.' And there is a moral here, if love strikes, or simply happens 'out of the blue' then all the girl needs to do is look out for it, be alert without actively seeking it. In fact this allows her, once again, to remain passive, she certainly can't approach a young man, only a coincidence may bring them together (though she may work on bringing about such a coincidence). At any rate she certainly can't hang about the bus-stop or street corner waiting to be picked up.

This convention of *place* also, by implication, deems leisure facilities for youth unnecessary. There is no need for them, if *your* boy is on the bus or train each morning. There are no stories set in youth clubs, community centres, even libraries or evening classes, and discos only appear as a backdrop where a girl is taken *to* by her boyfriend. Youth means individuals in search of or waiting for a partner and when this occurs all other leisure needs evaporate.

The third convention takes the idea of luck or coincidence one step further by introducing unambiguously *supernatural* devices. This way the reader is invited to share a fantasy, or 'dream come true'. These include magazines, leprechauns, magic lamps and dreams themselves.

But the dream or fantasy occupies a central place in the girls' life anyway – to an extent *all* the picture stories are fantasies, and escapist. Likewise real-life boys are frequently described as 'dreamy'. Daydreaming is an expected 'normal' activity on the part of girls, an adolescent phase. But dreaming of this sort is synonymous with passivity – and as we have already seen, romance is the language of passivity, *par excellence*. The romantic girl, in contrast to the sexual man, is *taken* in a kiss, or embrace. Writing on the development of female sexuality in little girls, Mitchell describes their retreat into the 'Oedipus complex' where the desire *to be loved* can be fulfilled in the comforting and secure environment of the home.[14] Likewise in *Jackie* stories the girl is *chosen*,

'Hmm, this mightn't be so bad after all – if I can get chatting to that little lady later' *is taken* in an embrace,

'Hmm, I could enjoy teaching you, love ... very, very much.'

And is herself waiting *to be loved.*

'I must be a nut! But I'm really crazy about Jay.
If only I could make him care.'

Finally there is the convention based round personal or domestic life. Here the girl is at odds with her family and siblings (who rarely appear in person) and eventually is *saved* by the appearance of a boyfriend. Thus we have a twin, madly jealous of her pretty sister, who tries to 'steal' the sister's boyfriend when she has to stay in bed with flu.

'Story of my life! Just Patsy's twin. He doesn't even know my name, I bet. Just knows me as the other one. The quiet one.'

Another common theme (echoed in the problem page) is the girl with the 'brainy' family. In one case such a girl is seen reading Shakespeare in the park, by a handsome young man. When he begins to take her out she insists on going to art galleries and museums, but gives herself away when his 'clever' friend shows that she doesn't know what she's talking about. Breaking down she admits to reading cheap romances inside the covers of highbrow drama! Through this humiliation and admission of inferiority (the daughter of another 'clever' family) she wins the true love of the boy. So much for *Jackie*'s anti-intellectualism. All the girl needs is a good personality, 'looks' and confidence. Besides which boys don't like feeling threatened by a 'brainy' girl.

Jackie asserts the absolute and natural separation of sex roles. Girls can take humiliation and be all the more attractive for it, as long as they are pretty and unassertive. Boys can *be* footballers, pop stars, even juvenile delinquents, but girls can only be feminine. The girl's life is defined through emotions – jealousy, possessiveness and devotion. Pervading the stories is an elemental fear, fear of losing your boy, or of never getting one. Romance as a code or a way of life, precipitates individual neurosis and prohibits collective action as a means of dealing with it.

By displacing all vestiges or traces of adolescent sexuality and replacing it with concepts of love, passion and eternity, romance gets trapped within its own contradictions, and hence we have the 'problem page'.

Once declared and reciprocated this love is meant to be lasting, and is based on fidelity and pre-marital monogamy. But the girl knows that where *she*, in most cases, will submit to these axioms, there is always the possibility that her boy's passion will, and can be, roused by almost any attractive girl at the bus-stop, outside the home, etc.

The way this paradox is handled is to introduce terms like resignation, despair, fatalism – it's 'all in the game'. Love has its losers, it must be admitted, but for the girl who has lost, there is always the chance that it will happen again, this time with a more reliable boy. Girls don't, then, fight back. Female 'flirts' always come to a 'bad end'; they are abandoned by their admirers who quickly turn their attention to the quiet, trusting best friend who had always been content to sit in the background.

Conclusion

What, then, are the central features of *Jackie* in so far as it presents its readers with an ideology of adolescent femininity? First it sets up, defines and focuses exclusively on 'the personal', locating it as the sphere of *prime* importance to the teenage girl. It presents this as a totality – and by implication all else is of secondary interest to the 'modern girl'. Romance problems, fashion, beauty and pop mark out the limits of the girl's concern – other possibilities are ignored or dismissed.

Second, *Jackie* presents 'romantic individualism' as the ethos, *par excellence*, for the teenage girl. The *Jackie* girl is alone in her quest for love; she refers back to her female peers for advice, comfort and reassurance *only* when she has problems in fulfilling this aim. Female solidarity, or more simply the idea of girls together – in *Jackie* terms – is an unambiguous sign of failure. To achieve self-respect, the girl has to escape the 'bitchy', 'catty' atmosphere of female company and find a boyfriend as fast as possible. But in doing this she has not only to be individualistic in outlook – she has to be prepared to fight ruthlessly – by plotting, intrigue and cunning, to 'trap her man'. Not surprisingly this independent-mindedness is short-lived. As soon as she finds a 'steady', she must renounce it altogether and capitulate to *his* demands, acknowledging his domination and resigning herself to her own subordination.

This whole ideological discourse, as it takes shape through the pages of *Jackie*, is immensely powerful. Judging by sales figures alone, *Jackie* is a force to be reckoned with by feminists. Of course this does not mean that its readers swallow its axioms unquestioningly. And indeed until we have a clearer idea of just how girls 'read' *Jackie* and encounter its ideological force, our analysis remains one-sided.

For feminists a related question must be how to go about countering *Jackie* and undermining its ideological power at the level of *cultural* intervention. One way of beginning this task would be for feminist teachers and youth leaders to involve girls in the task of 'deconstructing' this seemingly 'natural' ideology; and in breaking down the apparently timeless qualities of girls' and women's 'mags'.

Another more adventurous possibility would be the joint production of an alternative; a magazine where girls are depicted in situations other than the romantic, and where sexuality is discussed openly and frankly; not just contraception, masturbation and abortion, but the *social relations* of sexuality, especially the sexism of their male peers. Likewise girls would be encouraged to create their own music, learn instruments and listen to music without having to drool over idols. Their clothes would not simply reflect styles created by men to transform them into junior sex-objects, products of male imaginations and fantasies. But most of all, readers would be presented with an *active* image of female adolescence – one which pervades every page and is not just deceptively 'frozen' into a single 'energetic/glamorous' pose as in the fashion pages and Tampax adverts in *Jackie*.

Notes

Source: Stencilled Occasional Paper, Women Series SP No. 53, CCCS, Birmingham. © Centre for Contemporary Cultural Studies, University of Birmingham, and A. McRobbie.

1 See G.L. White, *Women's Magazines*, 1963–1968 (1970), Appendix IV.
2 See G. Rosei, 'The Private Life of Lord Snooty', *Sunday Times Magazine*, 29 July 1973, pp. 8–16.
3 L. Althusser, 'Ideology and Ideological State Apparatuses: Notes Toward an Investigation' in *Lenin and Philosophy, and Other Essays* (New Left Books, London, 1971), p. 163.
4 A. Dorfman and A. Mattelart, *How to Read Donald Duck* (I.G. Editions Inc., New York, 1975), p. 30.
5 P. Johnson, *New Statesman*, 1964.
6 C. Alderson, *The Magazines Teenagers Read* (Pergamon Press, Oxford, 1968), p. 3.
7 P. Willis, 'Symbolism and Practice: a Theory for the Social Meaning of Pop Music', Centre for Contemporary Cultural Studies, stencilled paper no. 2, p. 2.
8 Ibid., p. 1.

9 J. Clarke, S. Hall, T. Jefferson and B. Roberts (eds.), *Resistance Through Rituals* (Hutchinson, London, 1976), p. 55.

10 S. Hall, B. Lumley and G. McLennan, 'Politics and Ideology: Gramsci', *Working Papers in Cultural Studies*, no. 10 (1977), p. 51.

11 Ibid., p. 51.

12 R. Hoggart, *The Uses of Literacy* (Chatto and Windus, London, 1957), p. 51.

13 G. Greer, *The Female Eunuch* (Paladin, London, 1970), p. 173.

14 See J. Mitchell, *Psychoanalysis and Feminism* (Penguin, Harmondsworth, 1974).

7

Girls and Subcultures (1975)

with Jenny Garber

Very little seems to have been written about the role of girls in youth cultural groupings. They are absent from the classic subcultural ethnographic studies, the pop histories, the personal accounts and the journalistic surveys of the field. When girls do appear, it is either in ways which uncritically reinforce the stereotypical image of women with which we are now so familiar ... for example, Fyvel's reference, in his study of teddy boys,[1] to 'dumb, passive teenage girls, crudely painted' ... or else they are fleetingly and marginally presented:

It is as if everything that relates only to us comes out in footnotes to the main text, as worthy of the odd reference. We come on the agenda somewhere between 'Youth' and 'Any Other Business'. We encounter ourselves in men's cultures as 'by the way' and peripheral. According to all the reflections we are not really there.[2]

How do we make sense of this invisibility? Are girls really not present in youth subcultures? Or is it something in the way this kind of research is carried out that renders them invisible? When girls are acknowledged in the literature, it tends to be in terms of their sexual attractiveness. But this, too, is difficult to interpret. For example, Paul Willis comments on the unattached girls who hung around with the motor-bike boys he was studying, as follows: 'What seemed to unite them was a common desire for an attachment to a male and a common inability to attract a man to a long-term relationship. They tended to be scruffier and less attractive than the attached girls.'[3]

Is this simply a typically dismissive treatment of girls reflecting the natural rapport between a masculine researcher and his male respondents? Or is it that the researcher who is, after all, studying the motor-bike boys, finds it difficult not to take the boys' attitudes to and evaluation of the girls, seriously? He therefore reflects this in his descriptive language and he unconsciously adopts it in the context of the research situation. Willis later comments on the girls' responses to his questions. They are unforthcoming, unwilling to talk and they retreat, in giggles, into the background ... Are these responses to the man as a researcher or are they the result of the girls' recognition that 'he' identifies primarily with 'them'? Is this characteristic of the way in which girls customarily negotiate the spaces provided for them in a male-dominated and male-defined culture? And does this predispose them to retreat, especially when it is also a situation in which they are being assessed and labelled according to their sexual attributes?

It is certainly the case that girls do not behave in this way in all mixed-sex situations. In the classroom, for example, girls will often display a great show of feminine strength from which men and boys will retreat. It may well be that in Willis's case the girls simply felt awkward and self-conscious about being asked questions in a situation where they did not feel particularly powerful or important, especially if they were not the steady girl-friends of the boys in question.

What follows is a tentative attempt to sketch some of the ways we might think about and research the relationship between girls and subcultures. Many of the concepts utilised in the study of male subcultures are retained: for example, the centrality of class, the importance of school, work, leisure and the family: the general social context within which the subcultures have emerged, and the structural changes in postwar British society which partially define the different subcultures. Added to these issues are the important questions of sex and gender. The crucial question is: How does this dimension reshape the field of youth cultural studies as it has come to be defined?

It has been argued recently, for example, that class is a critical variable in defining the different subcultural options available to middle-class and working-class boys. Middle-class subcultures offer more full-time careers, whereas working-class subcultures tend to be restricted to the leisure sphere. This structuring of needs and options must also work at some level for girls. It might be easier for middle-class hippie girls, for example, to find an 'alternative' career in the counter-culture than it would be for working-class skinhead girls to find a job in that culture. Some subcultural patterns are therefore true for both boys and girls, while others are much more gender-divergent.

It might even be the case that girls are not just marginal to the postwar youth cultures but located structurally in an altogether different position. If women are marginal to the male cultures of work, it is because they are central and pivotal to a subordinate sphere. They are marginal to work because they are central to the family. The marginality of girls in these 'spectacular' male-focused subcultures might redirect our attention away from this arena towards more immediately recognisable teenage and pre-teenage female spheres like those forming around teenybop stars and the pop-music industry.

Bearing this in mind it is possible to identify a number of key questions to which subsequent work can be addressed:

- Are they present but invisible?
- Where present and visible, are their roles the same, but more marginal than boys, or are they quite different?
- Is the position of girls specific to the subcultural option, or do their roles reflect the more general social subordination of women in mainstream culture?
- If subcultural options are not readily available to girls, what are the different but complementary ways in which girls organise their cultural life?
- Are these, in their own terms, subcultural?

Girls' subcultures may have become invisible because the very term 'subculture' has acquired such strong masculine overtones.

Are Girls Really Absent from Subcultures?

The most obvious factor which makes this question difficult to answer is the domination of sociological work (as is true of most areas of scholarship) by men. Paradoxically, the exclusion of women was as characteristic of the new radical theories of deviance and delinquency as it had been of traditional criminology. The editors of *Critical Criminology* argue that the new deviancy theory often amounted to a 'celebration rather than an analysis of the deviant form with which the deviant theorist could vicariously identify – an identification by powerless intellectuals with deviants who appeared more successful in controlling events.'[4] With the possible exception of sexual deviance, women constituted an uncelebrated social category, for radical and critical theorists. This general invisibility was of course cemented by the social reaction to the more extreme manifestations of youth subcultures. The popular press and media concentrated on the sensational incidents associated with each subculture (for example, the teddy-boy killings, the Margate clashes between mods and rockers). One direct consequence of the fact that it is always the violent aspects of a phenomenon which qualify as newsworthy is that these are precisely the areas of subcultural activity from which women have tended to be excluded. The objective and popular image of a subculture is likely to be one which emphasises male membership, male focal concerns and masculine values. When women appear within the broad framework of a moral panic it is usually in more innocuous roles. The fears of rampant promiscuity which emerged with the hippy culture brought to the fore the involvement of girls and women in the 'love-ins' and 'orgies'. While this was roundly condemned and taken as a sign of declining moral values as well as of personal degradation and irresponsibility, the 'entertainment value', taken together with the lingering resonances of 1960s sexual liberalism, balanced out and even blunted the hard edge of the cries of horror of the moral guardians.

Are Girls Present but Invisible?

For all these reasons, female invisibility or partial visibility in youth subcultures takes on the qualities of the self-fulfilling prophecy. Perhaps women and girls have played only a minor role in these groupings. The exclusive attention paid to male expressions and male styles nonetheless reinforces and amplifies this image of the subculture as a male formation. Texts and images suggest, for example, that girls were involved with and considered themselves as part of the teddy-boy subculture. Girls can be seen in footage from the 1950s dancing with teddy-boys at the Elephant and Castle; they can also be seen in the background in the news pictures taken during the Notting Hill race riots of 1958. There are however many reasons why, to working-class girls in the late 1950s, this was not a particularly attractive option.

Though girls participated in the general rise in the disposable income available to youth in the 1950s, girls' wages were not as high as those of boys.[5] Patterns of spending were also structured in a different direction. Girls' magazines emphasised a particularly feminine mode of consumption and the working-class girl, though actively participating in the world of work, remained more focused on home and marriage than her male counterpart. Teddy-boy culture was an escape from the claustrophobia of the family, into the street and 'caff'. While many girls might adopt an appropriate way of dressing, complementary to the teds, they would be much less likely to spend the same amount of time hanging about on the streets. Girls had to be careful not to 'get into trouble' and excessive loitering on street corners might be taken as a sexual invitation to the boys. The double standard was probably more rigidly maintained in the 1950s than in any other time since then. The difficulty in obtaining effective contraception, the few opportunities to spend time unsupervised with members of the opposite sex, the financial dependency of the working-class woman on her husband, meant that a good reputation mattered above everything else. As countless novels of the moment record, neighbourhoods flourished on rumours and gossip and girls who spent too much time on the street were assumed to be promiscuous.[6]

At the same time the expanding leisure industries were directing their attention to *both* boys and girls. Girls were as much the subject of attention as their male peers when it came to pin-up pictures, records, and magazines. Girls could use these items and activities in a different context from those in which boys used them. Cosmetics of course were to be worn outside the home, at work and on the street, as well as in the dance-hall. But the rituals of trying on clothes, and experimenting with hair-styles and make-up were home-based activities. It might be suggested that girls' culture of the time operated within the vicinity of the home, or the friends' home. There was room for a great deal of the new teenage consumer culture within the confines of the girls' bedrooms. Teenage girls did participate in the new public sphere afforded by the growth of the leisure industries, but they could also consume at home, upstairs in their bedrooms.

The involvement of girls in the teddy-boy subculture was sustained therefore by a complementary but different pattern. What girls who considered themselves 'teddy-girls', did, and how they acted, was possibly exactly the same as their more conventional non-subcultural friends. It is gender therefore which structures differences rather than subcultural attachment. The same process can be seen at work in the emergence of rock and pop music. Girls and boys, in or out of subcultures, responded differently to this phenomenon. Boys tended to have a more participative and a more technically informed relationship with pop, where girls in contrast became fans and readers of pop-influenced love comics.

This pattern accelerates within the subcultures. If we look at a hard, male-oriented working-class subculture like the skinheads of the 1970s, we can see small groups of girls on the sidelines, as girlfriends or hangers-on. There is no evidence to suggest that these girls are as involved in 'aggro' as their male peers, even though their feminine image is a great deal more aggressive and less feminine than that of the teddy-girls was, some fifteen years earlier. If we follow the skinheads through their various evolutions, revivals and attachments up and down the country, the picture that emerges is one of an overwhelmingly male grouping. The recognition in the popular press that girls were present in some of the skinhead skirmishes tells us more about the increasing visibility of women in general in society, than it does about an upsurge in female violence.

What broad factors might have created a situation where girls could find subcultural involvement an attractive possibility? The emergence of a softer more feminised subculture in the 1960s, might well have opened the doors to female participation. There were certainly thousands of 'mod' girls who made their appearance in the nightclubs, on the streets, at work and even on the fringes of the clashes between the mods and rockers during the various Bank holiday weekends throughout the mid-1960s (and remembered in the film *Quadrophenia)*. It may well be that the mod preoccupation with style and the emergence of the unisex look and the 'effeminate' mod man, gave girls a more legitimate place in the subculture than had previously been the case.

This trend was confirmed and extended as mod moved towards the consumerist mainstream, and as it began to give way simultaneously to the hippy underground and psychedelia. In this space, inhabited largely though not exclusively by middle-class youth, we also find women taking on a much higher profile. As 1960s unisex gave way to hippie sexual ambiguity and then to mid-1970s high-camp glitter rock, we can see that both girls themselves and femininity as a representational form became more acceptable within the prevailing vocabulary of youth subcultures. However the feminising of the male image as seen in the iconography of Bowie or Jagger or even Gary Glitter, should not blind us to the asymmetry which remains in relation to the feminine image. There is much less sexual fluidity permitted to girls. The girl is by definition 'forever feminine.'

In short, the evidence about how active and present girls are in the main postwar subcultures is difficult to interpret conclusively. It seems to be the case that girls organise their social life as an alternative to the kinds of risks and qualifications involved in entering into the mainstream of male subcultural life.

Where Girls Are Visible, What Are Their Roles and Do These Reflect the General Subordination of Women in Culture?

Three selected images – the motor-bike girl, the 'mod' girl, and the hippy – will have to do here: where girls are present, but where the way they are present suggests that their cultural subordination is retained and reproduced.

Motor-bike girl

The motor-bike girl, leather-clad, a sort of subcultural pin-up heralding – as it appeared in the press – a new and threatening sort of sexuality. This image was often used as a symbol of the new permissive sexuality of the 1960s and was encapsulated in the figure of Brigitte Bardot astride a motor-bike with her tousled hair flying behind her. More mundanely this image encoded female sexuality in a modern, bold and abrasive way. With matte pan-stick lips, an insolent expression on her eyelined eyes and an unzipped jacket, the model looked sexual, numbed and unfeeling, almost expressionless. This was an image therefore at odds with conventional femininity and suggestive of sexual deviance. At the same time this very image was utilised in advertising and in soft pornography, an example of how – within the repertoire of subcultural representations – girls and women have always been located nearer to the point of consumerism than to the 'ritual of resistance.'

In rocker or motor-bike culture this sexualised image of a girl riding a bike remained a fantasy rather than a reality. Girls were rarely if ever seen at the handles and instead were ritualistically installed on the back seat. If Paul Willis is right, few girls ever penetrated to the symbolic heart of the culture – to the detailed knowledge of the machine, to the camaraderie and competition between the riders.[7] A girl's membership seemed to depend entirely on whose girlfriend she was. In the Hell's Angels groups, where the dynamics of the subculture were even more strenuously masculine, girls occupied particular, institutionalised roles. Hunter Thompson suggests that the Angels treated their women primarily as sexual objects. If they were not objects of the gang-bang' the only other role open to them was that of a 'Mama'.[8]

The mod girl

Mod culture offers a more complex subcultural opportunity for girls, if for no other reason than that it was located in and sprang from the mainstream of working-class teenage consumerism. In the mid- to late 1960s there were more teenage girls at work and there were new occupations in the distribution and service sector, particularly in the urban centres. Jobs in the new boutiques, in the beauty business and in clothing as well as in the white-collar sector all involved some degree of dressing up. It was from the mid-1960s onwards that the girls behind the counter in the new boutiques were expected to reflect the image of the shop and thus provide a kind of model or prototype for the young consumer. Glamour and status in these fields often compensated for long hours and low wages. Full employment and freedom to 'look the part' at work, encouraged greater freedom in domestic life. Tom Wolfe's accurate and vivid account of mod girls in London describes how many of these girls were living in flats and bedsits, a pattern hitherto unknown for working-class girls.[9] These factors made it more likely that girls got involved in mod culture than might otherwise have been the case.

Because mod style was in a sense quietly imperceptible to those unaware of its fine nuances, involvement was more easily accommodated into the normal routines of home, school and work. There was less likelihood of provoking an angry parental reaction since the dominant look was neat, tidy and apparently unthreatening. Parents and teachers knew that girls looked 'rather odd these days, with their white drawn faces and cropped hair', but as Dave Laing noted 'there was something in the way they moved which adults couldn't make out.'[10] The fluidity and ambiguity of the subculture meant that a girl could be around, could be a 'face' without necessarily being attached to a boy. Participation was almost wholly reliant on wearing the right clothes, having the right hair-style and going to the right clubs. With this combination right, the girl was a mod. Like her male counterpart, the mod girl demonstrated the same fussiness for detail in clothes, the same over-attention to appearance. Facial styles emphasised huge, darkened eyes and body-style demanded thinness.

It may be that mod girls came to the attention of the commentators and journalists because of the general 'unisex' connotations of the subculture. The much mentioned effeminacy of the boys drew attention to the boyish femininity of the girls, best exemplified in the early fashion shots of Twiggy. An absence of exaggerated masculinity like that displayed in the rocker subculture or by Willis's motor-bike boys, made the mod subculture both exciting and accessible to girls. Like their female counterparts, these boys were more likely to be employed in white-collar office work than in unskilled manual jobs. This greater visibility of girls in the subculture, single or attached, has also got to be seen in terms of the increasing visibility and confidence of teenage girls in the 1960s, working-class and middle class. Mod culture tippled easily into 'Swinging London' whose favourite image was the 'liberated' dolly-bird. The Brooke clinics opened in 1964 making the pill available to single girls and this facility also affected the sexual confidence not just of the middleclass girls in the universities but also of the working-class girls living in London's bedsitter-land.

However this new prominence and confidence should not be interpreted too loosely. The presence of 'girls' in the urban panoramas of trendy fashion photography, the new-found autonomy and sexual freedom, have got to be set alongside the other material factors which still shaped and determined their lives. This independence reflected short-term rather than long-term affluence. The jobs which provided the extra cash afforded immediate access to consumer goods, but few opportunities for promotion or further training. There is nothing to suggest that participation in the mod subculture changed the social expectations of girls, or loosened the bonds between mothers and daughters, even if they were living in flats. These girls had been educated under the shadow of the Newsom Report and had therefore been encouraged to consider marriage their real careers.[11]

The hippy

The term 'hippy' is of course an umbrella term, covering a variety of diverse groupings and tendencies. However it is most likely that girls would have entered this subculture through the social life afforded by the universities in the late 1960s and early 1970s. Access to prolonged higher education gives the middle-class girl the space, by right, which her working-class counterpart is denied or else gains only through following a more illegitimate route. The flat or the room in the hall of residence provides the female student with space to experiment, time of her own, and relatively unsupervised leisure. She also has three or four years during which marriage is pushed into the background. The lack of strict demarcation between work and leisure also allows for – indeed encourages – the development of a more uniquely personal style. The middle-class girl can express herself in dress without having to take into account the restrictions of work.

Nonetheless, traditional sex roles prevailed in the hippy subculture as numerous feminist authors have described. Femininity moved imperceptibly between the 'earth-mother', the pre-Raphaelite mystic, the kind of 'goddess' serenaded by Bob Dylan, and the dreamy fragility of Marianne Faithful. Media representations and especially visual images, of course, have to be read and interpreted with care. Moral panics around 'dirty hippies' frequently drew attention to the presence of girls and to the sexual immorality of commune-living. The images which linger tend also to suggest excessive femininity and 'quiet restraint' as demonstrated in the figure of Joni Mitchell. A still more dramatic rejection of the feminine image in the early 1970s carried a self-destructive element in it, as the addiction and eventual death of Janis Joplin shows. Although the range of available and acceptable images of femininity tended to confirm already-existing stereotypes, none the less the hippy under ground, set against a background of widespread social protest and youthful revolt, also represented an empowering space for women.

Within its confines and even on the pages of the underground press, the first murmurings of feminism were heard.[12]

Do Girls Have Alternative Ways of Organising Their Cultural Life?

The important question may not be the absence or presence of girls in male subcultures, but the complementary ways in which young girls interact among themselves and with each other to form a distinctive culture of their own, one which is recognised by and catered to in the girls' weekly comics and magazines. For example 'teenybopper' culture, based round an endless flow of young male pop stars, is a long-standing feature of post-war girls' culture. Where this kind of cultural form is markedly different from the male subcultures, is in its commercial origins. It is an almost totally packaged cultural commodity. It emerges from within the heart of the popmusic business and relies on the magazines, on radio and TV for its wide appeal. As a result it seems to carry less of the creative elements associated with the working-class youth subcultures considered by male sociologists like those mentioned above. However, teenybopper stars carry socially exclusive connotations and opportunities for their fans. The more other sectors of the population, including teenage boys, older adolescents, and parents, dislike and even despise these bland and pretty-looking young men, the more 11–13-year-old girls love them. The teenybopper phenomenon of the 1970s grew up around this very young age group who, it seemed, were not being addressed by the pop mainstream. At the same time the attraction of stars like David Cassidy for the media industries lay not just in the profits from songs but from the rights film and TV companies held over TV series and film appearances. Teenybopper was, and has been, big business from the start.

Mainstream taste like that evidenced in the popularity of stars like Cassidy and the Osmonds and, in Britain, the Bay City Rollers, could easily be seen as reflective therefore of a kind of cultural conservatism. Girls may be easy customers to please, they are happy to go along with the easiest, least aggressive, least rebellious and most manufactured kind of pop culture. This, however, is a much too simplistic way of accounting for what is in fact a much less passive (and much ridiculed) form of hero-worship. There is more to teenybopper culture than mere gazing in adoration at *Jackie* pin-ups. Even in so manufactured a form of pop culture we can locate a variety of negotiative processes at work:

1. Young pre-teen girls have access to less freedom than their brothers. Because they are deemed to be more at risk on the streets from attack, assault, or even abduction, parents tend to be more protective of their daughters than they are of their sons (who, after all have to learn to defend themselves at some point, as men). Teenybopper culture takes these restrictions into account. Participation is not reliant on being

able to spend time outside the home on the streets. Instead teeny-bopper styles can quite easily be accommodated into school-time or leisure-time spent in the home. Being a Cassidy fan or a Bay City Roller fan requires only occasional trips to live concerts (most of which finish conveniently early to allow the fans to get home).

2. There are few restrictions in relation to joining this mainstream and commercially based subculture. It carries no strict rules and requires no special commitment to internally generated ideas of 'cool'. Nor does it rely on a lot of money. Its uniforms are cheap, its magazines are well within the pocket-money weekly budget, its records are affordable and its concerts are sufficiently rare to be regarded as treats.

3. Membership carries relatively few personal risks. For girls of this age real boys remain a threatening and unknown quantity. Sexual experience is something most girls of all social classes want to hold off for some time in the future. They know, however, that going out with boys invariably carries the possibility of being expected to kiss, or 'pet'. The fantasy boys of pop make no such demands. They 'love' their fans without asking anything in return. The pictures which adorn bedroom walls invite these girls to look, and even stare at length, at male images (many of which emphasise the whole masculine physique, especially the crotch). These pin-ups offer one of the few opportunities to stare at boys and to get to know what they look like. While boys can quite legitimately look at girls on the street and in school, it is not acceptable for girls to do the same back. Hence the attraction of the long uninterrupted gaze at the life-size 'Donny Osmond Special'.

4. The kind of fantasies which girls construct around these figures play the same kind of role as ordinary daydreams. Narrative fantasies about bumping into David Cassidy in the supermarket, or being chosen out by him from the front row of a concert, both carry a strongly sexual element, and are also means of being distracted from the demands of work or school or other aspects of experience which might be perceived as boring or unrewarding.

5. Girls who define themselves actively within these teenybopper sub-cultures are indeed being *active*, even though the familiar iconography seems to reproduce traditional gender stereotypes with the girl as the passive fan, and the star as the active male. These girls are making

statements about themselves as consumers of music, for example. If the next record is boring or simply bad, the future of the star is in jeopardy. If the stars are seen to disregard the fans, they are likely to lose their place in both the charts and the popularity stakes. Finally and most importantly, teenybopper culture offers girls a chance to define themselves as different from and apart from both their younger and their older counterparts. They are no longer little girls and not yet teenage girls. Yet this potentially awkward and anonymous space can be, and is transformed into a site of active feminine identity.

Conclusion

Female participation in youth cultures can best be understood by moving away from the 'classic' subcultural terrain marked out as oppositional and creative by numerous sociologists. Girls negotiate a different leisure space and different personal spaces from those inhabited by boys. These in turn offer them different possibilities for 'resistance', if indeed that is the right word to use. Some of the cultural forms associated with pre-teenage girls, for example, can be viewed as responses to their perceived status as girls and to their anxieties about moving into the world of teenage sexual interaction. One aspect of this can be seen in the extremely tight-knit friendship groups formed by girls. A function of the social exclusiveness of such groupings is to gain private, inaccessible space. This in turn allows pre-pubertal girls, to remain seemingly inscrutable to the outside world of parents, teachers, youth workers and boys as well. Teenybopper subcultures could be interpreted as ways of buying time, within the commercial mainstream, from the real world of sexual encounters while at the same time imagining these encounters, with the help of the images and commodities supplied by the commercial mainstream, from the safe space of the all-female friendship group.

Notes

This article originally appeared in *Resistance through Rituals*, ed. Stuart Hall and Tony Jefferson, London, Hutchinson, 1976.

1 T. R. Fyvel, *The Insecure Offenders,* London, Chatto & Windus, 1963.
2 S. Rowbotham, *Woman's Consciousness, Man's World,* Harmondsworth, Pelican, 1973.

3 P. Willis, *Profane Culture,* London, Chatto & Windus, 1977.

4 I. Taylor, P. Walton and J. Young (eds), *Critical Criminology,* London, Routledge & Kegan Paul, 1975.

5 M. Abrams, *The Teenage Consumer,* London, Press Exchange, 1959.

6 See, for example, A. Sillitoe, *Saturday Night and Sunday Morning,* Harmondsworth, Penguin, 1959

7 Willis, *Profane Culture.*

8 H. Thompson, *Hell's Angels,* Harmondsworth, Penguin, 1967

9 T. Wolfe, 'The Noonday "Underground', in *The Pump House Gang,* Bantam Books, New York, 1968.

10 D. Laing, *The Sound of Our Time,* London, Sheed & Ward, 1969.

11 J. H. Newsom, *Half Our Future: A Report,* London, HMSO, 1963.

12 See, for example, issues of *Black Dwarf.*

8

Settling Accounts with Subculture: A Feminist Critique (1979)

Although 'youth culture' and the 'sociology of youth' – and particularly critical and Marxist perspectives on them – have been central strands in the development of cultural studies over the past fifteen years, the emphasis from the earliest work of the National Deviancy Conference (NDC) onwards has remained consistently on *male* youth cultural forms.[1] There have been studies of the relation of male youth to class and class culture, to the machinery of the State, and to the school, community and workplace. Football has been analysed as a male sport, drinking as a male form of leisure, the law and the police as patriarchal structures concerned with young male (potential) offenders. I do not know of a study that considers, never mind prioritises, *youth* and the family. This failure by subcultural theorists to dislodge the male connotations of 'youth' inevitably poses problems for those who are involved in teaching about those questions. As they cannot use the existing texts 'straight,' what other options do they have?

One is to dismiss the existing literature as irrevocably male-biased and to shift attention towards the alternative terrain of girls' culture, to the construction of ideologies about girlhood as articulated in and through various institutions and cultural forms – in schools, in the family, in law and in the popular media.[2] The danger of this course is that the opportunity may be missed of grappling with questions which, examined from a feminist perspective, can increase our understanding of masculinity, male culture and sexuality, and their place within class culture. This then is the other option: to combine a clear commitment to the analysis of girls' culture with a direct engagement with youth culture as it is constructed in sociological and cultural studies. Rather than simply being dismissed, the subcultural 'classics' should be re-read critically so that questions hitherto ignored or waved aside in embarrassment become central. An examination of their weaknesses and shortcomings can raise questions of immediate political relevance for feminists. What, for example, is the nature of women's and girls' leisure? What role do hedonism, fantasy escapes and imaginary solutions play in their lives? What access to these spheres and symbols do women have anyway?

In this article I am going to explore some questions about youth culture and subcultures by attempting this sort of feminist re-reading of two recent books, Paul Willis's *Learning to Labour* and Dick Hebdige's *Subculture*. The point, therefore, is not to condemn them – they represent the most sophisticated accounts to date of youth culture and style – but to read 'across' them to see what they say (or fail to say) about working-class male sexuality, bravado and the sexual ambiguity of style. Willis investigates the relation for a group of 'lads' between working-class-youth cultural gestures and the places to which they are allocated in production. The expressions of resistance and opposition which characterise this relation are fraught with contradiction. Willis suggests that the vocabulary articulating their distance from structures of authority in school and workplace simultaneously binds the 'lads' to the basically rigid positions they occupy in these spheres; their rowdy shouts of disaffiliation quickly become cries of frustration and incorporation. A particular mode of class culture is thus seen in a complex way to serve two masters ... capital *and* labour. The emphasis of Hebdige's *Subculture* is quite different. He focuses elliptically on subcultural style as *signifier* rather than as a series of distinct cultural expressions. Style, he claims, takes place several steps away from the material conditions of its followers' existence and continually resists precise historical analysis. One of its objectives, then, is to be forever out of joint with mainstream dominant culture: it evaporates just as it crystallises.

Willis and Hebdige both show how male adolescents take already-coded materials from their everyday landscapes (and, though this is not spelt out, from their fantasies) and mould them into desirable shapes, into social practices and stylish postures. Both accounts draw on the notion that control and creativity are exercised from within subordinate class positions and that, as a result of this subordination, cultural gestures often appear in partial, contradictory and even amputated forms. These insights can be taken further by focusing on the language of adolescent male sexuality embedded in these texts. Questions around sexism and working-class youth and around sexual violence make it possible to see how class and patriarchal relations work together, sometimes with an astonishing brutality and at other times in the 'teeth-gritting harmony' of romance, love and marriage. One of Willis's 'lads' says of his girlfriend, 'She loves doing fucking housework. Trousers I brought up yesterday, I took 'em up last night and her turned 'em up for me. She's as good as gold and I wanna get married as soon as I can.'[3] Until we come to grips with such expressions as they appear across the subcultural field, our portrayal of girls' culture will remain one-sided and youth culture will continue to 'mean' in uncritically masculine terms. Questions about girls, sexual relations and femininity in youth will continue to be defused or marginalised in the ghetto of Women's Studies.

Silences

One of the central tenets of the women's movement has been that the personal is political. Feminists recognise the close links between personal experience and the areas chosen for study – autobiographies invade and inform a great deal of what is written. Even if the personal voice of the author is not apparent throughout the text, she will at least announce her interest in, and commitment to, her subject in an introduction or foreword. Although few radical (male) sociologists would deny the importance of the personal in precipitating social and political awareness, to admit how their own experience has influenced their choice of subject-matter (the politics of selection) seems more or less taboo. This silence is particularly grating in the literature on the hippie and drug countercultures, where it seems to have been stage-managed only through a suspiciously exaggerated amount of methodological justification.[4]

It is not my intention here to read between the lines of writing about subcultures and unravel the half-written references, the elliptical allusions and the 1960s rock lyrics. The point is that this absence of self (this is quite different from the authorial 'I' or 'we') and the invalidating of personal experience in the name of the more objective social sciences goes hand in hand with the silencing of other areas, which are for feminists of the greatest importance. It is no coincidence, for example, that while the sociologies of deviance and youth were blooming in the early 1970s, the sociology of the family – still steeped in the structural-functionalism of Talcott Parsons – was everybody's least favourite option. If we look for the structured absences in this youth literature, it is the sphere of family and domestic life that is missing. No commentary on the hippies dealt with the countercultural sexual division of labour, let alone the hypocrisies of 'free love'; few writers seemed interested in what happened when a mod went home after a weekend on speed. Only what happened on the streets mattered.

Perhaps these absences should be understood historically. The sociology of crime/deviance/youth culture was one of the first areas from which the hegemony of Parsonianism was challenged. Many of the radical young sociologists in the vanguard of this attack were recruited from the New Left, from the student movement of the late 1960s and even from the hippie counterculture. At this time, before the emergence of the women's movement in the early 1970s, the notions of escaping from the family, the bourgeois commitments of children and the whole sphere of family consumption formed a distinct strand in left politics. Sheila Rowbotham has described how women were seen in some left-wing circles as a temptation provided by 'capital' to divert workers and militants alike from the real business of revolution, and she has also shown how hypocritical these anti-family, anti-women platitudes were.[5] Clearly things have changed since then but, although the work of the feminists has enabled studies of the family to transcend functionalism, the literature on subcultures and youth culture has scarcely begun to deal with the contradictions that patterns of cultural resistance pose in relation to women. The writers, having defined themselves as against the family and the trap of romance as well as against the boredom of the meaningless labour, seem to be drawn to look at other, largely working-class, groups who appear to be doing the same thing.

In documenting the temporary flights of the teds, mods or rockers, however, they fail to show that it is much more difficult for women to escape (even temporarily) and that these symbolic flights have often been at the expense of women (especially mothers) and girls. The lads may get by with each other alone on the streets but they did not eat, sleep or make love there. Their peer-group consciousness and pleasure frequently seem to hinge on a collective disregard for women and the sexual exploitation of girls. And in the literary sensibility of urban romanticism that resonates across most youth cultural discourses, girls are allowed little more than the back seat on a draughty motor-bike:

> Just wrap your legs around these velvet rims
> And strap your hands across my engines
> We'll run till we drop baby we'll never go back
> I'm just a scared and lonely rider
> But I gotta know how it feels.[6]

Writing about subcultures is not the same thing as being in one. Nonetheless, it is easy to see how it would be possible in sharing some of the same symbols – the liberating release of rock music, the thrill of speed, of alcohol or even of football – to be blinded in some of their more oppressive features.

I have oversimplified in this account, of course – there is a whole range of complicating factors. First, feminists also oppose the same oppressive structures as the radical sociologists and have visions of alternative modes of organising domestic life – although ones which are *primarily* less oppressive of women, because historically women have always suffered the greatest exploitation, the greatest isolation in the home. Second, to make sense of the literature on subculture *purely* in terms of male left identification with male working-class youth groups would mean devaluing the real political commitment behind the work and ignoring its many theoretical achievements. The attempts to explain the ways in which class fears on the part of the dominant class have been inflected during the postwar period onto sectors of working-class youth – and dealt with at this level – remains of vital significance; also important has been the ascription of a sense of dignity and purpose, an integrity and a rationale, to that section of youth commonly labelled 'animals' in the popular media. Third, there have been political and theoretical developments. The NDC of the late 1960s grew out of a libertarianism which rejected both reformist and old left politics in favour of 'grass-roots' politics (especially cultural and 'alternative' politics) and which emphasised the importance of community work and action research.[7] Many of these ideas have since been refined in an engagement with the work of Althusser and of Gramsci.

Yet the question of sexual division still remains more or less unexplored. In *Learning to Labour*, Paul Willis convincingly argues that the culture which the lads bring to the school and workplace and its consequent relation to the position they occupy in the labour hierarchy provides the key to many of the more contradictory aspects of male working-class culture. But what do these expressions mean for girls and female working-class culture? One striking feature of Willis's study is how unambiguously degrading to women is the language of aggressive masculinity through which the lads kick against the oppressive structures they inhabit – the text is littered with references of the utmost brutality. One teacher's authority is undermined by her being labelled a 'cunt'. Boredom in the classroom is alleviated by the mimed masturbating of a giant penis and by replacing the teacher's official language with a litany of sexual obscenities. The lads demonstrate their disgust for and fear of menstruation by substituting 'jam rag' for towel at every opportunity. What Willis fails to confront, I think, is the violence underpinning such imagery and evident in one lad's description of sexual intercourse as having 'a good maul on her'. He does not comment on the extreme cruelty of the lads' sexual double standards or tease out in sufficient detail how images of sexual power and domination are used as a kind of last defensive resort. It is in these terms that the book's closing lines can best be understood. When Paul Willis gently questions Joey about his future, he replies 'I don't know, the only thing I'm interested in is fucking as many women as I can if you really want to know.'

Although Willis shows how male manual work has come to depend on the elaboration of certain values – the cultural reproduction of machismo from father to son, the male pride in physical labour and contempt for 'pen-pushing' – he does not integrate these observations on masculinity and patriarchal culture into the context of the working-class family. The family is the obverse face of hard, working-class culture, the softer sphere in which fathers, sons and boyfriends expect to be, and are, emotionally serviced. It is this link between the lads' hard outer image and their private experiences – relations with parents, siblings and girlfriends – that still needs to be explored. Willis's emphasis on the cohesion of the tight-knit groups tends to blind us to the ways that the lads' immersion in and expression of working-class culture also takes place outside the public sphere. It happens as much around the breakfast table and in the bedroom as in the school and the workplace.

Shop-floor culture may have developed a toughness and resilience to deal with the brutality of capitalist productive relations, but these same 'values' can be used internally. They are evident, for example, in the cruel rituals to which the older manual workers subject school-leavers newly entering production.[8] They can also be used, and often are, against women and girls in the form of both wife and girlfriend-battering. A full *sexed* notion of working-class culture would have to consider such features more centrally.

Discourses of Disrespect

Because it constantly avoids reduction to one essential meaning and because its theses are almost entirely decentred, it is not easy to contain Dick Hebdige's *Subculture* within the normal confines of a critical review. Ostensibly his argument is that it is on the concrete and symbolic meeting-ground of black and white (implicitly male) youth that we have to understand the emergence and form of subcultural style, its syncopations and cadences. From an account of the 'Black Experience', he works outwards to the ways in which this culture has been taken up and paid homage to by white male intellectuals and by sections of working-class youth. At the heart of this process he places rock music – black soul and reggae, white rock (especially the music and style of David Bowie) and, of course, the 'mess' of punk. Acknowledging – and fleetingly pleading guilty to – the tendency to romanticism in such subcultural tributes, Hebdige stresses the danger that such hagiography can overlook the unmitigated ferocity of the oppression and exploitation which have created black culture as it is. He does not try to prove his case with a barrage of empirical facts, but presents his reading of style as one which the reader can take or leave. Yet the sheer partiality of extrapolating race as signifier *par excellence* makes that which he chooses *not* to deal with all the more shocking. Despite his emphasis on the neglect of race and racism in youth and subcultural work, he seems oblivious to the equal neglect of sexuality and sexism.

His book twists and winds its way around a variety of themes. At some moments it goes off into flights of densely referenced semisociological stream of consciousness. At others it addresses itself with forceful clarity to mainstream theoretical debates on youth culture: two of his arguments here are worth dwelling on in that a feminist critique would demand that they be pushed further than he is willing to do. From the start Hebdige acknowledges his debt to the theoretical overview in *Resistance through Rituals*, in particular its application of Gramsci's concept of 'hegemony' to the question of youth in postwar Britain, and places his own work broadly within the parameters defined by John Clarke's essay on 'Style' in that collection. The problem is that Hebdige's assumptions actually run counter to those of *Resistance through Rituals*. Briefly, he posits that the youth subculture is the sum of those attempts to define it, explain it away, vilify it, romanticise it and penalise it. The moral panic and smear campaign construct what the subculture 'becomes' just as much as the kids on the street. Linked to this is his important recognition that there is no necessary relation between the peculiarities of subcultural style and the area of (presumably) working-class life from which it is drawn, that 'one should not expect the subcultural response ... to be even necessarily in touch, in any immediate sense, with its material position in the capitalist system'.[9] Working-class self-images are just as constricted by the limitations and historical specificities of available codes as youth cultures. Their 'raw materials' may be material but they are never completely 'uncooked'.

In one of the most perceptive and exciting parts of the book, Hebdige uses punk to illustrate this. It is here, in spelling out his argument that punk was a response to already articulated 'noises' (especially in the popular press) of panic and crisis, that he contradicts the logic of the *Resistance through Rituals* position, which argued for the *deconstruction* of the ideological debris and clutter about youth and for the reconstruction from these ruins of a more adequately theorised account. The important point is that, precisely because it used a phenomenal forms/real relations model, *Resistance through Rituals* was unable to engage directly with the sort of concepts at play in Hebdige's account. The significance of 'outsider mythology', for example, or of representations of youth in film, literature or music, would have been consigned to the sphere of ideology or (worse) 'idealism', given the same logical, if not political, status as the 'moral panic' and therefore also in need of 'deconstruction'.

Hebdige, in contrast, argues that ultimately the radical/Marxist account is logically no more true than any other: it is valuable to the extent that it engages critically not only with the phenomenon in question but also with the inadequacies of the different existing accounts. Although its 'politics' cannot be read off – it may have little to say about youth politics in the activist sense – it nevertheless has a material political force in that it disrupts commonsense wisdoms about youth and their more respectable academic revisions. Whereas in *Resistance through Rituals* it is class that provides the key to unlocking subcultural meanings (though not, the authors stress, in a reductionist way) in *Subculture* style and race are selected as the organising principles for prising them open. Although neither book takes us very far in understanding youth and gender, Hebdige's account at least makes it possible to explore the theme without continual recourse to class and so may disrupt (in a positive sense) some of our own commonsense wisdoms about class and class culture. But although his method draws on the work of feminists like Kristeva and is one widely used by feminists working in media studies, Hebdige by and large reproduces yet another 'silence'. The pity is that he thereby misses the opportunity to come to grips with subculture's best-kept secret, its claiming of style as a male but never unambiguously masculine prerogative. This is not to say that women are denied style, rather that the style of a subculture is primarily that of its men. Linked to this are the collective celebrations of itself through its rituals of stylish public self-display and of its (at least temporary) sexual self-sufficiency. As a well-known ex-mod put it, 'You don't need to get too heavily into sex or pulling chicks, or sorts as they were called ... Women were just the people who were dancing over in the corners by the speakers.'[10] If only he had pushed his analysis of style further, Hebdige might well have unravelled the question of sexuality, masculinity and the apparent redundancy of women in most subcultures.

What is clear, though, is that Hebdige revels in style. For him it is a desirable mode of narcissistic differentiation – 'You're still doing things I gave up years ago', as Lou Reed put it. There's nothing inherently wrong with that; the problem is that as a signifier of desire, as the starting-point for innumerable fantasies or simply as a way of sorting friends from enemies, Hebdige's usage of 'style' structurally excludes women. This is ironic, for in mainstream popular culture it is accepted as primarily a female or feminine interest.[11] What is more, women are so obviously inscribed (marginalised, abused) within subcultures as static objects (girlfriends, whores or 'faghags'), that access to its thrills, to hard fast rock music, to drugs, alcohol and 'style', would hardly be compensation even for the most adventurous teenage girl. The signs and codes subverted and reassembled in the 'semiotic guerrilla warfare' conducted through style do not really speak to women at all. The attractions of a subculture – its fluidity, the shifts in the minutiae of its styles, the details of its combative bricolage – are offset by an unchanging and exploitative view of women.

Homages to Masculinity

Rather than just cataloguing the 'absences' in *Subculture*, I want to deal with three questions raised by a feminist reading: the extent to which subcultural bricoleurs draw on patriarchal meanings, the implications of ambiguous sexuality for youth cultures, and the question of gender and the moral panic.

Dick Hebdige claims that style breaks rules and that its refusals are complex amalgams taken from a range of existing signs and meanings. Their menace lies in the extent to which they threaten these meanings by demonstrating their frailty and the ease with which they can be thrown into disorder. But just as the agents who carry on this sartorial terrorism are inscribed as subjects within patriarchal as well as class structures, so too are the meanings to which they have recourse. These historical, cultural configurations cannot be free of features oppressive to women. Machismo suffuses the rebel archetypes in Jamaican culture which, Hebdige claims, young British blacks plunder for suitable images. The teds turned to the style of Edwardian gents. The mods, locating themselves within the 'modernism' of the new white-collar working class, looted its wardrobe as well as that of smart young blacks around town. The skins, similarly, turned simultaneously to both black style and that of their fathers and grandfathers. More tangentially, punks appropriated the 'illicit iconography of pornography', the male-defined discourse *par excellence*. Of course, it would be ludicrous to expect anything different. The point I am stressing is how highly differentiated according to gender, style (mainstream or subcultural) is – it is punk girls who wear the suspenders, after all.

If, following Eco's dictum,[12] we speak through our clothes, then we still do so in the accents of our sex. Although Hebdige does fleetingly mention sexual ambiguity in relation to style (and especially to the various personae of David Bowie), he does not consider it as a central feature right across the subcultural spectrum – for him subcultural style *is* Sta-prest trousers, Ben Sherman shirts or pork-pie hats. I am not suggesting that all subcultures value transvestism – but that subcultural formations and the inflections of their various 'movements' raise questions about sexual identity which Hebdige avoids. Does subcultural elevation of style threaten the official masculinity of straight society which regards such fussiness as cissy? Does the skinheads' pathological hatred of 'queers' betray an uneasiness about their own fiercely defended male culture and style? Are subcultures providing relatively safe frameworks within which boys and young men can escape the pressures of heterosexuality?[13]

For feminists the main political problem is to assess the significance of this for women. If subculture offers escape from the demands of traditional sex roles, then the absence of predominantly girl subcultures – their denial of access to such 'solutions' – is evidence of their deeper oppression and of the monolithic heterosexual norms which surround them and find expression in the ideology of romantic love. Whereas men who 'play around' with femininity are nowadays credited with some degree of power to choose, gender experimentation, sexual ambiguity and homosexuality among girls are viewed differently. Nobody explains David Bowie's excursions into female personae (see the video accompanying his single *Boys Keep Swinging*) in terms of his inability to attract women. But any indication of such ambiguity in girls is still a sure sign that they couldn't make it in a man's world. Failure replaces choice; escape from heterosexual norms is still synonymous with rejection. (Even the fashionable bisexuality among the women of the Andy Warhol set is less willingly dealt with in the popular press.) My point, then, is not to label subcultures as potentially gay, but to show that the possibility of escaping oppressive aspects of adolescent heterosexuality within a youth culture or a gang with a clearly signalled identity, remains more or less unavailable to girls. For working-class girls especially, the road to 'straight' sexuality still permits few deviations.

Finally I want to comment on the way in which Hebdige deals with the processes of reaction and incorporation accompanying the subcultural leap into the limelight of the popular press and media. He exposes with great clarity the inadequacies of the old moral panic argument and suggests that the Barthesian notion of trivialisation/exoticisation/domestication offers a better account of how youth cultures are 'handled'.[14] But again, because his model is not gendered, he fails to recognise that these are gender-specific processes. Ultimately the shock of subcultures can be partially defused because they can be seen as, among other things, boys having fun. That is, reference can be made *back* to the idea that boys should 'sow their wild oats' – a privilege rarely accorded to young women. This does not mean that the 'menace' altogether disappears, but at least there are no surprises as far as gender is concerned. Even male sexual ambiguity can be dealt with to some extent in this way. (Boys with ear-rings, dyed hair and mascara? ... They do it every week in *It Ain't Arf Hot, Mum.*) But if the Sex Pistols had been an all-female band spitting and swearing their way into the limelight, the response would have been more heated, the condemnation less tempered by indulgence. Such an event would have been greeted in the popular press as evidence of a major moral breakdown and not just as a fairly common, if shocking, occurrence.

Walking on the Wild Side – It is Different for Girls

Rather than dealing with more mainstream sociological criticisms of *Subculture* (it London-centredness, for example) or making my rather oversimplified comments on youth culture more specific (historically and in relation to such institutions as school, family and workplace), I now want to look briefly at some of the meanings ensconced within the objects and practices constituting the subcultural artillery.

Rock music has been so much part of postwar youth cultures that its presence has often just been noted by writers; the meanings signified by its various forms have not received the attention they deserve. Dick Hebdige does something to redress this, but again without developing a perspective sensitive to gender and sexual division. My points here are tentative and simple. Such a perspective would have to realise that rock does not signify alone, as pure sound. The music has to be placed within the discourses through which it is mediated to its audience and within which its meanings are articulated. Just as Elizabeth Cowie has shown how reviews construe the sense of a particular film in different ways,[15] so an album or concert review lays down the terms and the myths by which we come to recognise the music. One myth energetically sustained by the press is the overwhelming maleness of the rock scene. Writers and editors seem unable to imagine that girls could make up a sizeable section of their readership. Although at a grassroots level virulent sexism has been undermined by punk, Rock against Racism and Rock against Sexism, journalistic treatment remains unchanged. As the exception, women musicians are treated with a modicum of respect in the *New Musical Express* or *Melody Maker*, but women are dealt with more comfortably in the gossip column on the back page, as the wives or girlfriends of the more flamboyant rock figures.

The range of drug scenes characterising subcultures reveals a similar pattern. The inventory is familiar – alcohol for teds, rockers and skins, speed and other pills for mods and punks, hallucinogenics for hippies, cocaine and to a lesser extent heroin for other groups closer to the rock scene. So intransigently male are the mythologies and rituals attached to regular drug-taking that few women feel the slightest interest in their literary, cinematic or cultural expressions – from William Burroughs's catalogues of destructive self-abuse and Jack Kerouac's stream-of-consciousness drinking sprees to Paul Willis's lads and their alcoholic bravado. It would be foolish to imagine that women do not take drugs – isolated young housewives are amongst the heaviest drug-users and girls in their late teens are one of the largest groups among attempted suicides by drug overdose. Instead, I am suggesting that for a complex of reasons the imaginary solutions which drugs may offer boys do not have the same attraction for girls. One reason is probably the commonsense wisdom deeply inscribed in most women's consciousnesses – that boys do not like girls who drink, take speed and so on; that losing control spells sexual danger; and that drinking and taking drugs harm physical appearance. A more extreme example would be the way that the wasted male junkie in popular mythology, novels and films, can retain a helpless sexual attraction which places women in the role of potential nurse or social worker. Raddled, prematurely aged women on junk rarely prompt a reciprocal willingness.

The meanings that have sedimented around other objects, like motor-bikes or electronic musical equipment, have made them equally unavailable to women and girls. And although girls are more visible (both in numbers and popular representation) in punk than earlier subcultures, I have yet to come across the sight of a girl 'gobbing' (i.e. spitting). Underpinning this continual marginalisation is the central question of street visibility. It has always been on the street that most subcultural activity takes place (save perhaps for the more middle-class oriented hippies): it both proclaims the publicisation of the group and at the same time ensures its male dominance. For the street remains in some ways taboo for women (think of the unambiguous connotations of the term 'street walker'): 'morally dubious' women are the natural partners of street heroes in movies like Walter Hill's *The Warriors* and in rock songs from the Rolling Stones to Thin Lizzy or Bruce Springsteen. Few working-class girls can afford flats and so for them going out means either a date – an escort and a place to go – or else a disco, dance-hall or pub. Younger girls tend to stay indoors or to congregate in youth clubs; those with literally nowhere else to go but the street frequently become pregnant within a year and disappear back into the home to be absorbed by child-care and domestic labour.

There are of course problems in such large-scale generalisations. Conceptually it is important to separate popular public images and stereotypes from lived experience, the range of ideological representations we come across daily from empirical observation and sociological data. But in practice the two sides feed off each other. Everyday life becomes at least partly comprehensible within the very terms and images offered by the media, popular culture, education and the arts, just as material life creates the preconditions for ideological and cultural representation. This complexity need not paralyse our critical faculties altogether, however. It is clear from my recent research, for example, that girls are reluctant to drink precisely because of the sexual dangers of drunkenness. This does not mean that girls do not drink. Most available data suggests that they will drink with more confidence and less tension only when they have a reliable steady boyfriend willing to protect them from more predatory, less-scrupulous males. It is difficult to deal so schematically with drug usage, and especially involvement in hard-drug subcultures. Particularly interesting, however, are the warnings to girls against hard drugs in the West German media (the addiction rate there is much higher than in Britain). These are couched entirely in terms of the damage heroin can do to your looks, your body and your sexuality. They reinforce and spell out just how 'it is different for girls': a girl's self-evaluation is assumed to depend on the degree to which her body and sexuality are publicly assessed as valuable.

The Politics of Style – Two Steps Beyond

I noted earlier that a 'politics of youth' cannot simply be read off from Dick Hebdige's book. Although this hesitancy is preferable to the sloganising with which much writing on youth culture ends, it still barely disguises the pessimism deeply rooted in all structuralisms, the idea that codes may change but the scaffolding remains the same, apparently immutable. Hebdige's conclusion seems to point to a convergence between gloomy existentialism and critical Marxism as the gap between the 'mythologist' and the working class appears to expand. The sadness pervading the closing pages of *Subculture* hinges on this failure to communicate which, Hebdige claims, characterises the relation between intellectuals and the class about which they write. These facts need not lead to such pessimism. Instead we should develop a clearer idea of the sectors of 'youth' potentially responsive to Dick Hebdige's intervention (male ex-mods, hippies, skins and punks at Art Colleges, rock fans and young socialists ...?) and also a broader vision of our spheres of political competence.

Radical and feminist teachers could well, despite the usual resistances they encounter, popularise many of Hebdige's arguments (as well as some points of feminist critique). It is also conceivable that some young people may read the book unprompted by youth 'professionals' (teachers or community workers). After all, the *New Musical Express*, which sells over 200,000 copies, recently reviewed it in glowing terms and Hebdige's ideas have clearly influenced several of the paper's feature writers. So there is no doubt that, apart from being one of the most important books to date on the question of youth culture, it is also likely to reach, if often indirectly, an unprecedentedly wide audience. That is why its lack of attention to gender matters. It could have opened up questions of style *and* sexual politics. Also, had he addressed himself more directly to this potential audience, Hebdige might have made clearer the implications of the 'escape' from the working class into the subcultural bohemia of an art college or rock band, or simply into the independence of a rented flat. As it is, *Subculture* should become a landmark within the politics of culture inside the notoriously traditional art colleges because of its emphasis on style and image as *collective* rather than *individual* expressions and its investigation of the *social* meaning of style. The problem is just that Hebdige implies that you have to choose either style *or* politics and that the two cannot really be reconciled.

My own guess is that to understand these questions about youth culture and politics more fully, it will be necessary to supplement the established conceptual triad of class, sex and race with three more concepts – *populism, leisure* and *pleasure*. It is not possible to develop a full-blown justification for that project here, however. And as I opened this article by condemning the self-effacement of male writers, it would perhaps be appropriate to end on a personal note about the ambivalence of my own responses to subcultures and the possible links between youth subcultures and feminist culture. Collective public expressions of disaffiliation from authority and the hegemony of the dominant classes (by either sex) have an unambiguous appeal. Despite their often exaggerated romanticism and their (frequently sexist) politics, the 'spectacle' of these symbolic gestures has a personally 'thrilling' effect. (Sitting on a train in West Germany, surrounded by carefully coiffured businessman and well-manicured businesswoman, the sight of two 'Felliniesque' punks in the next compartment causes the sociologist to smile.)

In a similar way, punk is central to an understanding of the resurgence of 'youth politics' in Britain over recent years. It is not a *deus ex machina* which will banish the unpopularity of left politics but, as a set of loosely linked gestures and forms, it has proved a mobilising and energising force which has helped to consolidate developments like Rock against Racism. There have also been overlaps between the nuances of punk style and feminist style which are more than just coincidental. Although the stiletto heels, mini-skirts and suspenders will, despite their debunking connotations, remain unpalatable to many feminists, both punk girls and feminists want to overturn accepted ideas about what constitutes femininity. And they often end up using similar stylish devices to upset notions of 'public propriety'.

What this indicates is a mysterious symbiosis between aspects of subcultural life and style in postwar Britain and aspects of a 'new' left and even feminist culture. However precious or trivial the question of style may seem in contrast to concrete forms of oppression and exploitation (unemployment, for example, or the strengthening of the State apparatus), it cannot be hived off into the realm of personal hedonism. The sort of style

Dick Hebdige describes is central to the contradictory nature of working-class male culture, and it plays a visible role in the resistances by youth in Britain today. The style of black youth is as much an assault on authority as outright confrontation. For many girls *escaping* from the family and its pressures to act like a 'nice' girl, remains the first political experience. For us, the objective is to make this flight possible for all girls, and on a long-term basis.

I am not arguing that if girls were doing the same as some boys (and subcultures are always minorities) all would be well. The 'freedom' to consume alcohol and chemicals, to sniff glue and hang about the street staking out only symbolic territories is scarcely less oppressive than the pressures keeping girls in the home. Yet the classic subculture does provide its members with a sense of oppositional sociality, an unambiguous pleasure in style, a disruptive public identity and a set of collective fantasies. As a pre-figurative form and set of social relations, I cannot help but think it could have a positive meaning for girls who are pushed from early adolescence into achieving their feminine status through acquiring a 'steady'. The working-class girl is encouraged to dress with stylish conventionality; she is taught to consider boyfriends more important than girlfriends and to abandon the youth club or disco for the honour of spending her evenings watching television in her boyfriend's house, saving money for an engagement ring. Most significantly, she is forced to relinquish youth for the premature middle-age induced by childbirth and housework. It is not so much that girls do too much too young; rather, they have the opportunity of doing too little too late. To the extent that all-girl subcultures, where the commitment to the gang comes first, might forestall these processes and provide their members with a collective confidence which could transcend the need for 'boys', they could well signal an important progression in the politics of youth culture.

Notes

This article originally appeared in *Screen Education*, Spring 1980, no. 39.

1 Among the more important books are: J. Young, *The Drugtakers: The Social Meaning of Drug Use*, London, Paladin, 1971; S. Cohen, *Folk Devils and Moral Panics: The Creation of the Mods and Rockers*, London, MacGibbon & Kee, 1972; S. Hall and T Jefferson (eds) *Resistance through Rituals*, London, Hutchinson, 1976; D. Robbins and P. Cohen, *Knuckle*

Sandwich, Harmondsworth, Penguin, 1978; P. Corrigan, *Schooling the Smash Street Kids*, London, Macmillan, 1979; P. Willis, *Learning to Labour*, Aldershot, Saxon House, 1977; D. Hebdige, *Subculture: The Meaning of Style*, London, Methuen, 1979.

2 See, for example, S. Sharpe, *Just Like a Girl*, Harmondsworth, Penguin, 1977; A. M. Wolpe, *Some Processes in Sexist Education*, London, WRRC pamphlet, 1977; A. McRobbie, *The Culture of Working-Class Girls* and CCCS Women's Studies Group (eds) *Women Take Issue*, London, Hutchinson, 1978; D. Wilson, 'Sexual Codes and Conduct' in C. Smart and B. Smart (eds), *Women, Sexuality and Social Control*, London, Routledge & Kegan Paul, 1978.

3 P. Willis, *Learning to Labour*, Aldershot, Saxon House, 1977.

4 See, for example, Willis, *Profane Culture*; and also 'The Cultural Meaning of Drug Use' in Hall *et al.* (eds), *Resistance through Rituals*.

5 S. Rowbotham, *Woman's Consciousness, Man's World*, Harmondsworth, Penguin, 1973.

6 *Born to Run*, B. Springsteen, copyright.

7 This is well-documented in I. Taylor, P. Walton and J. Young (eds), *Critical Criminology*, London, Routledge & Kegan Paul, 1975.

8 Willis, *Learning to Labour, op. cit.*

9 See R. Coward's angry response to this debate, 'Culture and the Social Formation' in *Screen*, vol. 18, no. 1, Spring 1977.

10 Interview with P. Meaden, *New Musical Express*, 17 November 1979.

11 *Jackie* magazine, however, continues to warn girls against being too flamboyant in dress and personal style.

12 Quoted in Hebdige, *Subculture, op. cit.*

13 See, for example, N. Polsky, *Hustlers, Beats and Others*, Harmondsworth, Penguin, 1971.

14 R. Barthes, *Mythologies*, London, Paladin, 1972, quoted in Hebdige, *Subcultures, op. cit.*

15 E. Cowie, 'The Popular Film as a Progressive Text: A Discussion of Coma', Part I, in *M/F*, no. 3, 1979.

9

The Politics of Feminist Research: Between Talk, Text and Action (1981)

Forging a Feminist Culture

For feminists engaged in research – historical, anthropological, literary, sociological or otherwise – there is really no problem about answering the question, 'who do we do feminist research for?' Yet to state simply 'for women', is to obscure a whole range of issues which invariably rise to the surface in the course of a research project. Exactly how these issues are handled plays an important part in shaping the entire research procedure. That is to say, when a politics, its theory and aspects of its practice (in this case feminism) meet up with an already existing academic discipline, the convergence of the two is by no means unproblematic. Often the urgency and the polemic of politics, all the things about which we feel strongly and which we desperately want are quite at odds with the traditional requirements of the scholarly mode; the caution, the rigour and the measured tone in which one is supposed to present 'results' to the world. Frequently we worry about the extent to which we, unwittingly, impose our own culture-bound frame of reference on the data, and about how, so often, our personal preferences surface, as though by magic, as we write up the research.

My emphasis in this article is on a particular type of research, namely 'naturalistic' sociology, that branch of sociology which was, in many ways, appropriated by left academics in the early 1960s, and refashioned so as to become a kind of front line. Here accounts of how (mostly) working-class people made sense of their lives, jostled alongside the (often tortured) attempts of the sociologist as he too made sense. In fact this kind of sociology had a strong 'multicultural' heritage. It borrowed the term 'ethnography' from social anthropology; its methods, particularly 'participant observation', were strongly influenced by American sociologist Howard Becker; and its political force owed much to the work of E.P. Thompson and his 'history from below'. That is, the everyday histories of class resistance which mainstream 'History' otherwise condemns to silence. In fact feminist ethnographic sociology owes a great deal to this socialist tradition. What I want to single out for special attention here is the question of doing research *on* or *with* living human subjects, namely women or girls. But first some points which may well seem surprising but which I think warrant renewed attention.

In this country we take it very much for granted that research is based in and around the universities. Funding for research, regardless of where it comes from (the SSRC, DES, DHSS, EOC or the EEC) is almost invariably channelled through institutions of higher education. This means that, unlike in say West Germany, where research money is more often linked with grassroots projects, feminist research here has had a strongly academic rather than a practical bias. I shall be arguing against precisely this kind of distinction later – but I want to stress that insofar as such a division does exist, its results have been by no means negative.

For a start, an increasingly large number of women students have been, over the last few years, enrolling for higher (postgraduate) degrees – all of which entail the setting up of a research project. Slowly this has generated a feminist 'intellectual' culture, or to put it another way, a strongly feminist critique has found its way into the orthodoxies of sociology, history, psychology, politics and so on. Feminist research networks have been set up nationally, as have resource centres. Research-oriented groups, initially academically based but open to all women, meet regularly, and of course it is within this context that the journal *Feminist Review* must also be seen. At the risk of seeming oversimplistic, I think it is worth stating that possibly the most important achievement in these developments within the system of higher education, has been precisely the revealing of some of women's hidden oppressions – both past and present. Nor do the positive aspects of this drift towards educational establishments stop short at the point of producing interesting and politically valuable research. They also concern the way in which often 'mature' women – teachers, social workers and probation officers – are making use of the space which a period of time in education provides, in order to think through all those problems which tend to get dealt with automatically or hurriedly in the work situation. Gill Frith, an English teacher in a Coventry comprehensive school, for example, used her sabbatical year to consider more fully the sexual politics of teaching literature and – among other things – produced a definitive account of the way in which sexism pervades every aspect of literature teaching, from the choice of contents of the texts, to the achievements of the pupils (Frith, 1981).[1] Already this article is being consulted by other teachers grappling with the same problems. My own work on girls grew out of a commitment both to feminist politics in 1974, and to the value and usefulness of sociology as a discipline. I was also interested in 'history from below' and on how working people experience directly their own situation. My concern was with the way girls experienced all the pressures imposed on them to aspire to a model of femininity and how they lived this ideology on a day-to-day basis (McRobbie, 1978).[2]

But what is missing from all these research initiatives is the kind of locally funded social-policy-oriented projects found in almost every German city and town. Living in Germany and meeting many women involved in this kind of work certainly forced me to think more critically about the way we do our research here, particularly the way in which research has not really been able to feed into strategies in the community, the school, the workplace, and so on. It is true that these projects in West Germany (women and girls in relation to drugs and drug addiction, action research on street prostitution, women in prison, etc.) have often lacked a rigorous theoretical framework, but this is more than compensated in terms of the visible achievements. Four years of intensive local work with girls from disadvantaged social backgrounds, by a group of women in West Berlin, has resulted in their being given, by the local council, a huge hundred-roomed tenement to be restored in order to provide long-term housing for women and girls. The Women's House in the Potsdamer Strasse is already much more than a refuge or a hostel. In it prostitutes, delinquent girls, and battered wives mix with each other and with the women who set it up and who are increasingly able to play a much less directive role. However, this is also, officially, a research project. It has strong links with the University – offering places to women students, as well as having connections right through the network of local government. And its women workers are all involved in writing up annual reports, articles and proposals for further funding.

Wild Strategies

No research is carried out in a vacuum. The very questions we ask are always informed by the historical moment we inhabit – not necessarily directly or unambiguously, but in more subtle ways. The terms within which we set up a project will most likely reflect, among other things, the current level of debate and argument within the Women's Movement. Because in so many ways British feminism grew out of a left legacy and, in academic terms, out of a Marxist social-science tradition, for a long time the key question hinged on the relation between capitalism and patriarchy. The aim of so many studies carried out in the 1970s was somehow to show definitively how the two were linked to each other – with both shouldering equal responsibility for women's oppression. Not only was such a search often fruitless, but there was clearly a desperate edge to it, as though this engagement was somehow necessary for women researchers to prove their intellectual credibility. I certainly capitulated to such pressure and went to great lengths to grapple with both class and gender in my early study of 14-year-old girls in Birmingham.

I brought in class wherever I could in this study, often when it simply was not relevant. Perhaps I was just operating with an inadequate notion of class, but there certainly was a disparity between my 'wheeling in' class in my report and its almost complete absence from the girls' talk and general discourse. And this was something I did not really query. I felt that somehow my 'data' was refusing to do what I thought it should do. Being working-class meant little or nothing to these girls – but being a *girl* overdetermined their every moment. Unable to grapple with this uncomfortable fact, I made sure that, in my account anyway, class *did* count. If I had to go back and consider this problem now, I would go about it in a very different fashion. I would not harbour such a monolithic notion of class, and instead I would investigate how relations of power and powerlessness permeated the girls' lives – in the context of school, authority, language, job opportunities, the family, the community and sexuality. And from this I would begin once again, perhaps, to think about class. In many ways this marks exactly the shift which has taken place recently in feminist analysis; many radical feminist researchers have ditched class altogether, or else modified it out of recognition. One very positive result of this has been the space opened up to explore issues around class, rather than deal with it head-on. Recent feminist work has looked rather to the ways in which women are inscribed in unequal, passive and subordinate power relations – by the state, the law, and all those other spheres which have the ability to shape their subjects' lives for them.

Linked to this shift in priorities has to be our awareness of the changing function of research – the way it performs a vital role at certain moments, only to become outmoded the next (without of course being invalidated in the process). This happens when research is overtaken by events. For example, since the wide-scale setting up of girls' groups in schools and colleges, of girls' nights in youth clubs, of social work practice for girls and young women, the kind of research I did in 1975 is no longer reflective of gender relations in the school or in the youth service.[3] Research does not always have to be directly relevant or functional, but the chances are that we will nonetheless respond to current trends when we set up such a project. Thus in 1982 with massive youth unemployment, we are simply more likely to look to the meaning and consequences of unemployment for girls – than to seek out those girls *in work* and consider their situation. And yet I want to argue for the autonomy of research – it should not have to fit into agreed parameters of 'what is happening now'. Frequently the most exciting research flies in the face of convention; it asks new questions and applies wild strategies in a bid to force into action feminism's dynamic face. In retrospect now I can see how cautious I was in my own research initiatives. I was keen to be seen to be doing good sociology and I adopted often stilted and unhelpful tactics, hoping to come up with the right kind of data. I walked a nervous tightrope between positivist social science (and thereby trying to be 'scientific') and the more radical naturalistic sociology with its emphasis on the flow of interaction between sociologist and subject. I did not feel comfortable with questionnaires and samples but I did not want to fall into the 'bourgeois individualism' of lengthy case-study-oriented profiles. At the same time I recognised that as a discipline sociology had a lot to offer and that many of its contemporary figures – Basil

Bernstein and Stuart Hall, in Britain, and in America, Erving Goffman and Howard Becker had produced startlingly sensitive and intellectually rigorous work; work which could possibly provide a framework for looking at gender.

No longer is it necessary to define our research so tightly within an unreconstructed sociological framework. Feminism has changed the social sciences just as much as the social sciences have helped to form the frame of reference for many feminist projects. Equally, feminist writing outside academic social science has shown conclusively how feminist research can go beyond disciplinary boundaries without losing its drive and coherence.

From a Feminist Present to a Feminist Future

Research is historically located. This is true in terms of the questions it asks and the way it asks them. But how it is practised – and this includes all the social relations surrounding it – is much less clear. Many of its conventions – writing, archive work, interviewing or participant observation, and finally constructing arguments – go undiscussed or else are mystified as tricks of the trade. The points on which I want to concentrate here might seem simplistic and self-evident. Yet they continue to have real and complex implications for doing research.

Within feminism many of the resentments and hostilities between researchers and practitioners (youth and community workers, social workers and teachers) lie in the already existing division of labour where some skills and competencies are more highly regarded and carry higher status than others. Under this set of arrangements, those who have the privilege of 'stating'; those who write, those who discuss publicly and make pronouncements – these women are frequently subjected to recrimination by other feminist activists. They are criticised for 'representing' a movement which has no such official representatives. They are also accused of participating in a sphere of 'male' intellectual discourses whilst others are working every clay in the 'real world' of practical problems to which some sort of solutions have to be found.

In fact there are multiple problems raised by such a seemingly straightforward distinction. First there is the contradiction for women between the wish to gain themselves a career, a professional identity on a par with men and a right to earn their own living – whether as a university researcher or a community worker – and the more general feminist commitment to breaking down status hierarchies and changing the ways in which men have used their occupations as a way of competing with each other and of exercising power. Second, there is the problem of how we communicate. Which media do we use and on what terms? To maintain a continual flow of ideas, a cross-fertilisation of analysis and an ongoing exchange of descriptions, experiences and feelings, we need *words*. This may be in the form of rhetoric, feminist polemic or intellectual debate, journalism, research writing or official reporting. We need writing, printing, magazines, journals, pamphlets, books.

In the use of words, the tension arises between the anarchy and all-pervasiveness of talk and the order and formality of written words. We *all* talk, *all* the time. Few of us distil from all our discussions and arguments, the theories and analyses presented in print. Of course the two (talk and text) are absolutely interdependent. We know that to participate in the public sphere of politics, action goes hand in hand with the power of the written word. It is a vital part of attracting more women to the ideas of the women's movement and also of challenging the male dominance of the media, education, the law and all the other apparatuses of the State. We need words to 'speak' across institutions and structures and to address women (and men) both directly and through the medium of print, music or whatever.

The irony is that it is access to these very forms which have consistently been denied us. It is only recently that women have been demanding the right to acquire the skills necessary to communicate in this multiplicity of ways. This is a political struggle in itself. It amounts to an attempt to break out of the confines of talk, which is a comfortable but ultimately restricting ghetto. It is a form, called 'gossip', where women have been located throughout history. However, it is a particularly contradictory route outwards from the privatised local sphere of feminism to full-scale engagement in the public sphere. We have had to set up our own publishing networks, film cooperatives, magazines, pamphlets and resource centres, and this process is never simply a matter of making a grab for the necessary raw materials. Rather it involves continual engagements with the State (often the provider of both funds and employment), with education, the commercial media and the culture industry. And this often means operating on their terms. We want and need these resources, but frequently they demand walking an uneasy tightrope between capitulating to their established structures and values (it might mean becoming a 'star', a 'professional' and 'artist') and holding on to a commitment to those feminist values which oppose these statuses. If we are honest we probably want all of these things at once. In the meantime, we try to create a space to be effective and a work identity for ourselves, just as we try to democratise the structures which surround us in order to make them available for many more women and girls. Yet the distinction is made between those who are primarily involved in, and committed to, on the one hand 'the practical' and on the other 'the intellectual'. Women whose work involves periods of intense privatised labour, like writing, painting or reading, are seen as less committed than those who spend the entire working day, and often more, working with other women – battered women, delinquent girls, schoolgirls or isolated housewives.

So where do we meet? At what points are these disagreements overcome? I think it is when we recognise our shared interests. It is when our mutual dependence on each other is forced to the surface. A clear example is when a feminist project looks towards the future. Be it a hostel for runaway girls or setting up an older women's group in a community centre, its progress will be documented and charted, whether it is a resounding success or a dismal failure. If this is made available for wider circulation than only the women involved in setting it up, it can contribute to the 'noise' made by the women's movement, and to our effectiveness. These records – articles, reports and theses – make the difference between a small-scale feminist present and a wider female future.

But it is important not to ignore the differences within feminism. At what point do the areas of contention and dispute arise, for example, in the passage from local to national or from the private to the public feminist sphere? Frequently dissension arises at the point of representing the particular project or intervention. The 'account' cannot be objective. It is a political product, its construction comprising a set of explicitly ideological moves. To put it briefly, *representations* are *interpretations*. They can never be pure mirror images. Rather they employ a whole set of selective devices, such as highlighting, editing, cutting, transcribing and inflecting. Regardless of medium, literary or visual, these invariably produce new permutations of meaning. From this perspective, it is understandable that a researcher visiting a girls' project regularly and talking to the girls as a researcher, will come up with a different account of the girls and of the project than would the full-time worker. This is intrinsically neither good nor bad, but it does have consequences that must be recognised.

Failure to recognise the partiality of any account can lead to acrimonious disputes over who has got it right. In such cases often the girls or women themselves are used as arbiters, thus shifting the responsibility in the name of 'letting the girls speak out' and the spurious authenticity attached to this idea. Here again I am questioning the idea that what they say is somehow 'pure' or 'definitive'. True, there is something direct, immediate and concrete about such an account, but the girls or women themselves are a part of the social relations of the project. And even then, recorded speech goes through a number of transformations before it reaches its readers. The fact that it is 'uncommented on text' carries particular connotations, seeming the more 'pure' the less it is edited. In this way the intermediary processes fade into the background and fail to be recognised for what they are: activities which are as ideologically loaded and as saturated with 'the subjective factor' as anything else. My points, in summary, are these. First there is no such thing as 'pure' printed speech. By acting upon speech, it is invariably shaped in one way or another. Second, this directedness is not necessarily a bad thing which we should try to wipe out as if it is evidence of 'bias'. There are a range of distinct political positions within feminism and we must recognise them and work from there.

But perhaps my account disguises the most sensitive issue at stake – that is, the nature of the relationship between the researcher and the researched, a relationship paralleling in its unequal power that of social worker and client, or teacher and pupil. Feminists have been particularly aware of the exploitative or patronising propensity of these relationships and have asserted continuously that we must avoid such possibilities at all costs. It has also been argued that our shared gender, anyway, cuts across other divisions, uniting us on at least some counts. More directly we have all witnessed the way in which male sociologists have patronised their working-class client populations. Often in the name of research they have produced highly romanticised, even exoticised accounts, but depart from the 'field' leaving behind them only confusion, distrust or straightforward bewilderment. Frequently we have suspected such commentators of prioritising 'intellectual work' – the eventual book, or even the *a priori* theory and its fit with the material – over the politics of the situation they leave behind. We have, in short, accused them of flirting with working-class culture from the comfort and safety of the university environment. There has never really been any doubt about their status. A researcher is a researcher is a researcher and, we imagine, they have lost no sleep over their dealings with the school teachers, youth workers, social workers, and all those who mediate between them and their 'subjects'.

Feminist research which has concentrated on living human subjects has sought to subvert this academicism. Instead we have sought to treat our 'subjects' with respect and equality. We have studiously avoided entering 'their' culture, savouring it and then presenting it to the outside world as a subject for speculation. Feminism forces us to locate our own autobiographies and our experience inside the questions we might want to ask, so that we continually do *feel* with the women we are studying. So our own self-respect is caught up in our research relations with women and girls and also with other women field-workers. That aid, feminism should not be taken as a password mi leading us into a false notion of 'oneness' with all women purely on the ground of gender. No matter how much our past personal experience figures and feeds into the research programme, we cannot possibly assume that it necessarily corresponds in any way to that of the research 'subjects'. And is it desirable that research should be predicated on the often shaky notion of 'shared femininity'? Or the equally problematic objective of breaking down all barriers between women? For example, our project may be based on 'the girls' but why should we assume that we can actually *do* anything for *them*? Is this not an immensely patronising stance? How can *we* assume *they* need anything done for them in the first place? Or conversely that we have anything real to offer them? What then are the objectives of feminist research? Who do we do it for? Is there a case for arguing that some research works more effectively and avoids being condescending by addressing itself to, making demand of and challenging the institutions, structures and those who inhabit them, and occupy positions of power within them?

Pushing this line of argument one stage further we can question the making of assumptions about feminism which need not necessarily fit. How relevant is the contemporary women's movement to 'ordinary' women and girls? 1 f feminism is not an evangelical cause, then our research objectives can never be purely 'recruitist' – as though feminism naturally can solve all women's problems. We have to proceed much more cautiously – age, class, culture and race do create real barriers which have real effects. Invariably women researchers experience vast spaces between themselves and those they may be 'studying' – be they 15-year-old girl delinquents, or 70-year-old working-class militants reminiscing about their past lives. And this is precisely why research continues to be such an important feature of feminist struggle. We cannot possibly scrutinise, update and revise feminist politics without exploring all those regions inhabited by women who are socially and politically 'silent'. And there is no reason why this process of discovery has to be exploitative to it subject – or that it has to be conceptualised with the aim of doing something for them. This is inevitably a premature and preemptive claim. Research should first of all be directed towards existing feminist assumptions and practice. If we are to have any relevance to women and girls outside the movement today, we have to learn what they are thinking about and how they experience a patriarchal and sexist society. It is vital that these women speak back to *us* who are sometimes over-comfortably placed in a cosy feminist culture – about *their* discontents. It may well be that a whole range of our favourite principles and practices would be undermined if not wholly dislodged as a result.

To summarise: I have been suggesting that research is a historically charged practice; that it can never present more than a *partial* portrait of the phenomenon under study. I have also described how this fact often generates tensions within teams of women researchers, workers and teachers in terms of which 'account' is more or less accurate than any other – and in turn which version becomes official. Equally I have argued that whilst feminism ensures thoughtfulness, sensitivity and sisterhood, it cannot bind all women together purely on the grounds of gender. Such a cohesion would surely be spurious, misleading and short-lived. And indeed how are we to know that feminism, in its present form, is in itself a suitable instrument for overcoming all those obstacles which divide women? To make such a claim is to overload the potential of the women's movement and to underestimate the resources and capacities of 'ordinary' women and girls who occupy a different cultural and political space from us – by virtue of *age, class, race* and *culture* – to participate in their own struggles as women but quite autonomously.

In the next section I will be dealing more explicitly with the kinds of academic and political issues which arise in the course of research. Right now I will conclude here by mentioning some of the labels and misconceptions about feminist intellectual work which linger on. First there is the implication that such work involves purely *mental* labour, unlike work with girls in a youth club or centre which is thoroughly practical and even *manual*. This division in many ways reflects exactly the means by which different sectors of the traditional male working class were set apart from each other – the more skilled labour aristocracy, who often aspired to white-collar nonmanual positions, from the manual, unskilled workers. As popular mythology has it, women lecturers and researchers spend a lot of time thinking, reading, talking with their students and drinking coffee. On top of this there remain all the old connotations of élitism attached to intellectual work. All these images are quite ungrounded. If anything, women workers in institutes of higher education find themselves more involved in the very practical work of supervising, teaching, tutoring and interviewing than in many other fields. For a start there are still so few women employed in the universities and polytechnics. As 'token' feminists they are expected 'to be all things to all people'. They continually have to prove themselves intellectually and at the same time are expected to service the students through all their personal problems. Of course women recognise the dangers involved – yet it stands to reason that women will be more sympathetic, particularly with female students, and that they will also feel more committed to breaking down the hierarchies of status which separate staff from students.

It is difficult not to sound defensive when there are personal issues at stake, but there is a feeling in the women's movement that political work with other women outside the movement can only take place outside such (a) middle-class, (b) intellectual, and (c) formal structures as higher education. But the talk, discussion, argument and reading which takes place between feminist teachers and women students is as valid a mode of political engagement as any other. Young women may be at school or college because they have to be, or are privileged enough to be but that does not invalidate all attempts to raise feminist issues within the school, 'poly' or university. And, of course, just because the mechanisms of social control are less viable in the youth centre, the cafe or the club, does not mean they do not exist. For me teaching and research are not separate spheres. I am continually learning from my students in the same way as I hope they learn from me. Both research and teaching require thought, preparation, reading and discussion. These are not isolated activities. Instead they proceed out of – in this case – feminism and radical sociology. And in each case their movement and development is continually reflective and dialectic, continually strung out between texts, talk and action.

Odd Erotic Moments

So far I have presented what amounts to a justification for doing research and a defence of it. I have suggested that although research may be inscribed within an action-oriented programme, the work that it does has quite separate autonomous dimensions that may not speak directly to the subjects of the research themselves, but may rather be addressed towards institutions, policy-making bodies, academic debates, or feminist discussion groups. All this is quite abstract, and now I want to shift my attention to the more concrete aspects of research – how it is done and what it feels like, its awkwardnesses and its rewards. If research has to change the way that people look at things, to challenge the structures which determine the conditions of existence which, in this case, women and girls inhabit, then it has to be convincing. It has to display all those qualities typically linked with 'official' research; rigour, scholarliness, precision and lucidity. These features (for me, being located within a sociological framework) continue to have great relevance for those modes of operation linked with feminist research. They cannot be simply jettisoned as being part of a male practice, nor can they be mechanically replaced by more feminine qualities like intuition, imagination or 'feel'.

But what exactly does rigour mean, and how does one carry out scholarly research? Is it a matter of reading and referring to all the literature in the field? Or is it a matter of carefully selecting that which is most appropriate and applying its perspectives where necessary? And then there is the even more difficult question of how the argument is constructed, the moment when the raw material, all neatly set out in box files, on tape and in endless notebooks, is somehow transformed into something quite different. Strangely this is where the research feels more fragile, most personal and where most seems to be at stake, so much so that the validity of the whole project seems to rest on this mysterious object, the argument. Ideally there would be some infallible procedure which could be pulled out of a hat and which would guarantee the production of an endless stream of impressive, watertight theories and theses, written by women, and all contributing to our intellectual culture. The fact is that although this process is sweated over, it is rarely discussed. Nobody seems to know how it is done. Most work takes shape through the employment of a range of more-or-less systematic, more-or-less chaotic procedures, and there is no foolproof modus operandi. Instead there are the methods and prescriptions laid down by the discipline or subdiscipline we work within. Equally there remain the vital questions of who we are writing for and why.

Perhaps a more sensible way of going about dealing with this problem is to eliminate some of the wisdoms enshrined in the official research discourses – the idea, for example, that we learn always purely and directly from our experience in the field, that our arguments are the fruit of this intense foray into the 'unknown', and that our priorities must consequently be with this set of social relations. Not only is this unrealistic in the most orthodox types of research, but in a time of cut-backs, when, for women academics in particular, research is carried out on a part-time haphazard basis, crushed in between teaching, administrative work, child-care and domestic labour, it is unlikely to be the product of one untainted line of thought. And maybe this multiplicity of influence is in itself not a bad thing. Our own subjectivity can often add to the force of research, just as our precise political position will inflect our argument this way or that, as will our private fascinations, our personal obsessions, and our odd erotic moments. Why should we not be able to admit how we absorb ideas and apply them, from the films we see in our leisure to the 'other' books we read, whom we talk to in the pub and what we talk about with our friends, students, lovers or flatmates?

Paul Willis suggests that in ethnographic research the precise form the argument takes depends on those moments when the writer/researcher is taken by surprise (Willis, 1980), when the subjects temporarily 'hijack' the research and do the researchers' work for them.[4] In fact Willis's account of these moments tends to be a bit over-dramatised. It is as though he is describing a very literary or aesthetic experience, when for a few seconds everything miraculously falls into place. I think two things are going on here. First I think Willis is quite rightly asserting the importance of moments whose meaning cannot be captured accurately in the language of the 'social sciences'. And in this sense I would want to go even further and suggest that so-called sociology has been quite tyrannised by its reliance, at least officially, on mainstream sociological sources. Willis is absolutely right to point to the way in which the subjects' *language* and *talk* can often throw into crises the intellectual plan and all its baggage. And if this represents an incursion of the literary, the psychoanalytical, the linguistic or the non-sociological into the fieldwork, all the better. But I think that Willis is also here referring to the pleasure *he* experiences when he is unburdened by the research, when the subjects voluntarily and momentarily appropriate for themselves this often wearying and unrewarding activity.

What Willis is documenting are those points where the subjects provide a viewpoint which is simply beyond the intellectual horizons of the writer, a perspective he or she could not have anticipated regardless of how many books s/he had read, films seen or archives visited. Willis is in fact stumbling across the author's dependencies, the way in which, drawing on Barthes, the object of study 'writes' you as much as you 'write' it.[5] These moments force the researcher into a fresh humility, into an awareness of the limitations of one form of intellectual activity and its absolute dependence on these 'others'. This is to say that our research cannot ever be wholly ours, nor should we want it to be, just as it is never the product of privatised theory. And this is my final point on the research process: that traditionally, and certainly within a male-defined concept of doing research, it is presented as necessarily having to be new and innovative – the laying out of a *new* argument, the ordering of *new* research material, the presentation of a *new* thesis as a result of the discovery of 'hitherto unknown sources' ... But in fact if one casts a glance across the left/feminist/sociological horizon in this country, what one finds is often a lot less grand, much less self-assured and certainly not always new. That is to say most of these research discourses address themselves to already existing ones. Frequently research, feminist or otherwise, means presenting a new angle on an old question, a fresh perspective on a neglected topic, a mapping of the field (a favourite Centre for Contemporary Cultural Studies expression), an exploration, an enquiry, an interrogation or simply the following up of some interesting clues. Put this way the whole enterprise becomes much less daunting, much less subject to the mystifications of the professors.

But to return to the question of feminism meeting sociology. First, the ways in which traditional social science cannot prepare feminists for many of the discomforts of research and how in turn feminism can force sociology to face up to its own shortcomings. To begin with there is the awkwardness of forging a relationship with those women, girls (or men) who will provide the source material of the project. Without them and without their trust the research simply cannot proceed. More precisely, there are the ways in which we censor the asking of questions which may seem important for the research, but which feel unacceptably intrusive and nosy. One woman in Birmingham who was doing a short study of how girls read magazines found herself quite unable to ask the girls in question what their parents did for a living and what kind of house they lived in. Being female undoubtedly sensitises us to the discomforts and small humiliations which doing research can provoke. Sometimes indeed it does feel like 'holidaying on other people's misery'. This happened to me recently when I interviewed a 19-year-old woman whom I had known for some time in Birmingham, and who had been brought up in care. I was almost enjoying the interview, pleased it was going well and relieved that Carol felt relaxed and talkative. Yet there was Carol, her eyes filling up with tears as she recounted her life and how her mother had died and how desperate she was to find some man who would marry her and look after her. In fact two weeks after the interview Carol tried to commit suicide; a misunderstanding between her and her boyfriend prompted it. She recovered, is still waiting for him to propose, is unemployed and well-aware that her chances of a job are slender, hence marriage and children become all the more urgent.

Sociology does not prepare us for the humility of powerless women, for their often totally deferential attitude to the researcher. 'Why are *you* interested in *me*. I'm only a housewife?' Or else the surprise on the part of girls that any adults could be really interested in what *they* had to say, or indeed that adult women outside their immediate environment could be 'normal', might swear, be quite nice or interesting and lead exciting lives. Almost all feminist researchers have reported this sense of flattery on the part of the women subjects, as though so rarely in their lives have they ever been singled out for attention by anybody.

Of course this also relates to the way that 'ordinary' people, men and women, are excluded from the public sphere, from the world of politics, of participation, of decision-making and of making news rather than just watching it. And it is in this context that we can understand the football 'hooligans' and 'rioters' of 1981 carrying with them, as a kind of emblem of their fame and notoriety, press photographs of themselves throwing a brick at the police, or putting the boot in another skinhead. These mementoes are highly treasured. They are symbols of a momentary if fleeting engagement with society rather than a simple consumption of its goodies.

To those on the outside 'feminism' and 'research' represent precisely this more powerful arena. Funded by the state, representatives of higher education, well-spoken, self-confident and friendly as well, many women academics might as well be Martians. Unpleasant though it may be, we have not only to recognise this unequal distribution of privilege but also to draw out its consequences. Could it be that women are often such good research subjects because of their willingness to talk, which is in itself an index of their powerlessness? That, unlike men, they are never too busy. They can never *not* spare a moment, they never have such a pressing appointment, other than getting on with the housework or picking up the kids from school. And that even when interviewed in the workplace, they are more likely to squeeze in a quick chat with the researcher who is after all just doing her job? Or that, so used to caring for people, women are so bad at rejecting requests made of them to give themselves, are so bad at saying 'No, I'm sorry I'm not interested in talking to you.' And that class position also mediates in these patterns of deference and respect? After all, middle-class career women are much more difficult to pin down for an interview than elderly cleaners and domestic servants.

This point is nicely illustrated in the recent work of Ann Oakley (Oakley, 1981).[6] In an extremely suggestive and stimulating study of women going through childbirth, Oakley shows vividly the limitations and absurdity of orthodox sociological methods. She quotes one source which warns the sociologist of being drawn into the research process in an unprofessional manner and then of being asked questions by the respondents who are, of course, only expected to answer questions. In this situation the researcher is advised to look puzzled, and say something like 'Well, that's a hard one!' and hope that the person in question is put off asking any more. Oakley shows just how patronising is this stance. She also shows how, were she to have adopted such a silent role, her research would have got nowhere fast. Not only did the women on whom she did her research continually present her with a barrage of questions, they also became her friends, invited her to visit after both the birth and the research, and in some cases formed longstanding friendships with her. They also played an active role in the shaping of the research, discussing it in great detail as it was being written up.

But what I think Oakley fails to recognise is the way in which as a researcher she had everything going for her. At no time does she dwell on the question of their cooperation. She does not concern herself with the fact that pregnant, in hospital, often cut-off from family and relatives, the women were delighted to find a friendly, articulate, clever and knowledgeable woman to talk to about their experiences. Surrounded by distant and aloof doctors and over worked nurses, their extreme involvement in the research could also be interpreted as yet another index of their powerlessness.

What does this mean? Are women better at oral history, because of their historic hegemony over talk? Is this kind of feminist research parasitic on women' entrapment in the ghettoes of gossip? Or is *our* way with words something we must celebrate, something which need not simply be indicative of our imprisonment, but something we can use as a weapon of political struggle, an armament where we have an unambiguous advantage over men?

And if all of this is the case, how can we mobilise around it? How can we make talk walk? Possibly only by being modest about our own importance both as *bona fide* feminists and as researchers, and by recognising both the value and the limitations of the kind of work we do. By hoping for ripple effects rather than waves of support. By arguing for the articulation between different forms of feminist practice rather than the intrinsic merits of one over the other. Research on women in this sense would be one of a set of involvements. Even if it only finds its way onto the reading list of Community Studies degree courses, this still does not mean that it has been a purely intellectual activity. Through talk, textual production and even translation, research can help to transform the relations which characteristically divide thinking from acting.

Notes

First published in *Feminist Review*, no. 12, October 1982.

1 G. Frith, 'Little Women, Good Wives: Is English Good for Girls?', in A. McRobbie and T. McCabe (eds) *Feminism for Girls: An Adventure Story*, London, Routledge & Kegan Paul, 1981.
2 A. McRobbie (see Chapter 3 of this volume).
3 Ibid.
4 P. Willis, 'Notes on Method', in S. Hall *et al.* (eds), *Culture, Media*, London, Hutchinson, 1980, p. 88.
5 R. Barthes, *Image, Music, Text*, London, Fontana, 1980.
6 A. Oakley, 'Interviewing Women: A Contradiction in Terms', in H. Roberts (ed.), *Doing Feminist Research*, London, Routledge & Kegan Paul, 1981.

10

Rock and Sexuality (1981)

with Simon Frith

Of all the mass media rock is the most explicitly concerned with sexual expression. This reflects its function as a youth cultural form: rock treats the problems of puberty, it draws on and articulates the psychological and physical tensions of adolescence, it accompanies the moment when boys and girls learn their repertoire of public sexual behaviour. If rock's lyrics mostly follow the rules of romance, its musical elements, its sounds and rhythms, draw on other conventions of sexual representation, and rock is highly charged emotionally even when its direct concern is nonsexual. Rock is the everpresent background of dancing, dating, courting. 'Rock 'n' roll' was originally a synonym for sex, and the music has been a cause of moral panic since Elvis Presley first swivelled his hips in public. It has equally been a cause for the advocates of sexual permissiveness – the 1960s counter cul-turalists claimed rock as 'liberating', the means by which the young would free themselves from adult hangups and repression. For a large section of postwar youth, rock music has been the aesthetic form most closely bound up with their first sexual experiences and difficulties, and to understand rock's relationship to sexuality isn't just an academic exercise – it is a neces-sary part of understanding how sexual feelings and attitudes are learned.

Unfortunately, knowing that rock is important is not the same thing as knowing how it is important. The best writers on the subject state the contradictions without resolving them. On the one hand, there is some-thing about rock that is experienced as liberating – in Sheila Rowbotham's words, 1960s youth music was 'like a great release after all those super-consolation ballads.'[1] On the other hand, rock has become synonymous with a male-defined sexuality: 'Under my thumb', sang the Stones, the archetypical rock group, 'stupid girl'.

Some feminists have argued that rock is now essentially a male form of expression, that for women to make nonsexist music it is necessary to use sounds, structures, and styles that cannot be heard as rock. This raises important questions about form and content, about the effect of male domination on rock's formal qualities as a mode of sexual expression. These are more difficult questions than is sometimes implied. Lyrics are not a sufficient clue to rock's meanings, nor can we deduce rock's sexual message directly from the male control of its conditions of production. Popular music is a complex mode of expression. It involves a combination of sound, rhythm, lyrics, performance, and image, and the apparently straightforward contrast that can be drawn, for example, between Tammy Wynette's 'Stand By Your Man' (reactionary) and Helen Reddy's 'I Am Woman' (progressive) works only at the level of lyrics. It doesn't do justice to the overall meanings of these records: Tammy Wynette's country strength and confidence seem, musically, more valuable qualities than Helen Reddy's cute, show-biz self-consciousness. We will return to this comparison later.

There are few clues, then, in the existing literature as to *how* rock works sexually. Left accounts of popular music focus either on its political economy or on its use in youth subcultures. In the former approach, rock's ideological content is derived from its commodity form; rock is explained as just another product of the mass entertainment industry. But if we confine ourselves to this approach alone, we cannot distinguish between the sexual messages of, say, the Stranglers and Siouxsie and the Banshees. The contrast between the former's offensive attempts to reassert stereotypes of male domination and the latter's challenge to those stereotypes is lost if we treat them simply as equivalent bestselling products of multinational record companies. The problem of analysing the particular ideological work of a particular piece of music is avoided with the assumption that all commodities have the same effect.

In the subcultural approach rock's ideological meaning is derived, by contrast, from the culture of its consumers. The immediate difficulty here is that existing accounts of youth subcultures describe them as, on the one hand, exclusively male and, on the other hand, apparently asexual. But even a good culturalist account of rock would be inadequate for our purposes. Rock is not simply a cultural space that its young users can win for their own purposes. Rock, as an ideological and cultural form, has a crucial role to play in the process by which its users constitute their sexuality. It is that process we need to understand.

Our difficulty lies in the ease with which the analysis of rock as an aesthetic form can slip past the comparatively straightforward sociologies of record production and consumption. An obvious indication of this problem is the complex reference to the term 'rock' itself. As rock fans we know what we mean by rock empirically, but the descriptive criteria we use are, in fact, diverse and inconsistent. 'Rock' is not just a matter of musical definition. It refers also to an audience (young, white), to a form of production (commercial), to an artistic ideology (rock has a creative integrity that 'pop' lacks). The result of this confusion is constant argument as to whether an act or record is really rock – and this is not just a matter of subjective disagreement.

Records and artists have contradictory implications in themselves. The meaning of rock is not simply given by its musical form, but is struggled for. As a cultural product, a rock record has multiple layers of representation. The message of its lyrics may be undercut by its rhythmic or melodic conventions and, anyway, music's meanings don't reach their consumers directly. Rock is mediated by the way its performers are packaged, by the way it is situated as radio and dance music. Rock reaches its public via the 'gatekeepers' of the entertainment industry, who try to determine how people listen to it. The ideology of rock is not just a matter of notes and words.

One of the themes of this paper is that rock operates both as a form of sexual expression and as a form of sexual control. Expression and control are simultaneous aspects of the way rock works; the problem is to explain how rock gives ideological shape to its sexual representations. We reject the notion, central to the ideology of rock as counterculture, that there is some sort of "natural" sexuality which rock expresses and the blue meanies repress. Our starting point is that the most important ideological work done by rock is the *construction* of sexuality. We will describe rock's representations of masculinity and femininity and consider the contradictions involved in these representations. Our concern is to relate the effects of rock to its form – as music, as commodity, as culture, as entertainment.

Masculinity and Rock

Any analysis of the sexuality of rock must begin with the brute social fact that in terms of control and production, rock is a male form. The music business is male-run; popular musicians, writers, creators, technicians, engineers, and producers are mostly men. Female creative roles are limited and mediated through male notions of female ability. Women musicians who make it are almost always singers; the women in the business who make it are usually in publicity; in both roles success goes with a male-made female image. In general, popular music's images, values, and sentiments are male products.

Not only do we find men occupying every important role in the rock industry and in effect being responsible for the creation and construction of suitable female images, we also witness in rock the presentation and marketing of masculine styles. And we are offered not one definitive image of masculine sexuality, but a variety of male sexual poses which are most often expressed in terms of stereotypes. One useful way of exploring these is to consider 'cock rock', on the one hand, and 'teenybop', on the other.

By 'cock rock' we mean music making in which performance is an explicit, crude, and often aggressive expression of male sexuality – it's the style of rock presentation that links a rock and roller like Elvis Presley to rock stars like Mick Jagger, Roger Daltrey, and Robert Plant. Cock rock performers are aggressive, dominating, and boastful, and they constantly seek to remind the audience of their prowess, their control. Their stance is obvious in live shows; male bodies on display, plunging shirts and tight trousers, a visual emphasis on chest hair and genitals – their record sales depend on years of such appearances. In America, the Midwest concert belt has become the necessary starting point for cock rock success; in Britain the national popularity of acts like Thin Lizzy is the result of countless tours of provincial dance halls. Cock rock shows are explicitly about male sexual performance (which may explain why so few girls go to them – the musicians are acting out a sexual iconography which in many ways is unfamiliar, frightening, and distasteful to girls who are educated into understanding sex as something nice, soft, loving and private). In these performances mikes and guitars are phallic symbols; the music is loud, rhythmically insistent, built around techniques of arousal and climax; the

lyrics are assertive and arrogant, though the exact words are less significant than the vocal styles involved, the shouting and screaming.

The cock rock image is the rampant destructive male traveller,
smashing hotels and groupies alike. Musically, such rock takes off from
the sexual frankness of rhythm and blues but adds a cruder male physicality (hardness, control, virtuosity). Cock rockers' musical skills become
synonymous with their sexual skills (hence Jimi Hendrix's simultaneous status as stud and guitar hero). Cock rockers are not bound by the
conventions of the song form, but use their instruments to show 'what
they've got', to give vent to their macho imagination. These are the men
who take to the streets, take risks, live dangerously and, most of all, swag-
ger untrammelled by responsibility, sexual and otherwise. And, what's
more, they want to make this clear. Women, in their eyes, are either
sexually aggressive and therefore doomed and unhappy, or else sexually repressed and therefore in need of male servicing. It's the woman,
whether romanticized or not, who is seen as possessive, after a husband,
antifreedom, the ultimate restriction.

Teenybop, in contrast, is consumed almost exclusively by girls. What
they're buying is also a representation of male sexuality (usually in the
form of teen idols), but the nature of the image and the version of sexuality
on display is quite distinct from that of the cock rocker. The teenybop idol's
image is based on self-pity, vulnerability, and need. The image is of the
young boy next door: sad, thoughtful, pretty, and puppylike. Lyrically his
songs are about being let down and stood up, about loneliness and frustration; musically his form is a blend of pop ballad and soft rock; it is less
physical music than cock rock, drawing on older romantic conventions. In
teenybop, male sexuality is transformed into a spiritual yearning carrying
only hints of sexual interaction. What is needed is not so much someone
to screw as a sensitive and sympathetic soulmate, someone to support
and nourish the incompetent male adolescent as he grows up. If cock rock
plays on conventional concepts of male sexuality as rampant, animalistic,
superficial, and just for the moment, teenybop plays on notions of female
sexuality as serious, diffuse, and implying total emotional commitment.
In teenybop cults live performance is less significant than pinups, posters,
and TV appearances; in teenybop music, women emerge as unreliable,
fickle, more selfish than men. It is men who are soft, romantic, easily hurt,

loyal, and anxious to find a true love who fulfills their definitions of what female sexuality should be about.

The resulting contrast between, say, Thin Lizzy fans and David Soul fans is obvious enough, but our argument is not intended to give a precise account of the rock market. There are overlaps and contradictions. Girls put cock rock pinups on their bedroom walls, and boys buy teenybop records. Likewise there are a whole range of stars who seek to occupy both categories at once – Rod Stewart can come across just as pathetic, puppylike, and maudlin as Donny Osmond, and John Travolta can be mean and nasty, one of the gang. But our comparison of cock rock and teeny bop does make clear the general point we want to make: masculinity in rock is not determined by one all-embracing definition. Rather, rock offers a framework within which male sexuality can find a range of acceptable, heterosexual expressions. These images of masculinity are predicated on sexual divisions in the appropriation of rock. Thus we have the male consumer's identification with the rock performer; his collective experience of rock shows which, in this respect, are reminiscent of football matches and other occasions of male camaraderie – the general atmosphere is sexually exclusive, its euphoria depends on the absence of women. The teenybop performer, by contrast, addresses his female consumer as his object, potentially satisfying his sexual needs and his romantic and emotional demands. The teenybop fan should feel that her idol is addressing himself solely to her; her experience should be as his partner.

Elvin Bishop's 'Fooled Around', a hit single from 1975, captures lyrically the point we're making:

> I must have been through about a million girls
> I love 'em and leave 'em alone,
> I didn't care how much they cried, no sir,
> Their tears left me as cold as stone,
> But then I fooled around and fell in love ...

In rock conventions, the collective notion of fooling around refers explicitly to male experience; falling in love refers to the expectations of girls.

From this perspective, the contrast between cock rock and teenybop is clearly something general in rock, applicable to other genres. Male identity with the performer is expressed not only in sexual terms but also as a looser appropriation of rock musicians' dominance and power, confidence and control. It is boys who become interested in rock as music, who become hi-fi experts, who hope to become musicians, technicians, or music businessmen. It is boys who form the core of the rock audience, who are intellectually interested in rock, who become rock critics and collectors (the readership of *Sounds*, *New Musical Express*, and *Melody Maker* and the audience for the *Old Grey Whistle Test* are two-thirds male; John Peel's radio show listeners are 90 per cent male). It is boys who experience rock as a collective culture, a shared male world of fellow fans and fellow musicians.

The problems facing a woman seeking to enter the rock world as a participant are clear. A girl is supposed to be an individual listener, she is not encouraged to develop the skills and knowledge to become a performer. In sixth form and student culture, just as much as in teenybop music, girls are expected to be passive, as they listen quietly to rock poets, and brood to Leonard Cohen, Cat Stevens or Jackson Browne. Women, whatever their musical tastes, have little opportunity and get little encouragement to be performers themselves. This is another aspect of rock's sexual ideology of collective male activity and individual female passivity.

Music, Femininity, and Domestic Ideology

Male dominance in the rock business is evident in both the packaging and the musical careers of female rock stars. Even powerful and individual singers like Elkie Brooks can find success only by using the traditional showbiz vocabulary. Indeed, one of the most startling features of the history of British popular music has been the speed with which talented women singers, of all types, from Lulu through Dusty Springfield to Kate Bush, have been turned into family entertainers, become regulars on TV variety shows, fallen into slapstick routines, and taken their show-biz places as smiling, charming hostesses. Female musicians have rarely been able to make their own musical versions of the oppositional rebellious hard edges that male rock can embody.

Our argument is not that male stars don't experience the same pressures to be bland entertainers, but that female stars have little possibility of resisting such pressure. It may have been necessary for Cliff Richard and

Tommy Steele to become all-round entertainers in the 1950s, but one of the consequences of the rise of rock in the 1960s was that mass success was no longer necessarily based on the respectable conventions of show biz; sexual outrage became an aspect of rock's mass appeal. But for men only. The rise of rock did not extend the opportunities for women; notions of a woman's musical place have hardly changed. The one new success route opened to women was the singer/songwriter/folkie lady – long-haired, pure-voiced, self-accompanied on acoustic guitar – but whatever the ability, integrity, and toughness of Joan Baez, Judy Collins, Sandy Denny and the others, their musical appeal, the way they were sold, reinforced in rock the qualities traditionally linked with female singers – sensitivity, passivity and sweetness. For women rockers to become hard aggressive performers it was necessary for them, as Jerry Garcia commented on Janis Joplin, to become 'one of the boys'. Some women did make it this way – Grace Slick, Maggie Bell, Christine McVie – but none of them did it without considerable pain, frustration and, in the case of Janis Joplin, tragedy.

Perhaps the only way of resisting the pressures pushing women musicians into conventional stereotypes (and stereotyping is an inevitable result of commercialisation) was to do as Joni Mitchell did and avoid prolonged contact with the mass media. Since her success in the 1960s, Joni Mitchell has consistently refused to do TV appearances, rarely does concerts, turns down interviews with the music press, and exerts personal control over the making and production of her records. She, like Joan Armatrading, is rewarded with an 'awkward' reputation; despite their artistic achievements, theirs is not the popular image of the woman musician. For that we have to look at a group like ABBA. The boy/girl group is a common entertainment device in both pop and disco music (Coco, the Dooleys, on the one hand, Boney M and Rose Royce on the other). ABBA provides the clearest example of the sexual divisions of labour such groups involve: the men make the music (they write and arrange, play the guitars and keyboards), and the women are glamorous (they dress up and sing what they're told – their instruments are their 'natural' voices and bodies). *ABBA: The Movie* had a double plot; while a journalist pursued the men in the group, the camera lingered on Anna's bum – it was the movie's key visual image. In rock, women have little control of their music, their images, their performances; to succeed they have to fit into male grooves.

The subordination of women in rock is little different from their subordination in other occupations; as unskilled rock workers women are a source of cheap labour, a pool of talent from which the successes are chosen more for their appropriate appearance than for their musical talents.

But the problems of women in rock reach much further than those of surviving the business; oppressive images of women are built into the very foundations of the pop/rock edifice: into its production, its consumption, and even into its musical structures. Pop music reaches its public via a variety of gatekeepers – radio producers, TV producers and film producers. Disc jockeys at discos and dances, and writers in music papers and girls' magazines compete to interpret musical meanings. The Bay City Rollers, for example, were taken by girls' magazines to represent vocally and visually their own persuasive sexual ideology, were heard to articulate the comic strip vocabulary of true love.

Teenage magazines have used pop star images, male and female, to illustrate their romantic fantasies and practical hints since their origin in the 1950s. *Jackie*, for example, the highest-selling girls' weekly magazine in Great Britain, interprets music for its readers exclusively in terms of romance.[2] The magazine depends for its appeal on pop, carrying two or three large pop pinups each week; but it never actually deals with music. It doesn't review records and never hints that girls could learn an instrument or form a band, that they should take music seriously as either a hobby or a career. Music is reduced to its stars, to idols' looks and likes. Head-and-shoulder shots loom out of the centre and back pages, symbols of dreamily smiling male mastery. Nothing else in *Jackie* is allowed such uncluttered space – even the cover girl has to compete for readers' attention with the week's list of features and offers. Pop stars, in *Jackie*'s account of them, are not just pretty faces. Romance rests on more than good looks; the stars also have 'personality'. Each pinup uses facial expression and background location to tell readers something about the star's character – David Essex's pert cheekiness, David Cassidy's crumpled sweetness, Les McKeown's reassuring homeliness. There is an obvious continuity in the visual appeal of teenybop idols, from Elvis Presley to John Travolta – an unformed sensuality, something sulky and unfinished in the mouth and jaw, eyes that are intense but detached; sexiness – but sexiness that isn't physically rooted, that suggests a dreamy fantasy fulfillment. These images tell us more about the ideology of female than male sexuality; the plot is revealed in the home settings of *Jackie*'s photographs. Teenage music is not, after all, a matter of sex and drugs and carelessness; these stars are just like us – they're rich and successful and love their families, they come from ordinary pasts and have ordinary ambitions: marriage, settling down.

Girls are encouraged from all directions to interpret their sexuality in terms of romance, to give priority to notions of love, feeling, commitment and the moment of bliss. In endorsing these values girls prepare themselves for their lives as wives and mothers, where the same notions take on different labels – sacrifice, service and fidelity. In Sue Sharpe's words:

Women mean love and the home while men stand for work and the external world ... women provide the intimate personal relationships which are not sanctioned in the work organisation ... women are synonymous with softness and tenderness, love and care, something you are glad to come home from work to.[3]

Music is an important medium for the communication of this ideological message, and its influence extends much further than our analysis of teenybop has so far made clear. The BBC's daytime music shows on Radio 1 and 2, for example, are aimed primarily at housewives; their emphasis is consequently on mainstream pop, romantic ballads and a lightweight bouncy beat. On these shows there is little new wave music, few of the progressive, heavy, punk, or reggae sounds which creep into the playlists once the kids, the students, the male workers, are thought to be back from school and class and job. The BBC's musically interesting programmes are broadcast at night and the weekend, when men can listen, and this programming policy is shared by commercial stations. The recurrent phrase in radio producers' meetings remains: 'We can't really play *that* to housewives!'

Music has a function for women at work too, as Lindsay Cooper has pointed out.[4] Many employers provide piped music or Radio 1 for their female employees – indeed, piped music in a factory is a good indicator of a female workforce – and the service industries in which women work (offices, shops) also tend to have pop as a permanent backdrop. Music, like clean and pretty industrial design, is thought to soften the workplace, making it homey and personal, increasing female productivity and lessening female job dissatisfaction. Pop's romantic connotations are not only important for socializing teenagers, they also function to bring the sphere of the personal, the home, into the sphere of the impersonal, the factory. Music feminizes the workplace; it provides women workers with aesthetic symbols of their domestic identity; it helps them discount the significance of the boring and futile tasks on which they're actually engaged. If talk, gossip, passing round photos and displaying engagement rings indirectly help women overcome the tedium of their work, then the pop music supplied by management is a direct attempt to foster a feminine culture, in order to deflect women from more threatening collective activities as workers. Women's music at work, as much as girls' music at home, symbolises the world that is 'naturally' theirs – the world of the emotions, of caring, feeling, loving and sacrificing.

There's a feature on Simon Bates's morning Radio 1 show in which listeners send in the stories they attach to particular records. Records are used as aural flashbacks, and they almost always remind Bates's listening women of one of the following moments:

- when we first met;
- a holiday romance I'll never forget;
- when we broke up;
- when I told him I was pregnant;
- when we got together again;
- when he first kissed me/proposed/asked me out.

This request spot illustrates with remarkable clarity how closely music is linked with women's emotional lives and how important music is in giving sexual emotions their romantic gloss. The teenybop mode of musical appropriation has a general resonance for the ideology of femininity and domesticity.

A similar argument could be made with reference to cock rock and male sexuality, showing how the values and emotions that are taken to be 'naturally' male are articulated in all male-aimed pop music. But music is, in important respects, less important for male than for female sexual ideology. 'Maleness' gets much of its essential expression in work, both manual and intellectual; it isn't, as 'femaleness' is for women, confined to the aesthetic emotional sphere. Boys can express their sexuality more directly than girls; they are allowed to display physical as well as spiritual desire, to get carried away. The excitement of cock rock is suggestive not of the home and privacy but rather of the boozy togetherness of the boys who are, in Thin Lizzy's classic song, 'back in town'.

Of course male sex is no more 'naturally' wild and uncontrollable than feminine sexuality is passive, meek, and sensitive. Both are ideological constructs, but there is a crucial difference in the way the ideologies and the musics work. Cock rock allows for direct physical and psychological expressions of sexuality; pop in contrast is about romance, about female crushes and emotional affairs. Pop songs aimed at the female audience deny or repress sexuality. Their accounts of relationships echo the comic strips in girls' comics, the short stories in women's magazines. The standard plots in all these forms are the same: the 'ordinary' boy who turns out to be the special man, the wolf who must be physically resisted to be spiritually tamed, and so on. Ideologies of love are multimedia products, and teenage girls have little choice but to interpret their sexual feelings in terms of romance; few alternative readings are available.

This remains true even though we recognize that pop music is not experienced as an ideological imposition. Music is used by young people for their own expressive purposes, and girls, for example, use pop as a weapon against parents, schools and other authorities. At school they cover their books with pop pinups, carve their idols' names on their desks, slip out to listen to cassettes or radios in the toilets. In the youth club, music is a means of distancing girls from official club activities. They use it to detach themselves from their club leaders' attempts to make them participate in 'constructive' pursuits. The girls sit round their record players and radios, at home and school and youth club, and become unapproachable in their involvement with their music.

Music also gives girls the chance.to express a collective identity, to go out *en masse*, to take part in activities unacceptable in other spheres. Unlike their brothers, girls have little chance to travel about together; as groups of girls they don't go to football matches, relax in pubs, get publicly drunk. Teenage girls' lives are usually confined to the locality of their homes; they have less money than boys, less free time, less independence of parental control. A live pop concert is, then, a landmark among their leisure activities. The Bay City Rollers' shows, for instance, used to give girls a rare opportunity to dress up in a noisy uniform, to enjoy their own version of football hooligan aggression.

These moments of teenybop solidarity are a sharp and necessary contrast to the usual use of pop records in bedroom culture: as the music to which girls wash their hair, practice make-up, and daydream; and as the background music of domestic tasks (babysitting, housework) which girls unlike boys are already expected to do. But the ritual 'resistance' involved in these uses of music is not ideological. Rather, girls' use of teenybop music for their own purposes confirms the musical ideology of femininity. The vision of freedom on which these girls are drawing is a vision of the freedom to be individual wives, mothers, lovers, of the freedom to be glamorous, desirable male sex objects. For the contradictions involved in popular music's sexuality we have to look elsewhere, to the cock rock side of our ideal type distinction, to rock's ideological break with pop, to its qualities as beat music, its functions for dance.

Rock Contradictions

The audience for rock isn't only boys. If the music tends to treat women as objects, it does, unlike teenybop romance, also acknowledge in its direct physicality that women have sexual urges of their own. In attacking or ignoring conventions of sexual decency, obligation and security, cock rockers do, in some respects, challenge the way in which those conventions are limiting – to women as well as men. Women can contrast rock expression to the respectable images they are offered elsewhere – hence the feminist importance of the few female rock stars, such as Janis Joplin, hence the moral panics about rock's corrupting effects. The rock ideology of freedom from domesticity has an obvious importance for girls, even if it embodies an alternative mode of sexual expression.

There are ambiguities in rock's insistent presentation of men as sex objects. These presentations are unusually direct – no other entertainers flaunt their sexuality at an audience as obviously as rock performers. 'Is there anybody here with any Irish in them?' Phil Lynott of Thin Lizzy asks in passing on the *Live and Dangerous* LP, 'Is there any of the girls who would like a little more Irish in them?'

Sexual groupies are a more common feature of stars' lives in rock than in other forms of entertainment, and cock rock often implies female sexual aggression, intimates that women can be ruthless in the pursuit of *their* sex objects. Numerous cock rock songs – the Stones' for example – express a deep fear of women, and in some cases, like that of the Stranglers, this fear seems pathological, which reflects the fact that the macho stance of cock rockers is as much a fantasy for men as teeny-bop romance is for women.

Rock may be source and setting for collective forms of male toughness, roughness and noisiness, but when it comes to the individual problems of handling a sexual relationship, the Robert Plant figure is a mythical and unsettling model (in the old dance hall days, jealous provincial boys used to wait outside the dressing room to beat up the visiting stars who had attracted their women). Cock rock presents an ideal world of sex without physical or emotional difficulties, in which all men are attractive and potent and have endless opportunities to prove it. However powerfully expressed, this remains an ideal, ideological world, and the alternative teenybop mode of masculine vulnerability is, consequently, a complementary source of clues as to how sexuality should be articulated. The imagery of the cheated, unhappy man is central to sophisticated adult-oriented rock, and if the immediate object of such performers is female sympathy, girls aren't their only listeners. Even the most macho rockers have in their repertoires some suitably soppy songs with which to celebrate true (lustless) love – listen to the Stones' 'Angie' for an example. Rock, in other words, carries messages of male self-doubt and self-pity to accompany its hints of female confidence and aggression.

Some of the most interesting rock performers have deliberately used the resulting sexual ambiguities and ironies. We can find in rock the image of the pathetic stud or the salacious boy next door, or, as in Lesley Gore's 'You Don't Own Me', the feminist teenybopper. We can point too at the ambivalent sexuality of David Bowie, Lou Reed, and Bryan Ferry, at the camp teenybop styles of Gary Glitter and Suzi Quatro, at the disconcertingly 'macho' performances of a female group like the Runaways. These references to the uses made of rock conventions by individual performers lead us to the question of form: How are the conventions of sexuality we've been discussing embodied in rock?

This is a complex question, and all we can do here is point to some of the work that needs to be done before we can answer it adequately. First, then, we need to look at the *history* of rock. We need to investigate how rock 'n' roll originally affected youthful presentations of sexuality and how these presentations have changed in rock's subsequent development.

Most rock analysts look at the emergence of rock 'n' roll as the only event needing explanation; rock 'n' roll's subsequent corruption and 'emasculation' (note the word) are understood as a straightforward effect of the rock business's attempt to control its market or as an aspect of American institutional racism – and so Pat Boone got to make money out of his insipid versions of black tracks. But, from our perspective, the process of 'decline' – the successful creation of teenybop idols like Fabian, the sales shift from crude dance music to well-crafted romantic ballads, the late 1950s popularity of sweet black music and girl groups like the Shirelles – must be analysed in equal detail. The decline of rock 'n' roll rested on a process of 'feminization'.

The most interesting sexual aspect of the emergence of British beat in the mid-1960s was its blurring of the by then conventional teenage distinction between girls' music – soft ballads – and boys' music – hardline rock 'n' roll. There was still a contrast between, say, the Beatles and the Stones – the one a girls' band, the other a boys' band – but it was a contrast not easily maintained. The British sound in general, the Beatles in particular, fused a rough R&B beat with yearning vocal harmonies derived from black and white romantic pop; the resulting music articulated simultaneously the conventions of feminine and masculine sexuality, and the Beatles' own image was ambiguous, neither boys-together aggression nor boy-next-door pathos. This ambiguity was symbolized in Lennon and McCartney's unusual use of the third person: 'I saw *her* standing there', '*She* loves *you*'. In performance, the Beatles did not make an issue of their own sexual status; they did not, despite the screaming girls, treat the audience as their sexual object.

The mods from this period turned out to be the most interesting of Britain's postwar youth groups, offering girls a more visible, active, and collective role (particularly on the dance floor) than had previous or subsequent groups and allowing boys the vanity, the petulance, the soft sharpness that are usually regarded as sissy. Given this, the most important thing about late 1960s rock was not its well-discussed, countercultural origins, but the way in which it was consolidated as the central form of mass youth music in its cock rock form, as a male form of expression. The 'progressive' music of which everyone expected so much in 1967–68 became, in its popular form, the heavy metal macho style of Led Zeppelin, on the one hand, and the technically facile hi-fi formula of Yes, on the other. If the commercialization of rock 'n' roll in the 1950s was a process of 'feminisation', the commercialisation of rock in the 1960s was a process of 'masculinisation'.

In the 1970s, rock's sexual moments have been more particular in their effects but no less difficult to account for. Where did glam and glitter rock come from? Why did youth music suddenly become a means for the expression of sexual ambiguity? Rock was used this way not only by obviously arty performers like Lou Reed and David Bowie, but also by mainstream teenybop packages like the Sweet and by mainstream rockers like Rod Stewart.

The most recent issue for debate has been punk's sexual meaning. Punk involved an attack on both romantic and permissive conventions. In their refusal to let their sexuality be constructed as a commodity some punks went as far as to deny their sexuality any significance at all. 'My love lies limp', boasted Mark Perry of Alternative TV. 'What is sex anyway?' asked Johnny Rotten, 'Just thirty seconds of squelching noises'. Punk was the first form of rock not to rest on love songs, and one of its effects has been to allow female voices to be heard that are not often allowed expression on record, stage or radio – shrill, assertive, impure individual voices, the sounds of singers like Poly Styrene, Siouxsie, Fay Fife of the Rezillos, Pauline of Penetration; punk's female musicians have a strident insistency that is far removed from the appeal of most postwar glamour girls. The historical problem is to explain their commercial success, to account for the punks' interruption of the longstanding rock equation of sex and pleasure.

These questions can only be answered by placing rock in its cultural and ideological context as a form of entertainment, but a second major task for rock analysts is to study the sexual language of its musical roots – rhythm and blues, soul, country, folk, and so on. The difficulty is to work out the relationship of form and content. Compare, for example, Bob Dylan's and Bob Marley's use of supporting women singers. Dylan is a sophisticated rock star, the most significant voice of the music's cultural claims, including its claims to be sexually liberating. His most recent lyrics, at least, reflect a critical self-understanding that isn't obviously sexist. But musically and visually his backup trio are used only as a source of glamour, their traditional pop use. Marley is an orthodox Rastafarian, subscribes to a belief, an institution, a way of life in which women have as subordinate a place as in any other sexually repressive religion. And yet Marley's I-Threes sing and present themselves with grace and dignity, with independence and power. In general, it seems that soul and country musics, blatantly sexist in their organisation and presentation, in the themes and concerns of their lyrics allow their female performers an autonomous musical power that is rarely achieved by women in rock.

We have already mentioned the paradoxes in a comparison of Tammy Wynette's 'Stand By Your Man' and Helen Reddy's 'I Am Woman'. The lyrics of 'Stand By Your Man' celebrate women's duty to men, implore women to enjoy subordinating themselves to men's needs – lyrically the song is a ballad of sexual submissiveness. But the female authority of Tammy Wynette's voice involves a knowledge of the world that is in clear contrast to the gooey idealism of Helen Reddy's sound. 'Sometimes it's hard to be a woman', Tammy Wynette begins, and you can hear that it's hard and you can hear that Tammy Wynette knows why – her voice is a collective one. 'I am woman', sings Helen Reddy, and what you hear is the voice of an idealised consumer, even if the commodity for consumption in this instance is a package version of women's liberation.

This comparison raises the difficult issue of musical realism. It has long been commonplace to contrast folk and pop music by reference to their treatments of 'reality'. Pop music is, in Hayakawa's famous formula, a matter of 'idealization/frustration/demoralization'; a folk form like the blues, in contrast, deals with 'the facts of life'.[5] Hayakawa's argument rested on analysis of lyrics, but the same point is often made in musical terms – it is a rock-critical cliché, for example, to compare the 'earthy' instrumentation of rhythm and blues with the 'bland' string arrangements of Tin Pan Alley pop. A. L. Lloyd rests his assessment of the importance of folk music (contrasted with the 'insubstantial world of the modern commercial hit') on its truth to the experience of its creators. If folk songs contain 'the longing for a better life', their essence is still consolation, not escapism:

Generally the folk song makers chose to express their longing by transposing the world on to an imaginative plane, not trying to escape from it, but colouring it with fantasy, turning bitter, even brutal facts of life into something beautiful, tragic, honourable, so that when singer and listeners return to reality at the end of the song, the environment is not changed but they are better fitted to grapple with it.[6]

Consolation derived not just from folk songs' lyrical and aesthetic effects, but also from the collective basis of their creation and performance: women's songs, for example, became a means of sharing the common experience of sexual dependence and betrayal. This argument can be applied to the realistic elements of a commercial country performance like Tammy Wynette's. But the problem remains: Is musical realism simply a matter of accurate description and consequent acceptance of 'the way things are', or can it involve the analysis of appearances, a challenge to 'given' social forms?

In analysing the sexual effects of rock, a further distinction needs to be made between rock realism – the use of music to express the experience of 'real' sexual situations – and rock naturalism – the use of music to express 'natural' sexuality. An important aspect of rock ideology is the argument that sexuality is asocial, that music is a means of spontaneous physical expression which is beset on all sides by the social forces of sexual repression. Rhythm, for example, the defining element of rock as a musical genre, is taken to be naturally sexual.

What this means is unclear. What would be the sexual message of a cock rock dancing classic like 'Honky Tonk Women' if its lyrics were removed? Rock's hard beat may not, in itself, speak in terms of male domination, power or aggression, but the question is whether it says anything, in itself. Rock critics describe beat as 'earthy' or 'bouncy' or 'sensual' or 'crude', and so reach for the sorts of distinctions we need to make, but such descriptive terms reflect the fact that rhythmic meaning comes from a musical and ideological context.

We can best illustrate the complexities of musical sexuality with another comparison – between Kate Bush's 'Feel It' and Millie Jackson's 'He Wants to Hear the Words'. Kate Bush is the English singer/songwriter who became famous with 'Wuthering Heights'. 'Feel It' is a track on her debut album, *The Kick Inside*, and is, lyrically, a celebration of sexual pleasure:

> After the party, you took me back to your parlour
> A little nervous laughter, locking the door
> My stockings fall on the floor, desperate for more
>
> Nobody else can share this
> Here comes one and one makes one
> The glorious union, well, it could be love,
> Or it could be just lust but it will be fun
> It will be wonderful.

But, musically, the track draws on conventions that are associated not with physical enjoyment but with romantic self-pity. Kate Bush performs the song alone at her piano. She uses the voice of a little girl and sounds too young to have had any sexual experience – the effect is initially titillating; her experience is being described for *our* sexual interest. But both her vocal and her piano lines are disrupted, swooping, unsteady; the song does not have a regular melodic or rhythmic structure, even in the chorus, with its lyrical invocation of sexual urgency. Kate Bush sings the lyrics with an unsettling stress – the words that are emphasised are 'nervous', 'desperate', 'nobody else'. The effect of the performance is to make listeners voyeurs, but what we are led to consider is not a pair of lovers but an adolescent sexual fantasy. The music contradicts the enjoyment that the lyric assert. Kate Bush's aesthetic intentions are denied by the musical conventions she uses.

Millie Jackson is a black American musician who has made a career out of the celebration of adult sexual pleasure. Her performances are put together around long risqué raps and her stance, in the words of *Spare Rib*, is somewhere between Wages for Housework and *Cosmopolitan*. 'He Wants to Hear the Words' is a routine song on Millie Jackson's LP *Get It Outcha' System*. She sings the song to a new lover; 'he' is the man she lives with:

> He wants to hear the words, needs to know that it's for real.
> He wants to hear me say that I love him in every way,
> Though he knows he's got a hold on me and I will stay.
> How can I tell him what I told you last night?

The song has a pretty tune, a gentle beat, and a delicate string arrangement. It has the conventional sound of an unhappy romantic ballad. But the passivity of this form is contradicted by the self-conscious irony of Millie Jackson's own performance. She gives the corny situation an interest that is not inherent in the song itself. She uses gospel conventions to express direct emotion, she uses her own customary mocking tone of voice to imply sexual need, and the effect is not to make the song's situation seem 'real' (the usual way in which great soul singers are said to transcend banal musical material) but to reverse its meaning. Millie Jackson is so obviously in control of her torn-between-two-lovers life that it is the man she lives with who becomes the figure of pathos – so desperate for deception, so easy to deceive. Millie Jackson's contempt for her man's dependence on romance becomes, implicitly, a contempt for the song itself, and its own expression of romantic ideology. It is impossible to listen to her performance without hearing it as a 'performance'. Millie Jackson contradicts the sexual meaning of the song's musical form in her very use of it.

Sexual Expression/Sexual Control

The recurrent theme of this essay has been that music is a means of sexual expression and as such is important as a mode of sexual control. Both in its presentation and in its use, rock has confirmed traditional definitions of what constitutes masculinity and femininity, and reinforces their expression in leisure pursuits. The dominant mode of control in popular music (the mode which is clearly embodied in teenybop culture) is the ideology of romance, which is itself the icing on the harsh ideology of domesticity. Romance is the central value of show biz and light entertainment, and in as far as pop musicians reach their public through radio, television and the press, they express traditional show-biz notions of glamour, femininity, and so forth. These media are crucial for establishing the appeal of certain types of pop star (Tom Jones, Gilbert O'Sullivan, Elton John, etc.), and they are particularly significant in determining the career possibilities of female musicians, as discussed earlier in this essay.

It was against this bland show-business background that rock was, and is, experienced as sexually startling. Rock, since its origins in rock 'n' roll, has given youth a more blatant means of sexual expression than is available elsewhere in the mass media and has therefore posed much more difficult problems of sexual control. Rock's rhythmic insistence can be heard as a sexual insistence, and girls have always been thought by mass moralists to be especially at risk; the music so obviously denies the concept of feminine respectability. In short, the ideology of youth developed in the 1960s by rock (among other media) had as its sexual component the assumption that a satisfying sexual relationship meant 'spontaneity', 'free expression', and the 'equality of pleasure'; sex in many ways came to be thought of as *best* experienced outside the restrictive sphere of marriage, with all its notions of true love and eternal monogamy. The point is, however, that this was a male-defined principle and at worst simply meant a greater emphasis on male sexual freedom. Rock never was about unrestricted, unconfined sexuality. Its expression may not have been controlled through the domestic ideology basic to pop as entertainment, but it has had its own mode of control, a mode which is clearly embodied in cock rock and which can be related to the general ideology of permissiveness that emerged in the 1960s: the 'liberated' emphasis on everyone's right to sexual choice, opportunity and gratification.

One of the most important activities to analyse if we're going to understand how sexual ideology works is dancing. The dance floor is the most public setting for music as sexual expression, and it is the place where pop and rock conventions overlap; for teenybop girls music is for dancing, and rock, too, for all its delusions of male grandeur, is still essentially a dance form. Girls have always flocked to dance halls, and their reason haven't just been to find a husband; dance is the one leisure activity in which girls and young women play a dominant role. Dancing for them is creative and physically satisfying. But more than this, dancing is also a socially sanctioned sexual activity – at least it becomes so when the boys, confident with booze, leave the bar and the corners to look for a partner from the mass of dancing girls.

One function of dance as entertainment, from Salome to Pan's People, has been to arouse men with female display, but this is not a function of most contemporary youth dancing – it remains an aspect of girls' own pleasure, even in the cattle-market context of a provincial dance hall. The girls are still concerned with attracting the lurking boys, but through their clothes, makeup and appearance – not through their dancing. This is equally true of boys' dances – their energy and agility are not being displayed to draw girls' attention; the most dedicated young dancers in Britain, the Northern soul fans, are completely self-absorbed.

The concept of narcissism, like that of realism, raises more difficult questions than we can answer here, but we do need to make one concluding point: rock's sexual effect is not just on the construction of femininity and masculinity. Rock also contributes to the more diffuse process of the sexualization of leisure.

The capitalist mode of production rests on a double distinction: between work and pleasure, between work and home. The alienation of the worker from the means of production means that the satisfaction of her or his needs becomes focused on leisure, on the one hand, and family on the other. Under capitalism, sexual expression is constituted as an individual leisure need – compare precapitalist modes of production, in which sexual expression is an aspect of a collective relationship with nature. This has numerous con sequences – the exchange of sex as a commodity, the exchange of commodities as sex – and means that we have to refer mass entertainment (films as well as music) to a theory of leisure as well as to a theory of ideology.

In writing this paper we have been conscious of our lack of an adequate theory of leisure. Underlying our analysis of rock and sexuality have been some nagging questions. What would non-sexist music sound like? Can rock be non-sexist? How can we counter rock's dominant sexual messages? These issues aren't purely ideological, matters of rock criticism. The sexual meaning of rock can't be read off independently of the sexual meaning of rock consumption, and the sexual meaning of rock consumption derives from the capitalist organization of production. In this essay we have described the ways in which rock constitutes sexuality for its listeners. Our last point is that sexuality is constituted in the very act of consumption.

Notes

This article first appeared in *Screen Education*, 29 (1978), London.

1 S. Rowbotham, *Woman's Consciousness, Man's World*, London, Penguin, 1973, pp. 14–15.
2 A 1967 issue of *Petticoat* magazine went so far as to urge girls to stop buying records and spend the money they saved on clothes, holidays and makeup. 'Borrow records from your boyfriend instead', the magazine suggested.
3 S. Sharpe, *Just Like a Girl*, London, Penguin, 1976.
4 L. Cooper, 'Women, Music, Feminism', *Musics*, October 1977.
5 S. I. Hayakawa, 'Popular Songs vs. the Facts of Life', in B. Rosenberg and D. M. White (eds), *Mass Culture*, New York, Free Press, 1957.
6 A. L. Lloyd, *Folk Song in England*, London, Paladin, 1975, p. 170.

11

Second-Hand Dresses and the Role of the Ragmarket (1985)

Miss Brooke had that kind of beauty which seems to be thrown into relief by poor dress. Her hand and wrist were so finely formed that she could wear sleeves not less bare of style than those of which the Blessed Virgin appeared to Italian painters.

—*Middlemarch*, George Eliot

She's dressed in old European clothes, scraps of brocade, out-of-date old suits, old curtains, odd oddments, old models, moth-eaten old fox furs, old otterskins, that's her kind of beauty, tattered, chill, plaintive and in exile, everything too big, and yet it looks marvellous. Her clothes are loose, she's too thin, nothing fits yet it looks marvellous. She's made in such a way, face and body, that anything that touches her shares immediately and infallibly in her beauty.

—*The Lover*, Marguerite Duras

Introduction

Several attempts have been made recently to understand 'retrostyle'. These have all taken as their starting point that accelerating tendency in the 1980s to ransack history for key items of dress, in a seemingly eclectic and haphazard manner. Some have seen this as part of the current vogue for nostalgia while others have interpreted it as a way of bringing history into an otherwise ahistorical present. This article will suggest that second-hand style or 'vintage dress' must be seen within the broader context of post-war subcultural history. It will pay particular attention to the exis-tence of an entrepreneurial infrastructure within these youth cultures and to the opportunities which second-hand style has offered young people, at a time of recession, for participating in the fashion 'scene'.

Most of the youth subcultures of the post-war period have relied on second-hand clothes found in jumble sales and ragmarkets as the raw material for the creation of style. Although a great deal has been written about the meaning of these styles little has been said about where they have come from. In the early 1980s the magazine *iD* developed a kind of *vox pop* of street style which involved stopping young people and asking them to itemise what they were wearing, where they had got it and for how much. Since then many of the weekly and monthly fashion publications have followed suit, with the result that this has now become a familiar feature of the magazine format. However, the act of buying and the processes of looking and choosing still remain relatively unexamined in the field of cultural analysis.

One reason for this is that shopping has been considered a feminine activity. Youth sociologists have looked mainly at the activities of adolescent boys and young men and their attention has been directed to those areas of experience which have a strongly masculine image. Leisure spheres which involve the wearing and displaying of clothes have been thoroughly documented, yet the hours spent seeking them out on Saturday afternoons continue to be overlooked. Given the emphasis on street culture or on public peer-group activities, this is perhaps not surprising, but it is worth remembering that although shopping is usually regarded as a private activity, it is also simultaneously a public one and in the case of the markets and second-hand stalls it takes place in the street. This is particularly important for girls and young women because in other contexts their street activities are still curtailed in contrast to those of their male peers. This fact has been commented upon by many feminist writers but the various pleasures of shopping have not been similarly engaged with.[1] Indeed, shopping has tended to be subsumed under the category of domestic labour with the attendant connotations of drudgery and exhaustion. Otherwise it has been absorbed into consumerism where women and girls are seen as having a particular role to play. Contemporary feminism has been slow to challenge the early 1970s orthodoxy which saw women as slaves to consumerism. Only Erica Carter's work has gone some way towards dislodging the view that to enjoy shopping is to be passively feminine and incorporated into a system of false needs.[2]

Looking back at the literature of the late 1970s on punk, it seems strange that so little attention was paid to the selling of punk, and the extent to which shops like the *Sex* shop run by Malcolm McLaren and Vivienne Westwood functioned also as meeting places where the customers and those behind the counter got to know each other and met up later in the pubs and clubs. In fact, ragmarkets and second-hand shops have played the same role up and down the country, indicating that there is more to buying and selling subcultural style than the simple exchange of cash for goods. Sociologists of the time perhaps ignored this social dimension because to them the very idea that style could be purchased over the counter went against the grain of those analyses which saw the adoption of punk style as an act of creative defiance far removed from the mundane act of buying. The role of McLaren and Westwood was also downgraded for the similar reason that punk was seen as a kind of collective creative impulse. To focus on a designer and an art-school entrepreneur would have been to undermine the 'purity' or 'authenticity' of the subculture. The same point can be made in relation to the absence of emphasis on buying subcultural products. What is found instead is an interest in those moments where the bought goods and items are transformed to subvert their original or intended meanings. In these accounts the act of buying disappears into that process of transformation. Ranked below these magnificent gestures, the more modest practices of buying and selling have remained women's work and have been of little interest to those concerned with youth cultural resistance.[3]

The literature on youth culture provides by no means the only point of entry to the question of second-hand fashion. It retains a usefulness, however, in its emphasis on the wider social and historical factors which frame youth cultural expressions and in the emphasis on the meaning and significance of the smallest and apparently most trivial of gestures and movements. Second-hand style has, in fact, a long history in British culture, but it was Peter Blake's sleeve for the Beatles' *Sgt Pepper* album which marked the entrance of anachronistic dressing into the mainstream of the pop and fashion business. In their luridly coloured military uniforms, the Beatles were at this point poised midway between the pop establishment and hippy psychedelia. The outfits, along with John Lennon's 'granny' spectacles and the other symbols of 'flower power' depicted on the cover, comprised a challenge to the grey conformity of male dress and an impertinent appropriation of official regalia for civilian anti-authoritarian, hedonistic wear.

Military uniforms were first found alongside the overalls and greatcoats in army surplus stores and on second-hand rails of shops such as

'Granny Takes a Trip', in the King's Road. Metalrimmed glasses added a further element to that theme in the counter-culture suggesting an interest in the old, the used, the overtly cheap and apparently unstylish. Standard male glasses had been until then black and horn-rimmed. National Health Service gold-coloured rims retained the stigma of poverty and the mark of parental will imposed on unwilling children. Lennon's cheap, shoddy specs became one of his trade marks. At the same time they came to represent one of the most familiar anti-materialist strands in hippy culture. They suggested a casual disregard for obvious signs of wealth, and a disdain for 'the colour of money'.

Stuart Hall saw in this 'hippy movement' an 'identification with the poor', as well as a disavowal of conventional middle-class smartness.[4] His comment touches on issues which are still at the heart of any analysis of second-hand style because the relationship to real poverty, or to particular stylised images of poverty, remains central. At an early point in its evolution the hippy subculture denounced material wealth and sought some higher reality, expressing this choice externally through a whole variety of old and second-hand clothes. None the less, these clothes were chosen and worn as a distinctive style and this style was designed to mark out a distance both from 'straight' and conventional dress, and from the shabby greyness of genuine poverty. A similar thread runs right through the history of post-war second-hand style. This has raised questions engaged with at a journalistic level by Tom Wolfe and then more recently by Angela Carter[5] ... Does rummaging through jumble sales make light of those who search in need and not through choice? Does the image of the middle-class girl 'slumming it' in rags and ribbons merely highlight social class differences? Wolfe poked fun at the *arriviste* young middle classes of America in the 1960s who were so well off that they could afford to look back and play around with the *idea* of looking poor. Almost twenty years later Angela Carter made the same point in relation to the 'ragamuffin look' favoured by post-punk girls, an image which held no attraction, she claimed, for working-class girls whose role-model was Princess Diana. Each of these writers see in second-hand style a kind of unconsciously patronising response to those who 'dress down' because they have to. It is an act of unintended class condescension.

While it is still the case that students and young 'bohemians' who possess what Pierre Bourdieu has called 'cultural capital' can risk looking poor and unkempt while their black and working-class counterparts dress up to counter the assumption of low status, there have been crucial social shifts which confuse this simple divide. Not all students in the 1980s are white, affluent and middle-class. Nor is it any longer possible to pose the world of street style or second-hand style against that of either high fashion or high street fashion. A whole range of factors have intervened to blur these divisions. For example, the street markets have themselves come into prominence and have been subjected to greater commercial pressure, while high street retailing has been forced to borrow from the tactics of the street trader. The sharpest illustration of these overlaps and cross-fertilisations lies, at present, in the wardrobes of the so-called young professionals, male and female. Those 'new' items which now make up his or her wardrobe were almost, to the last sock or stocking, discovered, restored and worn by the young men and women who worked in, or hung around, Camden Market and a whole series of provincial ragmarkets, in the late 1970s and early 1980s.

The ladies' suit announced as the high fashion item of summer 1988, is a reworking of the early 1960s Chanel suit worn by Jackie Kennedy and others. A bouclé wool version in pink and orange can be found on the rails of Next this season, but it is not simply a 1980s revamp of the Chanel original, because it was in the late 1970s, as part of her war on conventional femininity, that Poly Styrene first wore this most unflattering of outfits, the ladies' two-piece found in the jumble sale or ragmarket in abundance for 50p. Exactly the same process can be seen at work in the recent 'respectabilisation' of the classic gents' lightweight poplin raincoat. Designed by Jasper Conran and retailing at £350 in expensive department stores, with the cuffs turned up to reveal a quality striped lining, these were first found by great numbers of second-hand shoppers on the rails at Camden or even cheaper in the charity shops. Finally, there is the so-called 'tea dress', heavily advertised in the summers of both 1987 and 1988 by Laura Ashley, Next, Miss Selfridge and Warehouse. These are new versions of the high quality 1930s and 1940s printed crêpes sought out by girls and young women for many years, for the fall of their skirts and for their particularly feminine cut.

The parasitism of the major fashion labels on the post-punk subcultures is a theme which will be returned to later in this chapter. While fashion currently trades on the nostalgia boom, it also, more specifically, reworks the already recycled goods found in the street markets. It produces new and much more expensive versions of these originals in often poor quality fabrics and attempts to sell these styles, on an unprecedented scale, to a wider section of the population than those who wander round the ragmarkets. To understand more precisely the mechanisms through which this predatory relation reproduces itself, it would be necessary to examine questions which are beyond the scope of this article. In the concluding section they will be referred to briefly. They include the dependence of the fashion industry on media 'hype' and the consequent prominence of the 'designer' fresh out of college and surviving, in fact, on the Enterprise Allowance Scheme but none the less featured regularly in *Elle*; the huge explosion of the media industries in the 1980s and their dependence on an endless flow of fashion images again on an unprecedented scale; and finally, with this, a broader process sometimes described as 'the aestheticisation of culture'. This refers to the media expansion mentioned above, and with it the renunciation by some young people of the grey repertoire of jobs offered in the traditional fields of youth opportunities, and their preference for more self-expressive 'artistic' choices ... part time or self-employed work which offers the possibility of creativity, control, job satisfaction and perhaps even the promise of fame and fortune in the multimedia world of the image or the written word.

The Role of the Ragmarket

Second-hand style owes its existence to those features of consumerism which are characteristic of contemporary society. It depends, for example, on the creation of a surplus of goods whose use value is not expended when their first owners no longer want them. They are then revived, even in their senility, and enter into another cycle of consumption. House clearances also contribute to the mountain of bric-à-brac, jewellery, clothing and furniture which are the staple of junk and second-hand shops and stalls. But not all junk is used a second time around. Patterns of taste and discrimination shape the desires of second-hand shoppers as much as they do those who prefer the high street or the fashion showroom. And those who work behind the stalls and counters are skilled in choosing their stock with a fine eye for what will sell. Thus although there seems to be an evasion of the mainstream, with its mass-produced goods and marked-up prices, the 'subversive consumerism' of the ragmarket is in practice highly selective in what is offered and what, in turn, is purchased. There is in this milieu an even more refined economy of taste at work. For every single piece rescued and restored, a thousand are consigned to oblivion. Indeed, it might also be claimed that in the midst of this there is a thinly veiled cultural élitism in operation. The sources which are raided for 'new' second-hand ideas are frequently old films, old art photographs, 'great' novels, documentary footage and textual material. The apparent democracy of the market, from which nobody is excluded on the grounds of cost, is tempered by the very precise tastes and desires of the second-hand searchers. Second-hand style continually emphasizes its distance from second-hand clothing.

The London markets and those in other towns and cities up and down the country cater now for a much wider cross-section of the population. It is no longer a question of the *jeunesse dorée* rubbing shoulders with the poor and the down-and-outs.[6] Unemployment has played a role in diversifying this clientele, so also have a number of other less immediately visible shifts and changes. Young single mothers, for example, who fall between the teen dreams of punk fashion and the reality of pushing a buggy through town on a wet afternoon, fit exactly with this new constituency.[7] Markets have indeed become more socially diverse sites in the urban landscape. The Brick Lane area in London, for example, home to part of the Bangladeshi population settled in this country, attracts on a Sunday morning, young and old, black and white, middle-class and working-class shoppers as well as tourists and the merely curious browsers. It's not surprising that tourists include a market such as Brick Lane in their itinerary. In popular currency, street markets are taken to be reflective of the old and unspoilt, they are 'steeped in history' and are thus particularly expressive of the town or region.

The popularity of these urban markets also resides in their celebration of what seem to be pre-modern modes of exchange. They offer an oasis of cheapness, where every market day is a 'sale'. They point back in time to an economy unaffected by cheque cards, credit cards and even set prices. Despite the lingering connotations of wartime austerity, the market today promotes itself in the language of natural freshness (for food and dairy produce) or else in the language of curiosity, discovery and heritage (for clothes, trinkets and household goods). There is, of course, a great deal of variety in the types of market found in different parts of the country. In London there is a distinction between those markets modelled on the genuine fleamarkets, which tend to attract the kind of young crowd who flock each weekend to Camden Lock, and those which are more integrated into a neighbourhood providing it with fruit, vegetables and household items. The history of these more traditional street markets is already well documented. They grew up within the confines of a rapidly expanding urban economy and played a vital role in dressing (in mostly second-hand clothes), and feeding the urban working classes, who did not have access to the department stores, grocers or other retail outlets which catered for the upper and middle classes. As Phil Cohen has shown, such markets came under the continual surveillance of the urban administrators and authorities who were concerned with 'policing the working class city.'[8] The street markets were perceived by them as interrupting not only the flow of traffic and therefore the speed of urban development, but also as hindering the growth of those sorts of shops which would bring in valuable revenue from rates. These were seen as dangerous places, bringing together unruly elements who were already predisposed towards crime and delinquency; a predominantly youthful population of costermongers had to be brought into line with the labour discipline which already existed on the factory floor.

The street market functioned, therefore, as much as a daytime social meeting place as it did a place for transactions of money and goods. It lacked the impersonality of the department stores and thrived instead on the values of familiarity, community and personal exchange. This remains the case today. Wherever immigrant groups have arrived and set about trying to earn a living in a largely hostile environment, a local service economy in the form of a market has grown up. These offer some opportunities for those excluded from employment, and they also offer some escape from the monotony of the factory floor. A drift, in the 1970s and 1980s, into the micro-economy of the street market is one sign of the dwindling opportunities in the world of real work. There are now more of these stalls carrying a wider range of goods than before in most of the market places in the urban centres. There has also been a diversification into the world of new technology, with stalls offering cut-price digital alarms, watches, personal hi-fis, videotapes, cassettes, 'ghetto-blasters' and cameras. The hidden economy of work is also supplemented here by the provision of goods obtained illegally and sold rapidly at rock-bottom prices.

This general expansion coincides, however, with changing patterns in urban consumerism and with attempts on the part of mainstream retailers to participate in an unexpected boom. In the inner cities the bustling markets frequently breathe life and colour into otherwise desolate blighted areas. This, in turn, produces an incentive for the chain stores to reinvest, and in places such as Dalston Junction in Hackney, and Chapel Market in Islington, the redevelopment of shopping has taken place along these lines, with Sainsbury's, Boots the Chemist and others, updating and expanding their services. The stores flank the markets, which in turn line the pavements, and the consumer is drawn into both kinds of shopping simultaneously. In the last few years many major department stores have redesigned the way in which their stock is displayed in order to create the feel of a market place. In the 'Top Shop' basement in Oxford Street, for example, there is a year-round sale. The clothes are set out in chaotic abundance. The rails are crushed up against each other and packed with stock, which causes the customers to push and shove their way through. This intentionally hectic atmosphere is heightened by the disc jockey who cajoles the shoppers between records to buy at an even more frenzied pace.

Otherwise, in those regions where the mainstream department stores are still safely located on the other side of town, the traditional street market continues to seduce its customers with its own unique atmosphere. Many of these nowadays carry only a small stock of second-hand clothes. Instead, there are rails of 'seconds' or cheap copies of high street fashions made from starched fabric which, after a couple of washes, are ready for the dustbin. Bales of sari material lie stretched out on counters next to those displaying make-up and shampoo for black women. Reggae and funk music blare across the heads of shoppers from the record stands, and hot food smells drift far up the road. In the Ridley Road market in Hackney the hot bagel shop remains as much a sign of the originally Jewish population as the eel pie stall reflects traditional working-class taste. Unfamiliar fruits create an image of colour and profusion on stalls sagging under their weight. By midday on Fridays and at weekends the atmosphere is almost festive. Markets like these retain something of the pre-industrial gathering.

For the crowd of shoppers and strollers the tempo symbolises time rescued from that of labour, and the market seems to celebrate its own pleasures. Differences of age, sex, class and ethnic background take on a more positive quality of social diversity. The mode of buying is leisurely and unharassed, in sharp contrast to the Friday afternoon tensions around the checkout till in the supermarket.

Similar features can be seen at play in markets such as Camden Lock on Saturday and Sunday afternoons. Thousands of young people block Camden's streets so that only a trickle of traffic can get through. The same groups and the streams of punk tourists can be seen each week, joined by older shoppers and those who feel like a stroll in the sun, ending with an ice cream further along Chalk Farm Road. Young people go there to see and be seen if for any other reason than that fashion and style invariably look better worn than they do on the rails or in the shop windows. Here it is possible to see how items are combined with each other to create a total look. Hairstyles, shoes, skirts and 'hold-up' stockings; all of these can be taken in at a glance. In this context shopping is like being on holiday. The whole point is to amble and look, to pick up goods and examine them before putting them back. Public-school girls mingle with doped-out punks, ex-hippies hang about behind their Persian rug stalls as though they have been there since 1967, while more youthful entrepreneurs trip over themselves to make a quick sale.

Subcultural Entrepreneurs

The entrepreneurial element, crucial to an understanding of street markets and second-hand shops, has been quite missing from most subcultural analysis. The vitality of street markets today owes much to the hippy counter-culture of the late 1960s. It was this which put fleamarkets firmly back on the map. Many of those which had remained dormant for years in London, Amsterdam or Berlin, were suddenly given a new lease of life. In the years following the end of World War Two the thriving black markets gradually gave way to the fleamarkets which soon signalled only the bleakness of goods discarded. For the generation whose memories had not been blunted altogether by the dizzy rise of post-war consumerism, markets for old clothes and jumble sales in the 1960s remained a terrifying reminder of the stigma of poverty, the shame of ill-fitting clothing, and the fear of disease through infestation, rather like buying a second-hand bed.

Hippy preferences for old fur coats, crêpe dresses and army great-coats, shocked the older generation for precisely this reason. But they were not acquired merely for their shock value. Those items favoured by the hippies reflected an interest in pure, natural and authentic fabrics and a repudiation of the man-made synthetic materials found in high street fashion. The pieces of clothing sought out by hippy girls tended to be antique lace petticoats, pure silk blouses, crêpe dresses, velvet skirts and pure wool 1940's-styled coats. In each case these conjured up a time when the old craft values still prevailed and when one person saw through his or her production from start to finish. In fact, the same items had also won the attention of the hippies' predecessors, in the 'beat culture' of the early 1950s. They too looked for ways of by-passing the world of ready-made clothing. In the rummage sales of New York, for example, 'beat' girls and women bought up the fur coats, satin dresses and silk blouses of the 1930s and 1940s middle classes. Worn in the mid-1950s, these issued a strong sexual challenge to the spick and span gingham-clad domesticity of the moment. By the late 1960s, the hippy culture was a lot larger and much better off than the beats who had gone before them. It was also politi-cally informed in the sense of being determined to create an alternative society. This subculture was therefore able to develop an extensive semi-entrepreneurial network which came to be known as the counter-culture. This was by no means a monolithic enterprise. It stretched in Britain from hippy businesses such as Richard Branson's Virgin Records and Harvey Goldsmith's Promotions to all the ventures which sprang up in most cities and towns, selling books, vegetarian food, incense, Indian smocks, san-dals and so on. It even included the small art galleries, independent cin-emas and the London listings magazine *Time Out*.

From the late 1960s onwards, and accompanying this explosion of 'alternative' shops and restaurants, were the small second-hand shops whose history is less familiar. These had names like 'Serendipity', 'Cobwebs' or 'Past Caring' and they brought together, under one roof, all those items which had to be discovered separately in the jumble sales or fleamarkets. These included flying jackets, safari jackets, velvet curtains (from which were made the first 'loon' pants) and 1920s flapper dresses.

These second-hand goods provided students and others drawn to the sub-culture, with a cheaper and much more expansive wardrobe. (The two looks for girls which came to characterise this moment were the peasant 'ethnic' look and the 'crêpey' bohemian Bloomsbury look. The former later became inextricably linked with Laura Ashley and the latter with Biba, both mainstream fashion newcomers.) Gradually hippie couples moved into this second-hand market, just as they also moved into antiques. They rapidly picked up the skills of mending and restoring items and soon learnt where the best sources for their stock were to be found. This meant scouring the country for out-of-town markets, making trips to Amsterdam to pick up the long leather coats favoured by rich hippy types, and making thrice-weekly trips to the dry cleaners. The result was loyal customers, and if the young entrepreneurs were able to anticipate new demands from an even younger clientele, there were subsequent generations of punks, art students and others.

The presence of this entrepreneurial dynamic has rarely been acknowledged in most subcultural analysis. Those points at which subcul-tures offered the prospect of a career through the magical exchange of the commodity have warranted as little attention as the network of small-scale entrepreneurial activities which financed the counter-culture. This was an element, of course, vociferously disavowed within the hippy culture itself. Great efforts were made to disguise the role which money played in a whole number of exchanges, including those involving drugs. Selling goods and commodities came too close to 'selling out' for those at the heart of the subculture to feel comfortable about it. This was a stance reinforced by the sociologists who also saw consumerism within the counter-culture as a fall from grace, a lack of purity. They either ignored it, or else, employ-ing the Marcusian notion of recuperation, attributed it to the intervention of external market forces.[9] It was the unwelcome presence of media and other commercial interests which, they claimed, laundered out the politics and reduced the alternative society to an endless rail of cheesecloth shirts.

There was some dissatisfaction, however, with this dualistic model of creative action followed by commercial reaction. Dick Hebdige[10] and others have drawn attention to the problems of positing a raw and undi-luted (and usually working-class) energy, in opposition to the predatory youth industries. Such an argument discounted the local, promotional activities needed to produce a subculture in the first place. Clothes have to be purchased, bands have to find places to play, posters publicising these concerts have to be put up ... and so on. This all entails business and managerial skills even when these are displayed in a self-effacing manner. The fact that a spontaneous sexual division of labour seems to spring into being is only a reflection of those gender inequalities which are prevalent at a more general level in society. It is still much easier for girls to develop skills in those fields which are less contested by men than it is in those already occupied by them. Selling clothes, stage-managing at concerts, handing out publicity leaflets, or simply looking the part, are spheres in which a female presence somehow seems natural.[11]

While hippy style had run out of steam by the mid-1970s the alternative society merely jolted itself and rose to the challenge of punk. Many of those involved in selling records, clothes and even books, cropped their hair, had their ears pierced and took to wearing tight black trousers and Doctor Martens boots. However, the conditions into which punk erupted and of which it was symptomatic for its younger participants were quite different from those which had cushioned the hippy explosion of the 1960s. Girls were certainly more visible and more vocal than they had been in the earlier subculture, although it is difficult to assess exactly how active they were in the do-it-yourself entrepreneurial practices which accompanied, and were part of, the punk phenomenon. Certainly the small independent record companies remained largely male, as did the journalists and even the musicians (though much was made of the angry femininity of Poly Styrene, The Slits, The Raincoats and others). What is less ambiguous is the connection with youth unemployment, and more concretely, within punk, with the disavowal of some of the employment which was on offer for those who were not destined for university, the professions or the conventional career structures of the middle classes.

Punk was, first and foremost, cultural. Its self-expressions existed at the level of music, graphic design, visual images, style and the written word. It was therefore engaging with and making itself heard within the terrain of the arts and the mass media. Its point of entry into this field existed within the range of small-scale youth industries which were able to put the whole thing in motion. Fan magazines (fanzines) provided a training for new wave journalists, just as designing record sleeves for unknown punk bands offered an opportunity for keen young graphic designers. In the realm of style the same do-it-yourself ethic prevailed and the obvious place to start was the jumble sale or the local fleamarket. Although punk also marked a point at which boys and young men began to participate in fashion unashamedly, girls played a central role, not just in looking for the right clothes but also in providing their peers with a cheap and easily available supply of second-hand items. These included 1960s' cotton print 'shifts' like those worn by the girls in The Human League in the early 1980s (and in the summer of 1988 'high fashion' as defined by MaxMara and others), suedette sheepskin-styled jackets like that worn by Bob Dylan on his debut album sleeve (marking a moment in the early 1960s when he too aspired to a kind of 'lonesome traveller' hobo look), and many other similarly significant pieces.

This provision of services in the form of dress and clothing for would-be punks, art students and others on the fringe, was mostly participated in by lower middle-class art and fashion graduates who rejected the job opportunities available to them designing for British Home Stores or Marks and Spencer. It was a myth then, and it is still a myth now, that fashion houses are waiting to snap up the talent which emerges from the end-of-term shows each year. Apart from going abroad, most fashion students are, and were in the mid-1970s, faced with either going it alone with the help of the Enterprise Allowance Schemes (EAS), or else with joining some major manufacturing company specialising in down-market mass-produced fashion. It is no surprise, then, that many, particularly those who wanted to retain some artistic autonomy, should choose the former. Setting up a stall and getting a licence to sell second-hand clothes, finding them and restoring them, and then using a stall as a base for displaying and selling newly designed work, is by no means unusual. Many graduates have done this and some, like Darlajane Gilroy and Pam Hogg, have gone on to become well-known names through their appearance in the style glossies like *The Face*, *Blitz* and *iD*, where the emphasis is on creativity and on fashion-as-art.

Many others continue to work the markets for years, often in couples and sometimes moving into bigger stalls or permanent premises. Some give up, re-train or look round for other creative outlets in the media. The expansion of media goods and services which has come into being in the last ten years, producing more fashion magazines, more television from independent production companies, more reviews about other media events, more media personalities, more media items about other media phenomena, and so on, depends both on the successful and sustained manifestation of 'hype' and also on the labour power of young graduates and school leavers for whom the allure of London and metropolitan life is irresistible. For every aspiring young journalist or designer there are many thousands, however, for whom the media remains tangible only at the point of consumption. Despite the lingering do-it-yourself ethos of punk, and despite 'enterprise culture' in the 1980s, this bohemian world is as distant a phenomenon for many media-struck school-leavers as it has always been for their parents. 'Enterprise subcultures' remain small and relatively privileged metropolitan spaces.

Baby Dresses and Girls in Men's Suits

Nonetheless, the 'implosionary' effect of the mass media means that in the 1980s youth styles and fashions are born into the media. There is an 'instantaneity' which replaces the old period of subcultural incubation. The relentless forces of consumerism now operate at the style-face with teams of stylists being sent out by the magazines each month to scour the market places and end-of-term fashion shows for commercial ideas. Students who start off working on the stalls move, often to their own labels, within a year of leaving college, with the help of the EAS and a bank loan. They provide magazines and journalists with strong images and lively copy and the whole system reproduces itself at an increasingly frenzied speed. Thanks to the vitality of the style glossies, the fashion business becomes more confident about and more conversant with fashion language. As more column inches are given over to fashion in the daily and weekly quality newspapers (adding a dash of colour to the black and white format and catering for the 'new' women readers at the same time) fashion learns to talk about itself with a new fluency, it can even mock itself.[12]

Mainstream fashion has a lot to thank youth subcultures for. It can gesture back in time knowing that its readers have been well educated, through the media, in post-war pop culture history. Often it is enough just to signal Brian Jones's hairstyle, or Jimi Hendrix's hat and scarf, or Cathy

McGowan's floppy fringe, as though they have already been immortalised as Andy Warhol prints. They remain recognisable as traces, signs or even as fragments of signs. This instant recall on history, fuelled by the super-fluity of images thrown up by the media, has produced in style a non-stop fashion parade in which 'different decades are placed together with no historical continuity'.[13] Punk do-it-yourself fashion has transformed fash-ion into pop art, and collecting period fashion pieces into a serious hobby.

From the mid-1970s punk girls salvaged shockingly lurid lurex minis of the sort worn in Italian 'jet-set' films of the mid-1960s. They reinstated the skinny-rib jumper and plastic earrings (worn by Pauline of Penetration and Fay Fife of The Rezillos) as well as any number of 'shift' dresses into the fashion mainstream. They also reclaimed tarty fishnet stockings, black plastic mini skirts and, of course, ski pants. When Debbie Harry first appeared in this country she was dressed in classic New York hooker style with white, knee-length, 'these boots are made for walkin'' boots, micro skirt and tight black jumper. Television shows, even puppet TV shows, as well as 1960s movies such as *Blow Up* and, of course, all the old James Bond films, were continually raided by the 'new' stylists in search of ideas. Paul Weller, for example, joined this rush in the early 1980s and uncov-ered old pieces of 1960s 'Mod' clothing which were then installed as part of the 1980s 'soulboy' wardrobe ... Jon Savage has described this plunder-ing of recent style history displayed each week at Camden Lock as fol-lows: 'Fashion, cars, buildings from the last hundred years piled up in an extraordinary display ... a jungle where anything could be so worn, driven, even eaten as long as it was old.'[14] Savage reinforces Frederic Jameson's gloomy prognosis of the post-modern condition in this 'mass flight into nostalgia'.[15] Loss of faith in the future has produced a culture which can only look backwards and re-examine key moments of its own recent his-tory with a sentimental gloss and a soft focus lens. Society is now incapa-ble of producing serious images, or texts which give people meaning and direction. The gap opened up by this absence is filled instead with cultural bric-à-brac and with old images recycled and reintroduced into circula-tion as pastiche.

It is easy to see how this argument can be extended to include second-hand style, which in the early and mid-1980s did indeed appear to the observer like a bizarre pantomime parade where themes and strands from recognisable historical moments seemed to be combined at random. Against Savage and Jameson however, it might be argued that these styles are neither nostalgic in essence nor without depth. Nostalgia indicates a desire to recreate the past faithfully, and to wallow in such mythical representations. Nostalgia also suggests an attempt at period accuracy, as in a costume drama. While both of these are true, for example, of Laura Ashley fashions, they are certainly not apparent in contemporary second-hand style. This style is marked out rather by a knowingness, a wilful anarchy and an irrepressible optimism, as indicated by colour, exaggeration, humour and disavowal of the conventions of adult dress.

The best known examples of this are the two girl groups, Bananarama and Amazulu, and the pop presenter Paula Yates. The wardrobes of Yates and the others are still drawn in spirit, if not in practice, from the jumble sale or the second-hand market. Paula Yates's 'silly' dresses and gigantic hair bows are like outfits salvaged from a late 1950s children's birthday party. The huge baggy trousers worn by Bananarama, tied round the waist 'like a sack of potatoes', their black plimsolls and haystack hairstyles caught up with straggly cotton headscarves are equally evocative of an urchin childhood or a 'Grapes of Wrath' adolescence. It is as though the Bananarama girls tumbled out of bed and put on whatever came to hand without their mothers knowing. Amazulu's gypsy dresses worn with cascades of hair ribbons and Doctor Martens boots creates a similar effect. Again and again they gesture back to a childhood rummage through a theatrical wardrobe and the sublime pleasure of 'dressing up'. There is a refusal of adult seriousness and an insistence on hedonism and hyperbole. The 1950s ball-gown glamour sought out by Paula Yates is undercut by the sheer excessiveness of it. Paula Yates's wardrobe exists within the realms of high camp. Her style of presentation and style of dress create an image of pure pastiche.

However this pastiche is celebratory rather than reflective of a sterile and depthless mainstream culture. It plays with the norms, conventions and expectations of femininity, post feminism. Each item is worn self-consciously with an emphasis on the un-natural and the artificial. Madonna remains the other best-known exemplar of this rags, ribbons and lace style. She wore her mid-1980s image like a mask and with what Kaja Silverman has described as a sense of 'ironic distance'.[16]

The other most influential image in the fashion horizons of the 1980s which also drew on second-hand style flirted with the idea of androgyny. Punk androgyny was never unambiguously butch or aggressive, it was slim, slight and invariably 'arty'. The Robert Mapplethorpe cover of Patti Smith's first album made a strong impression on those who were less keen on studs, chains and bondage trousers. Smith appeared casual, unmade-up with a jacket slung over her shoulders and a tie loosened at her neck. The cuffs of her shirt were visibly frayed and she faced the camera direct with a cool, scrutinizing gaze. This cautious but somehow threatening androgyny had a much greater resonance than, for example, Diane Keaton's very feminine take-up of the male wardrobe in the Woody Allen film *Annie Hall*. She too ransacked the traditional gents' wardrobe but her image was New York 'kooky' and eccentric (ex-hippy), and not even vaguely menacing. Smith was unmistakably from the New York underground. She was pale-faced, dark, undernourished, intense and 'committed'.

Patti Smith sent bohemian girls off in search of these wide, baggy and unflattering clothes, while *Annie Hall* alerted others to the feminine potential of the male wardrobe. She made the do-it-yourself look attractive to those less familiar with the ragmarket, and balanced her shirts and ties with a soft, floppy, feminine hat. Suddenly all those male items which had lain untouched for years in second-hand shops, charity shops and street markets came to life. Nothing was left untouched including cotton pyjama tops, shirts, jackets, evening suits and tuxedos, overcoats, raincoats, trousers and even the occasional pair of shiny black patent evening shoes, small enough to fit female feet. Men's jackets replaced early 1970s figure-hugging jackets with an inverted pyramidic line. The exaggerated shoulders narrowed slowly down to below the hips creating a strong but none the less slimming effect. This was immediately taken up by fashion writers as 'liberating'. It covered all 'irregularities' in size, imposing instead a homogenously baggy look. It was a style open to all, not just the size 10s and 12s. As a result these jackets began to appear 'new', in chain stores and exclusive boutiques up and down the country. They were soon being worn by high-flying businesswomen as well as by secretaries, professionals and others. These 'new' jackets imitated what had been a necessary alteration on those bought second-hand. Instead of shortening male-length sleeves, these had simply been turned up revealing the high quality, soft, striped silk lining. Again, the effect of this was to lighten an otherwise dark and fairly heavy image. The same feature appeared in the second-hand winter coats found in 'Flip' and in markets like that at Camden Lock. The huge surplus of tweed overcoats kept prices low and the range of choice extensive. These too were adapted for female use by turning up the sleeves, as were their summer equivalents, the lightweight cotton raincoats of which there was, and still is, a vast discarded 'mountain'. This effect was soon copied in new overcoats for both men and women. It can be seen in outlets as exclusive as Joseph's and Paul Smith's and also in Warehouse and Miss Selfridge. However, the cost of such garments in fabric comparable to that found in their second-hand equivalents makes them prohibitively expensive. This in itself forces a much wider range of shoppers, including the so-called young professionals, back towards Flip and Camden Lock.

These items of male clothing never conferred on girls and women a true androgyny. There was instead a more subtle aesthetic at work. The huge, sweeping greatcoats imposed a masculine frame on what was still an unmistakably feminine form. All sorts of softening devices were added to achieve this effect – diamante brooches, lop-sided berets, provocatively red lipstick, and so on. A similar process took place round the appropriation of the male shirt. It too seemed baggy and egalitarian and thus in keeping with 1970s feminist critiques of fashion. But these shirts were tightly tucked into a thick waistband which just as surely emphasised the traditional hour-glass figure. Men's shirts ushered in the new shape for female clothing. Their sleeve line fell far below the shoulder on women, often connecting with the body of the garment halfway down the arm. This produced a 'batwing' effect which in turn was taken up by manufacturers and marketed as such. The inverted pyramid shape here took the form of an elongated arm and shoulder line narrowing down at each side to a small and feminine waist.

Alongside these, other 'stolen' items began to appear in the high street. Tuxedos (favoured by Princess Diana), bow ties, silk evening shirts, and for everyday wear, flat, black patent, lace-up shoes. For two consecutive winters these were as ubiquitous as leggings were in the summer. And in both cases the point of origin was the man's wardrobe. Indeed, leggings offer a good example. These first appeared alongside the gent's vests, in a cream-coloured knitted cotton fabric, as winter underpants, again in places like Camden Market. They had an elasticated waistband and button opening at the front. Punk girls began to buy them as summer alternatives to their winter ski pants. Dyed black, they created a similar effect. Then, the stall-holders dyed them and sold them in a dark, murky, grey-black shade. But they still suffered from the design faults which arise from adapting male lower garments for women. They were cut too low at the waist and frequently slid down. The fly front cluttered the smooth line across the stomach and they were often too short at the crotch. It was not long, therefore, before the same stall-holders were making up their own models in the professionally dyed brushed cotton fabric popularised through consumer demand for track suits and sweatshirts. By the summers of 1985 and 1986 these were being worn by what seemed to be the entire female population aged under thirty. They were combined with wide, baggy male-shaped shirts, headscarves knotted on top 1940s munitions-worker style, children's black plimsolls (or else smart walking shoes) and lightweight cotton jackets.

The popularity of the male wardrobe therefore reflects a similar confusion of meanings as those thrown up by second-hand 'baby' dressing. In this apparently androgynous context these meanings highlight an appreciation of high-quality fabrics of the sort rarely found in mass-produced goods, a desire also to reinstate them to their former glory, and even a desire to wear something 'socially useful'. By recycling discarded pieces of clothing new wearers are not only beating the system by finding and defining high fashion cheaply, they are also making good use of the social surplus. An ecological ideal thus resides alongside the desire for artifice, decoration and ambiguous, double-edged femininity.

The Death of the Designer

Writing in the early 1970s Tom Wolfe offered one of the few fragments on the subject of second-hand dress when he labelled this style, along with that ethnic look made fashionable for whites by the Black Panthers, 'radical chic'. This meant dressing down, looking righteous and wearing 'jeans of the people ... hod carrier jeans ... and woolly green socks, that kind you get at the Army surplus at two pair for twenty nine cents'.[17] For those seeking to achieve the white equivalent of Afro-style this meant going natural: 'God knows Panther women don't spend thirty minutes in front of the mirror shoring up their eye holes with contact lenses, eyeliner, eye shadow, eyebrow pencil... .'[18]

Wolfe went on to suggest that on a grander scale *'nostalgie de la boue'* marked the arrival of a thrusting new middle class sufficiently confident culturally and socially to outrage their stuffier class equals by asserting in an upfront way where they have come from, through dressing in the 'styles of the lower orders'. These 'Peter, Paul and Mary' hippy types and with their apparently unwashed appearance and preference for old, discarded clothes brought out, on the part of the urbane Wolfe, a tone of slight disdain: 'She didn't wear nylons, she didn't wear make up, she had bangs and long straight hair down below her shoulders ...'[19] The point which Wolfe made is one commonly enough asserted, that this 'poverty dressing' is both insulting to 'the people' and ill judged: '... today the oppressed, the hard core youth of the ghetto, they aren't into ... Army surplus socks. If you tried to put one of those lumpy lumberjack shirts on them, they'd vomit.'[20]

In a much more recent piece in *New Society*, Angela Carter makes the same point.[21] The focus here is on an image widely displayed in the city centre hoardings and in the London Underground in 1983 to advertise the magazine *19*. The model is dressed in an assortment of wide, baggy clothes, in this case new but drawn in spirit from the ragmarket: 'But if you didn't know she was a fashion model, the girl in the poster ... would in fact look like nothing so much as a paper bag lady (or rather person), in her asexually shaped jacket, loose trousers, sagging socks, with a scarf of dubious soiled colour wrapped round her head like a bandage, beneath a hat jammed firm down ... .'[22] Carter sees this as a style favoured, once again, by the rich who can afford to play at looking poor: '... it is ironic that rich girls (such as students) swan about in rancid long johns with ribbons in their hair, when the greatest influence on working class girls would appear to be Princess Di... .'[23] Both Angela Carter and Tom Wolfe recognise that for working-class people the structure of the working day, the tyranny of the clock, and the monotony of work, with its uniforms, overalls and aprons, conspire to produce in leisure an overwhelming desire to mark out distance from the factory floor. In contrast, the middle classes, who can achieve individuality in dress on a day-to-day basis, have no need for a 'Sunday best'. Likewise, because they have to dress up during the working day for their professional roles, they are able to dress down in leisure and to 'slop about' as students.

The problem is that this is now being changed by forces beyond the control of either of the two groups. In the 1980s, for old and young alike, the discipline of the factory clock no longer prevails. The unemployed and semi-employed have been cast adrift, and for many young men and women their attention has turned inwards towards the body. Wild peacock punk dressing of the type seen on the streets in the early 1980s signified this body politics, this making strange through an excessive masquerade, a 'quotidien marvellous'.[24]

There have been changes on both sides of the class divide. Students are not, as Angela Carter suggests, 'rich girls'. Many are barely scraping along on their grants with no parental back-up. This is even more true for the ranks of the student body who would once have proceeded into training or an apprenticeship but are now finding their way into further and higher education. This too marks the increasing fluidity across the old class lines which previously distinguished working-class from middle-class youth. Of course, it does not mean that all young people now dress in what Carter labelled 'recession style'. There are as many girls who still aspire to the Princess Di look as there are boys who model themselves on the 'casual' elegance of Italian style. It does mean however that there is a much wider constituency for ragmarket shopping than was once the case.

This fluidity is reflected across all the other social sites and fashion spheres engaged with here. The high street emulates the style of the market-place and takes up the ideas of those who produce for the markets. At the same time, for the do-it-yourself 'designers' and stall-holders the lure of the mainstream is not altogether unattractive. Many sell simultaneously to the department stores and to the passing crowds at Camden or Kensington Market. Self-employment of this sort is both an attempt to participate in an economy unwilling to open itself up to school leavers and graduates alike and an act of evasion, an evasion of those sorts of dull jobs which are promised at the end of a work experience programme. All of the styles described above have been seen as part of the contemporary interest in 'retro'. They have therefore been linked with other visual images which draw on and 'quote' from past sources or earlier genres. These are now most prominent in the world of advertising and in pop videos where some nebulous but nonetheless popular memory is evoked in the swirl of a petticoat or the sweep of a duster coat. It is unwise however to place second-hand style unproblematically within that cultural terrain marked out by Frederic Jameson as the sphere of post modernity. This would be to conflate retro-dressing as merely yet another cultural re-run, no different from the nostalgic re-makes of 1940s 'B' movies, or the endless re-releases and revivals of old hit records.

These trends, including that of second-hand dress, require much more specific analysis. While pastiche and some kind of fleeting nostalgia might indeed play a role in second-hand style, these have to be seen more precisely within the evolution of post-war youth cultures. Second-hand style in this context reveals a more complex structure offering, among other things a kind of internal, unofficial job market within these 'enterprise subcultures'. Girls and young women have played a major role, not just in providing youth subcultures with their items of style and dress, but also in re-discovering these items and imaginatively re-creating them. Despite being at the vanguard of style in this respect, these young women have been passed over and eclipsed in the fashion pages by the young 'geniuses' of fashion in the 1980s like John Galliano or John Flett. In fact fashion designers play a much less central role in setting fashion trends than is commonly imagined. There is even a case to be made for the 'death of the designer', since the main impetus for changes in fashion and in contemporary consumer culture, as this article has argued, comes from below, from those who keep an eye open for redeemable pieces which are then re-inscribed into the fashion system.

Notes

Originally published in *Zoot Suits and Second-Hand Dresses*, ed. A. McRobbie, Macmillan, Basingstoke, 1989.

1 P. Cohen, 'Policing the Working Class City' in B. Fine *et al.*, *Capitalism and the Rule of Law*, London, Hutchinson, 1979.
2 E. Carter, 'Alice in Consumer Wonderland' in A. McRobbie and M. Nava (eds), *Gender and Generation*, London, Macmillan, 1979.
3 S. Hall *et al.*, *Resistance through Rituals*, London, Hutchinson, 1977 and D. Hebdige, *Subculture: The Meaning of Style*, London, Methuen, 1979.
4 S. Hall, 'The Hippies: An American Moment', CCCS Stencilled Papers, University of Birmingham, 1977.

5 T. Wolfe, *Radical Chic and Man Maning the Flak Catchers*, New York, Bantam Books, 1974, and A. Carter, 'The Recession Style', *New Society*, January, 1983.

6 Paddy's Market in Glasgow, in the early 1970s, offered one of the best examples of absolute social polarity in second-hand shopping.

7 The Birmingham Ragmarket in the late 1970s provided many similar examples of social diversity in second-hand shopping.

8 P. Cohen (1979).

9 J. Clarke, 'Style' in S. Hall (ed.) *et al., Resistance through Rituals*, London, Hutchinson, 1977.

10 D. Hebdige (1979) and A. McRobbie, 'Settling the Accounts with Subcultures: A Feminist Critique' in *Screen Education* no. 34, reprinted in T. Bennett (ed.), *Culture, Ideology and Social Process*, London, Academia Press, 1981.

11 A. McRobbie and J. Garber, 'Girls and Subcultures: An Exploration' in S. Hall *et al., Resistance through Rituals*, London, Hutchinson, 1977.

12 Sally Ann Lasson reviewed Nicholas Coleridge's *The Fashion Conspiracy* by poking fun at her own profession which specialises in lines like 'Paris was awash with frothy femininity', *Observer*, 20 March 1988.

13 J. Savage, 'Living in the Past', *Time Out*, February 1983.

14 J. Savage (1983).

15 F. Jameson, 'Postmodernism, the Cultural Logic of Capital' in H. Foster (ed.) *Postmodern Culture*, London, Pluto Press, 1985.

16 K. Silverman, 'Fragments of a Fashionable Discourse', in T. Modeleski *Studies in Entertainment: Critical Approaches to Mass Culture*, Bloomington and Indianapolis, Indiana University Press, 1986.

17 T. Wolfe (1974).

18 Ibid.

19 Ibid.

20 Ibid.

21 A. Carter (1983).

22 Ibid.

23 Ibid.

24 A. Breton, *What Is Surrealism?*, London, Pluto Press, 1981.

12

Rethinking 'Moral Panic' for Multi-Mediated Social Worlds (1995)

with Sarah L. Thornton

'Moral panic' is now a term regularly used by journalists to describe a process which politicians, commercial promoters and media habitually attempt to incite. It has become a standard interview question to put to Conservative MPs: are they not whipping up a moral panic as a foil to deflect attention away from more pressing economic issues? It has become a routine means of making youth-orientated cultural products more alluring; acid house music was marketed as 'one of the most controversial sounds of 1988' set to outrage 'those who decry the glamorization of drug culture.'[1] Moreover, as moral panics seem to guarantee the kind of emotional involvement that keeps up the interest of, not just tabloid, but broadsheet newspaper readers, as well as the ratings of news and true crime television, even the media themselves are willing to take some of the blame. Sue Cameron, discussing 'new juvenile crime' on BBC2's *Newsnight*, asks, 'Is it not the media itself which has helped to create this phenomenon?'

Moral panics, once the unintended outcome of journalistic practice, seem to have become a goal. Rather than periods to which societies are subject 'every now and then' (Cohen 1972/80: 9), moral panics have become the way in which daily events are brought to the attention of the public. They are a standard response, a familiar, sometimes weary, even ridiculous rhetoric rather than an exceptional emergency intervention. Used by politicians to orchestrate consent, by business to promote sales in certain niche markets, and by media to make home and social affairs newsworthy, moral panics are constructed on a daily basis.

Given their high rate of turnover and the increasing tendency to label all kinds of media event as 'moral panic', we think it is time to take stock of the revisions, then consider the strengths and weaknesses of this key concept. Although both the original model of moral panics and the reformulations which introduced notions of ideology and hegemony were exemplary interventions in their time, we argue that it is impossible to rely on the old models with their stages and cycles, univocal media, monolithic societal or hegemonic reactions. The proliferation and fragmentation of mass, niche and micro-media and the multiplicity of voices, which compete and contest the meaning of the issues subject to 'moral panic', suggest that both the original and revised models are outdated in so far as they could not possibly take account of the labyrinthine web of determining relations which now exist between social groups and the media, 'reality' and representation.

The Original Theory of Moral Panics

Although the argument that media coverage can have an active role in creating deviant behaviour owes its existence to symbolic interactionist theories of 'labelling' (cf. Becker 1963; Wilkins 1964), it was the pioneering studies of Jock Young (1971) on the social meaning of drug-taking and Stanley Cohen (1972/1980) on the media-inspired confrontations between mods and rockers, and their edited collections (Cohen 1971; Cohen and Young 1973) which developed and effectively launched the concept of 'moral panic'. Not only did their studies explore how agents of social control like the police played a role in 'amplifying' deviance, but they developed a vocabulary for understanding the powerful part played by the media. This meant going beyond the sociological accounts which looked at patterns of ownership and control as signs of complicity between media and government. Attention was now being paid to the ideological role of the media and the active construction of certain kinds of meaning.

In addition, this work explored how deviant behaviour was interactive rather than absolutist. It was more often the outcome of complex chains of social interaction than the product of young people with a predisposition, individually or environmentally, towards crime or rule-breaking behaviour. Finally this approach challenged moral guardians by suggesting that their overreaction was counterproductive. The media coverage of deviance acted as a kind of handbook of possibilities to be picked over by new recruits. Worse still, segregating young people away from the community created a greater risk of long-term social disorder since 'a society can control effectively only those who perceive themselves to be members of it' (Young 1971: 39). Overreaction, therefore, contributed to further polarization, though this might have been the desired effect, as Stuart Hall *et al.* (1979) later argued.

Cohen's *Folk Devils and Moral Panics* is rightfully a classic of media sociology, embracing a greater degree of complexity than the many summaries of the work indicate. He acknowledges that social control is uneven and much less mechanistic than the model of deviancy amplification suggests. Indeed one group of respondents (drawn from the non-mod, non-rocker public) criticizes the media for over-reporting the clashes, while others describe how they came down to the beach to have a look at the 'fun'. Cohen has a sophisticated grasp of how these events fed into popular folklore ('Where are the mods and rockers today?' was a question he was repeatedly asked while carrying out his fieldwork) and when the panic had finally run its course and de-amplification had set in, the characters in this drama settled into history as recognizable social types belonging to a particular period, sometimes referred to, even by the agents of social control, with a hint of nostalgia.

Hooligans, History, and Hegemony

Engaging directly with the law and other rhetoric of Thatcherism in the late 1970s and into the 1980s, Geoff Pearson's *Hooligans: A History· of Respectable Fears* (1983) focuses on the way moral panics often entail looking back to a 'golden age' where social stability and strong moral discipline acted as a deterrent to delinquency and disorder. However, twenty years previously, the same process could be seen in operation: the 'kids' were seen as unruly and undisciplined, unlike their counterparts of the previous decade. The same anxieties appear with startling regularity; these involve the immorality of young people, the absence of parental control, the problem of too much free time leading to crime, and the threat which deviant behaviour poses to national identity and labour discipline. Pearson shows how, during the 1940s, there were scares about 'cosh boys' and Blitz kids and how, in the 1930s, there were a string of moral panics about the misuse of leisure time and the decline of the British way of life through the popularity of Hollywood cinema. Pursuing this chain of investigation back through the nineteenth century, Pearson argues that the nature of the complaints and the social response to them provides a normative and consensual language for understanding the turbulence of social change and discontinuity. The value of this historical study is to cast a critical shadow over any claims about the dramatic rise in violent crimes carried out by young people. Instead, it shows how moral panics in society act as a form of ideological cohesion which draws on a complex language of nostalgia.

The studies of Cohen, Young and Pearson show moral panics as acting on behalf of the dominant social order. They are a means of orchestrating consent by actively intervening in the space of public opinion and social consciousness through the use of highly emotive and rhetorical language which has the effect of requiring that 'something be done about it'. The argument about deviancy amplification is precisely that where such strategies are indeed followed by social and legislative action, they also reassure the public that there is strong government and strong leadership.

It is only with theories of ideology that the idea of the media's moral panics as defining and distorting social issues gives way to a more integrated and connective understanding of the construction of meaning across the whole range of media forms and institutions. *Policing the Crisis* (1979) by Stuart Hall and his colleagues at the Centre for Contemporary Cultural Studies (CCCS), University of Birmingham, marks a turning point in this respect. They introduced a more Marxist and a more theoretical vocabulary to the terrain, which was more palatable to British sociologists than much of the structuralist and semiological analysis of the mass media which followed it, first, because it drew on the empirical model of the moral panic and, second, because of its concern for history and political culture. As a result, *Policing the Crisis* can be seen as bridging the gap between sociology and cultural studies.

Policing the Crisis introduced the Gramscian concept of hegemony to analyse the way in which moral panics around mugging and the alleged criminality of young Afro-Caribbean males created the social conditions of consent which were necessary for the construction of a society more focused towards law and order and less inclined to the liberalism and 'permissiveness' of the 1960s. This particular analysis of the moral panic shows it not to be an isolated phenomenon but a connective strategy, part of the practice of hegemony which enlarges the sphere of influence which Gramsci labelled 'civil society'. The moral panic then becomes an envoy for dominant ideology. In the language of common sense, it operates as an advance warning system, and as such it progresses from local issues to matters of national importance, from the site of tension and petty anxieties to full-blown social and political crisis. The authors are alert to the complexity of historical and social breakdown which, they claim, can then be managed only through the escalation of the control and coercion. This begs many questions in relation to the scale of social control, but what is particularly important is the recognition that ideology is a suffusive social process, and that it is not a simple question of the distortion of truth, but rather that ideology is a force which works continuously through the mobilization of 'common sense'.

Despite the pivotal position *Policing the Crisis* occupies in the history of the concept of moral panic, the panoramic sweep of its Gramsci-influenced argument across the entire landscape of post-war Britain makes it more a work of classic neo-Marxist scholarship than a sociology of deviance. Critical response has thus been divided between those sociologists who take issue with the study's empirical claims, suggesting as Waddington does that

the evidence cited in support of the view that the situation with regard to crime in general and 'muggings' in particular was not getting dramatically worse, and in some respects shows an improvement, does not in fact support this contention. (Waddington 1986: 257)

and writers like Paul Gilroy who draw from the study a vocabulary for developing further an analysis of race and ethnicity, relocating *Policing the Crisis* within a more distinctly Cultural Studies perspective (Gilroy 1987). More recently Schlesinger and Tumber (1994) have returned to the sociology of crime reporting and both responded to Hall *et al.* (1981) and re-visited moral panic theory as a whole.

As its title suggests, Simon Watney's *Policing Desire* (1987) looks not at crime but at so-called deviant sexual practice, taking the debates of *Policing the Crisis* further by providing a foundation for a better understanding of how controversial social and sexual issues become inscribed with certain kinds of meaning across a wide variety of media forms. Watney rightly points out that the gradual and staged creation of a 'folk devil' as described by moral panic theorists applies to neither gay men and lesbians nor people who are HIV positive. Instead there is a whole world of 'monstrous' representations. Since sexuality is subjected to regulation and control through a multiplicity of institutions each with their own distinctive discursive practices and textual strategies, moral panics are not, as some have suggested, the key to understanding fears and anxieties about AIDS. As Watney puts it

the theory of moral panics is unable to conceptualise the mass media as an industry intrinsically involved with excess, with the voracious appetite and capacity for substitutions, displacements, repetitions and signifying absences. Moral panic theory is always obliged in the final instance to refer and contrast 'representation' to the arbitration of 'the real', and is hence unable to develop a full theory concerning the operations of ideology within all representational systems. Moral panics seem to appear and disappear, as if representation were not the site of *permanent* struggle of the meaning of signs. (Watney 1987: 41)

Classic moral panic theorists would ignore the daily endorsement (not to say enjoyment) of heterosexuality as an ideological norm and the consequences this has for those who are excluded. Policies and practices which are concerned with 'policing desire' do not, according to Watney, emanate from one or two centralized agencies of social control. They are endemic in media and society, and in this context the moral panic is best seen as a local intensification or 'the site of the current front line' rather than a sudden, unpleasant and unanticipated development (Watney 1987: 42). Watney suggests that our understanding of moral panics might be fruitfully informed by psychological models which seek to understand the ambivalence, excessive interest and even fascination displayed by moral guardians for the objects of their distaste.

Through considering the meanings which have developed around AIDS and homosexuality, Watney replaces the vocabulary of the moral panic with that of representation, discourse and the 'other'. In so doing, he is able to bring to his work concepts drawn from fields of psychoanalysis, film studies and cultural studies to produce a deeper account of processes of exclusion and regulation than that available in the traditional sociology of social control.

Contesting 'Society' and 'Hegemony'

British society and media, youth culture and 'deviance' have changed considerably since the 1960s, and these historical transformations bring to light some of the theoretical and methodological limits of these various studies. In original moral panic theory, 'society' and 'societal reactions' were monolithic and, as others have already argued, ultimately function-alist. Similarly, Hall *et al.*, Pearson and Watney perhaps over-state hege-mony and overlook the counter-discourses from which they draw and to which they contribute. In the 1990s, when social differentiation and audi-ence segmentation are the order of the day, we need to take account of a plurality of reactions, each with their different constituencies, effectivities and modes of discourse.

Given the kinds of moral panic to which they attend, it is problematic that Cohen's 'society', Pearson's description of collective memory and Hall *et al.*'s 'hegemony' exclude youth. Ethnographies of contemporary youth culture (cf. Thornton 1995) find that youth are inclined *not* to lament a safe and stable past *but* to have overwhelming nostalgia for the days when youth culture was genuinely transgressive. The 1990s youth culture is steeped in the legacy of previous 'moral panics'; fighting mods and rock-ers, drug-taking hippies, foul-mouthed punks and gender-bending New Romantics are part of their celebrated folklore. Whether youth cultures espouse overt politics or not, they are often set on being culturally 'radi-cal'. Moral panic can therefore be seen as a culmination and fulfillment of youth cultural agendas in so far as negative news coverage baptizes trans-gression. What better way to turn difference into defiance, lifestyle into social upheaval, leisure into revolt?

Disapproving mass media coverage legitimizes and authenticates youth cultures to the degree that it is hard to imagine a British youth 'move-ment' without it. For, in turning youth into news, mass media both frame subcultures as major events and disseminate them; a tabloid front page *is* frequently a self-fulfilling prophecy. Sociologists might rightly see this in terms of 'deviancy amplification', but youth have their own discourses which see the process as one in which a 'scene' is transformed into a 'movement'. Here youth have a point, for what gets amplified is not only a 'deviant' activity, but the records, haircuts and dance styles which *were said* to accompany the activities.

Knowledge of this youth-culture ethos is such that its exploitation has become a routine marketing strategy of the publishing and recording industries. For example, the 'moral panic' about 'Acid House' in 1988, 1989 and 1990 began with a prediction on the back of the album that launched the music genre. The sleeve notes described the new sound as 'drug induced', 'sky high' and 'ecstatic' and concluded with a prediction of moral panic: 'The sound of acid tracking will undoubtedly become one of the most controversial sounds of 1988, provoking a split between those who adhere to its underground creed and those who decry the glamorization of drug culture.' In retrospect, this seems prescient, but the statement is best understood as hopeful. Moral panics are one of the few marketing strategies open to relatively anonymous instrumental dance music. To quote one music monthly, they amount to a 'priceless PR campaign' (*Q*, January 1989).[2]

Following London Records' sleeve notes, the youth-orientated music and style press repeatedly predicted that a moral panic about Acid House was 'inevitable'.[3] Innuendo, then full-blown exposés about Ecstacy use in British clubs, appeared in the music press for months before the story was picked up by the tabloids. By the end of August, many magazines were wondering why the tabloids were ignoring the issue, while others, confident of eventual moral panic, imagined possible headlines like 'London Gripped by Ecstacy!' or 'Drug Crazed New Hippies in Street Riot' (*Time Out* 17–24 August 1988). In September 1988, during the 'silly season', the tabloids finally took the bait and subjected the culture to the full front-page treatment. The government, Labour opposition *and* the police were keen to ignore the topic for as long as they possibly could, only belatedly making statements, arrests and recommending legislation. This moral panic was incited by a couple of culture industries (e.g. recording and magazine publishing) well versed in the 'hip' ideologies of youth subcultures.

In addition to the difficulty we have in excluding rather large social groups and industrial activities from accounts of 'society' or 'consensus', so we can't ignore the many voices which now contribute to the debate during moral panics. In the 1990s, interest groups, pressure groups, lobbies and campaigning experts are mobilized to intervene in moral panics. For example, the spokeswoman of the National Council for One Parent Families, Sue Slipman, played a leading role, on an almost weekly basis over a period of three or six months, in diminishing the demonization by the Tories of young single mothers for having children without being married.

One of the main aims of pressure groups is timely intervention in relevant moral panics – to be able to respond instantly to the media demonization of the group they represent, and to provide information and analysis designed to counter this representation. The effectiveness of these groups and in particular their skills at working with the media and providing highly professional 'soundbites' more or less on cue make them an invaluable resource to media machinery working to tight schedules and with increasingly small budgets. They allow the media to be seen to be doing their duty by providing 'balance' in their reporting. At the same time, they show how 'folk devils' can and do 'fight back.'

This phenomenon of becoming an expert, having been a deviant, has a long history in the field of serious crime, drug abuse and juvenile delinquency. However, the proliferation of groups recently set up to campaign on behalf or with folk devils and the skill with which they engage with media is an extremely important development in political culture. When Labour and Conservatives take the same line on law and order, arguing for 'effective punishment' and the need for the moral regeneration of society, many media are inclined to give voice to other, sometimes dissenting, groups. In the absence of an immediate and articulate response from Labour, such groups occasionally function as a virtual form of opposition to the government. A new political sociology, taking into account the prominence of the media, might fruitfully explore the precise sphere of influence and the effectiveness of these organizations.

This marks a series of developments which have occurred perhaps in response to the impact of moral panic theory itself,[4] i.e. the sociologist as expert. At least some of the agents of social control must have been listening when figures like Jock Young and Geoff Pearson were invited to add their voices to these debates, because in recent incidents where there have been fears that disorder or outbreaks of rioting might spread to other areas or to other cities, the playing down of the scale of such incidents has been a recurrent feature and a point of recommendation by the police in relation to the media.

Although moral panics are anti-intellectual, often characterized by a certain religious fervour, and historically most effectively used by the right, only a predominantly right-wing national press arguably stops them from being amenable to the current left. Of course, government is always advantaged, due to higher number of authoritative news sources and to institutionalized agenda-setting. But, there is always the possibility of backfire. For example, when John Major attempted to build upon the moral panic around 'single mothers' (if not initiated, then certainly fuelled by government spokespeople because it helped legitimize welfare cutbacks) with his 'Back to Basics' campaign, the media, followed by Labour, deflected the empty rhetoric back onto the Tory party, turning the campaign into an ad-hoc investigation into the personal morality and sexual practices of Tory MPs.

The delicate balance of relations which the moral panic sociologists saw existing between media, agents of social control, folk devils and moral guardians, has given way to a much more complicated and fragmented set of connections. Each of the categories described by moral panics theorists has undergone a process of fissure in the intervening years. New liaisons have been developed and new initiatives pursued. In particular, two groups seem to be making ever more vocal and 'effective' intervention: pressure groups have, among other things, strongly contested the vocality of the traditional moral guardians; and commercial interests have planted the seeds, and courted discourses, of moral panic in seeking to gain the favourable attention of youthful consumers.

This leads us to query the usefulness of the term 'moral panic' – a metaphor which depicts a complex society as a single person who experiences sudden fear about its virtue. The term's anthropomorphism and totalization arguably mystify more than they reveal. Its conception of morals overlooks the youthful ethics of abandon and the moral imperatives of pressure groups and vocal experts. In the 1990s, we need to acknowledge the perspectives and articulations of different sectors of society. New sociologies of social regulation need to shift attention away from the conventional points in the circuit of amplification and control and look instead to these other spaces.

Moral Panics for Every Medium

Not only need the attitudes and activities of different social groups and organizations be taken into account and not subsumed under a consensual 'society', but also the disparate perspectives of different mass, niche and micro-media need to be explored. Britain saw a remarkable 73 per cent increase in consumer magazine titles during the 1980s – the result of more detailed market research, tighter target marketing and new technologies like computer mailing and desk-top publishing (*Marketing* 13 August 1993). Crucially, the success of many of these magazines has been in the discovery and effective representation of niches of opinion and identity.

As seen above, moral panic is a favourite topic of the youth press. When the mass media of tabloids and TV become active in the 'inevitable' moral panic about 'Acid House', the subcultural press were ready. They tracked the tabloids every move, re-printed whole front pages, analysed their copy and decried the *misrepresentation* of Acid House. Some 30 magazines now target and speak up for youth.

Another area of development is the gay and lesbian press who are represented by several national and regional, weekly and monthly papers, magazines and free sheets, some of which have become sub-divided by age, like the long-established *Gay News* which takes a different editorial line from the younger, less political *Boyz*. Of course, these developments are very much dependent on the development of a 'pink economy' and the commercial recognition of the presence and persistence of high levels of gay discretionary income.

Despite their proliferation and diversification, however, the media are obviously not a positive reflection of the diversity of Britain's social interests. This is partly because there are large groups of people in which the media are not economically, and, therefore, editorially interested – crucially, the D and E 'social grades' which are categorized by the *National Readership Survey* as the unskilled working class and 'those at the lowest levels of subsistence', in other words, the long-term employed and poorly pensioned. But even here, there are glimmers of hope. The *Big Issue* is now perceived as the newspaper voice of the homeless. Other groups and agencies produce a never-ending flow of newsletters and press releases many of which are written in a house-style customized to the needs of the journalists on national and local media. So-called folk devils now produce their own media as a counter to what they perceive as the biased media of the mainstream.

Moreover, these niche and micro-media can even attempt to incite their own moral panics. Take, for example, two rival political groups, the Socialist Workers Party (SWP) and the British National Party (BNP) – both of which have their own tabloid papers, which speak to their members and attempt to reach out beyond. In the wake of the election of a BNP councillor in Tower Hamlets in autumn 1993, the fascist BNP paper wrote hysterically about the lost neighbourhoods of the white working class and vilified members of the Anti-Nazi League (ANL, a branch of the SWP) as 'ANAL' scum. The SWP paper, on the other hand, recounted how fascism was sweeping the country and full-out Nazism was just around the corner, due to the actions of their chief 'folk devil', not the BNP hooligan, but the police – those 'traitors' to the working class who gave the BNP the protection of the state. Both attempted to fuel violent political action with their respective moral panic discourses – arguably with a measure of success. This case suggests that moral panics, of this localized variety, are not necessarily hegemonic.

But one needn't turn to specialist magazines and newspapers to find the plurality and divergences of opinion that characterize today's (and probably yesterday's) 'moral panics'. Even the national dailies have dependably different stances. The paper whose tone and agenda is closest to 1960/ 1970s-style moral panic is probably the *Daily Mail*. During the Thatcher years, the *Daily Mail* practised and perfected the characteristics of hegemony, in a way which was in uncanny harmony with Thatcherism. It was a daily process of reaching out to win consent through endlessly defining and redefining social questions and representing itself as the moral voice of the newly self-identified middle class as well as the old lower-middle class. The fact that the *Mail* is the only national daily with more female than male readers – if only 51 per cent female – undoubtedly informs its respectable girl's brand of moral indignity. Hence, hysteria about single and teenage mothers is perfect material for a *Daily Mail* moral panic.

Tabloids like the *Sun* prefer to espouse an altogether different brand of moral outrage. With a topless sixteen year old on page 3 and a hedonistic pro-sex editorial line, their moralism need be finely tuned. But that doesn't stop them from being the most preachy and prescriptive of Britain's daily papers, with page after page of the '*Sun* says ...' However, the *Sun*'s favourite moral panics are of the 'sex, drugs and rock 'n' roll' variety – stories about other people having far *too much* fun, if only because the paper is set on maintaining a young (and not graying) readership. Moreover, these kinds of story have the advantage of allowing their readers to have their cake and eat it too; they can vicariously enjoy and/or secretly admire the transgression one moment, then be shocked and offended the next. When considering the way moral panics work within different publications, one need keep in mind that *Sun* readers take their paper a good deal less seriously than *Mail* readers take theirs. As Mark Pursehouse discovered in interviewing *Sun* readers, one of the key pleasures in reading the *Sun* is the process of estimating what part of a story is true, what parts exaggerated or totally invented. (cf. Pursehouse 1991)

In the last few years, the broadsheets have not only made use of more visual and colour material, they also seem to have adopted tabloid-style headlines to accompany their tabloid supplements. For example, the covers of the *Guardian* G2 section frequently sport exaggerated, sensational headlines. 'BLOOD ON THE STREETS: They're Packing Pistols in Manchester' announces a story about the increasing use of firearms by young drug dealers on mountain bikes in Manchester's Moss Side (*Guardian* 9 August 1993). Given the more measured copy which follows, the *Guardian* would seem to be using this 'shock horror' language to lighten up the story – the capital letters signifying an ironic borrowing of tabloid style. But, as the *Sun*'s language is understood by many of its readers as tongue-in-cheek, the *Guardian*'s irony gives it an alibi, but not absolution. Moreover, these mixtures of outrage and amusement point to the 'entertainment value' of moral panics – something mentioned but not really integrated into previous models. (cf. Curran and Sparks 1991 for a critique of the 'astigmatic perspective' of accounts of politics and the press which overlook entertainment.)

In considering the *Daily Mail*, the *Sun* and the *Guardian*, we've found that each paper has its own style of in-house moralism. As the British press becomes more competitive, one strategy for maintaining healthy circulation figures is for a newspaper to cast itself in the role of moral guardian, ever alert to new possibilities for concern and indignation. It would seem that professional journalistic style, carefully attuned to the popularity of 'human interest' stories, draws on a moralistic voice which, for the purposes of variety, it is willing to undercut with occasional irony, jokes, etc.

Although the multiplicity of contemporary moral panics is perhaps best demonstrated in relation to print media, the same tendencies can be found in radio and television. Even with only four terrestrial channels, new definitions of youth programming have opened a space for counter-discourses. Television producer Janet Street-Porter, drawing on the cut-up graphic style of punk and indicating a new commitment on the part of broadcasters to take youth seriously, pioneered 'Youth TV' in the mid-eighties through her *Def II* series on BBC2. In keeping with this commitment, several of these programmes were explicitly aimed at countering youthful folk devils and moral panics, particularly around drugs. Thus an informative and rational BBC2 *Reportage* programme on the use of Ecstasy in rave culture can be set against the much more traditional sensational and fearful *Cook Report* (ITV) on the same subject (1992).

Mediated Social Worlds

In addition to unpacking 'society', on the one hand, and the 'media', on the other, the third consideration in updating models of 'moral panic' need be that the media is no longer something separable from society. Social reality is experienced through language, communication and imagery. Social meanings and social differences are inextricably tied up with representation. Thus when sociologists call for an account which tells how life actually is, and which deals with the real issues rather than the spectacular and exaggerated ones, the point is that these accounts of reality are already representations and sets of meanings about what they perceive the 'real' issues to be. These versions of 'reality' would also be impregnated with the mark of media imagery rather than somehow pure and untouched by the all-pervasive traces of contemporary communications.

The media have long been seen to be embedded in the fabric of society. What may be constitutively new is the degree to which media have become something with which the social is continuously being defined. For example, characterizations like '*Mirror* reader' or '*Times* reader' often give us as good an indication of social class as the mention of a particular occupation. Social age and generation (rather than biological age) are played out in the relation between Radios One and Two or Capital FM and

Capital Gold. Subtle differences of gender identity are negotiated when, say, a working-class woman says she dislikes all soap operas, preferring instead news, sport and nature programmes. Similarly, at the risk of being cliché, for a man to admit his devotion to the films of Joan Crawford and Judy Garland is, in some contexts, tantamount to 'coming out'.

At another level, the hard and fast divide between media professionals and media 'punters' seems to have broken down to some extent. The ownership of home video-cameras, the new space for broadcasting home video material on national television (in series like *Video Diaries*), the existence of 'right to reply' programmes, the possession of degrees in media studies all point in this direction. Audiences can be credited with possessing a greater degree of 'media literacy' than they did in the past. Also important here is the introduction of a distinctively amateurish (rather than professional) style of presentation, developed by Channel Four's *The Tube* in the early 1980s and best reflected in the 'fluffed' mannerism of its two presenters, Jools Holland and Paula Yates. Finally, the increasing reliance on the audience as a resource for successful television, either as visualized participants or audible internal audiences, seems to give a positive place to the audience in the process of programme production.

The strength of the old models of moral panic was that they marked the connection between 'the media' and 'social control'. But, nowadays, most political strategies *are* media strategies. The contest to determine news agendas is the first and last battle of the political campaign. Moreover, the kinds of social issues and political debates which were once included on the agendas of moral panic theorists as sites of social anxiety, and even crisis, could now be redefined as part of an endless debate about who 'we' are and what 'our' national culture is. These are profoundly 'home affairs'. The daily intensity and drama of their appearance and the many voices now heard in the background but in the foreground, punctuating and producing reality, point more to the reality of dealing with social difference than to the unity of current affairs (cf. Hall, Connell and Curtis 1981).

Conclusions

What has been argued here is that the model of moral panic is urgently in need of updating precisely because of its success. While the theory began its life in radical sociology, the strength of the argument quickly found its way into those very areas with which it was originally concerned, influencing social policy and attitudes to deviance generally. As a result, the police, as agents of social control now show some awareness of the dangers of overreaction, while sectors of the media regularly remind viewers of the dangers of moral panic and thus of alienating sections of the community by falsely attributing to them some of the characteristics of the so-called folk devils.

Crucially, the theory has, over the years, drawn attention to the importance of empowering folk devils so that they or their representatives can challenge the cycle of sanctions and social control. Pressure groups, lobbies, self-help and interest groups have sprung up across the country and effectively positioned themselves as authoritative sources of comment and criticism. They now contribute to the shape of public debate, playing a major role in contesting what they perceive as dangerous stereotypes and popular misconceptions.

The theory has also influenced business practice, albeit through an undoubtedly more circuitous route. Culture industry promotions and marketing people now understand how, for certain products like records, magazines, movies and computer games, nothing could be better for sales than a bit of controversy – the threat of censorship, the suggestion of sexual scandal or subversive activity. The promotional logic is twofold: first, the cultural good will receive a lot of free, if negative, publicity because its associations with moral panic have made it newsworthy; second, rather than alienating everyone, it will be attractive to a contingent of consumers who see themselves as alternative, avant-garde, radical, rebellious or simply young. In the old models of moral panic, the audience played a minor role and remained relatively untheorized. With few exceptions, they were the space of consensus, the space of media manipulation, the space of an easily convinced public. A new model need embrace the complex realm of reception – readers, viewers, listeners and the various social groups categorized under the heading of public opinion cannot be read off the representation of social issues.

The moral panics we have been discussing here are less monolithic than those the classic model implied. Recent moral panics do remain overwhelmingly concerned with moral values, societal regularities and drawing of lines between the permissible and the less acceptable. However, hard and fast boundaries between 'normal' and 'deviant' would seem to be less common – if only because moral panics are now continually contested. Few sociologists would dispute the expansion over the last decade of what used to be called, quite simply, the mass media. The diversification of forms of media and the sophisticated restructuring of various categories of audience require that, while a consensual social morality might still be a political objective, the chances of it being delivered directly through the channels of the media are much less certain.

Notes

This article was first published in the *British Journal of Sociology*, December 1995, vol. 46, no. 4.

1 Sleeve notes of *The House Sound of Chicago Volume III: Acid Tracks* released in January 1988 by London Records (a label of Polygram International).
2 This may not, in fact, be new. Perhaps the first publicity campaign intentionally to court moral outrage was conducted by Andrew Loog Oldman who, back in the 1960s, promoted the Rolling Stones as dirty, irascible, rebellious and threatening (cf. Norman 1993).
3 Cf. 'New Acid Daze', *New Musical Express* (6 February 1988); 'Acid Daze', *Record Mirror* (20 February 1988); 'Acid Daze', *Melody Maker* (27 February 1988); Darren Reynolds 'Acid House', *Soul Underground* (April 1988). The repetition of the phrase 'Acid Daze' suggests the stories were PR led.
4 Cohen's *Folk Devils and Moral Panics* and Young's *The Drugtakers* have been on the syllabi of many A-level sociology courses and university courses in sociology, social policy, social work, and more recently media studies.

Bibliography

Becker, H. 1963. *The Outsiders,* New York: Free Press.

Cohen, S. (ed.) 1971. *Images of Deviance*, Harmondsworth: Penguin.

Cohen, S. 1972/1980. *Folk Devils and Moral Panics: The Creation of the Mods and the Rockers*, Oxford: Basil Blackwell.

Cohen, S. and Young, J. (eds) 1973. *The Manufacture of the News: Deviance, Social Problems and the Mass Media*, London: Constable.

Curran, J. 1978. 'The Press as an Agency of Social Control: An Historical Perspective' in G. Boyce *et al.* (eds) *Newspaper History*, London: Constable.

Curran, J. and Sparks, C. 1991. 'Press and Popular Culture', *Media, Culture and Society* 13: 215–37.

Gilroy, P. 1987. *There Ain't No Black in the Union Jack: The Cultural Politics of Race and Nation*, London: Hutchison.

Hall, S. *et al.* 1979. *Policing the Crisis: Mugging, the State and Law and Order*, London: MacMillan.

Hall, S., Connell, I. and Curti, L. 1981. 'The "Unity" of Current Affairs Television' in Tony Bennett *et al.* (eds) *Popular Television and Film*, London: BFI.

Pearson, G. 1983. *Hooligans: A History of Respectable Fears*, London: MacMillan.

Pursehouse, M. 1991. 'Looking at the *Sun:* Into the Nineties with a Tabloid and its Readers', *Cultural Studies from Birmingham* 1: 88–133.

Schlesinger, P. and Tumber, H. 1994. *Reporting Crime: The Media Politics of Criminal Justice*, Oxford: Oxford University Press.

Thornton, S. L. 1995. *Club Culture: Music, Media and Subcultural Capital*, Oxford: Polity.

Waddington, P.A.J. 1986. 'Mugging as a Moral Panic: A Question of Proportion', *British Journal of Sociology* 37(2): 245–59.

Watney, S. 1987. *Policing Desire: Pornography, AIDS and the Media,* London: Methuen.

Wilkins, L. T. 1964. *Social Deviance: Social Policy, Action and Research*, London: Tavistock.

Young, J. 1971. *The Drugtakers: The Social Meaning of Drug Use*, London: Paladin.

References

Adburgham, A. 1972. *Women in Print: Writing Women and Women's Magazines From the Restoration to the Accession of Victoria*. London: Allen and Unwin.

Ahmed, S. 2012. *On Being Included: Racism and Diversity in Institutional Life*. Durham, NC: Duke University Press.

Akomfrah, J. (dir). 1986. *Handsworth Songs*. London: Smoking Dog Productions.

Akomfrah, J. (dir). 1998. *Goldie: When Saturn Returnz*. London: Smoking Dog Productions.

Albertine, V. 2014. *Clothes, Clothes, Clothes, Music, Music, Music, Boys, Boys, Boys*. London: Faber.

Althusser, L. 1971. 'Ideology and Ideological State Apparatuses'. In *Lenin and Philosophy and Other Essays*. London: NLB.

Ayres, J. 2021. 'Enterprising Fashion: The Political Economy of Vintage, Secondhand Clothes, and Secondary Markets'. PhD diss., New York University.

Back, L. 1996. *New Ethnicities and Urban Culture: Racism and Multiculture in Young Lives*. London: Routledge.

Back, L. 2007. *The Art of Listening*. London: Routledge.

Bain, V. 2019. 'Counting the Music Industry: The Gender Gap: A Study of Gender Inequality in the UK Music Industry'. https://vbain.co.uk/research/.

Banet-Weiser, S. 2018. *Empowered: Popular Feminism and Popular Misogyny*. Durham, NC: Duke University Press.

Barron, C. 2019. *Dance Nation Oberon Modern Plays*. New York: Oberon.

Barthes, R. 1957/1972. *Mythologies*. London: Jonathan Cape.

Bauman, Z. 1999. *Liquid Modernity*. Oxford: Wiley.

Bauman, Z. 2001. *The Individualised Society*. Cambridge: Polity Press.

Bayer, T. 2021. *Textilwirtschaft*. Germany. https://www.textilwirtschaft.de/suche/schlagworte/Tobias+Bayer/.

Baym, N. 2000. *Tune In, Log On: Soaps, Fandom and Online Community*. London: Sage.

Benjamin, W. 1979. *Berlin Chronicle 1932*. London: NLB Books.

Bennett, T. 2018. ' "The Whole Feminist Taking Your Clothes Off Thing": Negotiating the Critique of Gender and Inequality in the UK Music Industry'. *Iaspm@Journal* 8 (1).

Berlant, L. 2011. *Cruel Optimism*. Durham, NC: Duke University Press.

Bettie, J. 2003. *Women without Class: Girls, Race and Identity*. Berkeley: University of California Press.

Bey, M. 2022. 'All In'. *Representations* 158 (1): 42–56.

Bhabha, H.K. 1986. *The Location of Culture*. London: Routledge.

Black, P. 2011. *Black by Design: An A to Z Two Tone Memoir*. London: Profile Books.

Bobie, A.O. 2022. 'The Politics of Sustainability'. Paper delivered at *Global Fashion and Social Change Conference*, Loughborough University, London Campus, 6 July.

Born, G. 2010. 'The Social and the Aesthetic: For a Post-Bourdieuian Theory of Cultural Production'. *Cultural Sociology* 4 (2): 171–208.

Bourdieu, P. 1984. *Distinction: A Social Critique of the Judgement of Taste*. Translated by Richard Nice. London: Routledge.

Brah, A. 1996. *Cartographies of Diaspora: Contesting Identities*. London: Routledge.

Brown, W. 2015. *Undoing the Demos: Neoliberalism's Stealth Revolution*. Cambridge, MA: MIT Press.

Brunsdon, C. 1978. *Everyday Television-Nationwide*. London: BFI.

Butler, J. 1990. *Gender Trouble: Feminism and the Subversion of Identity*. London: Routledge.

Butler, J. 1993. *Bodies That Matter: On the Discursive Limits of 'Sex'*. New York: Routledge.

Butler, J. 1997. *The Psychic Life of Power Theories in Subjection*. Palo Alto, CA: Stanford University Press.

The Care Collective. 2020. *The Care Manifesto: The Politics of Interdependence*. London: Verso.

Carey, M. 2021. *Black Girlhood in 20th-Century America*. Oxford: Oxford University Press.

Centre for Contemporary Cultural Studies. 1982. *The Empire Strikes Back: Race and Racism in 70s Britain*. London: Routledge.

Clayton, A. 2022. 'Going through Torture'. *Guardian*, 14 December. https://www.theguardian.com/music/2022/dec/13/megan-thee-stallion-testify-tory-lanez-los-angeles-court.

Cochrane, L. 2022. 'Cool Kids Want to Dress Like Old Crunchy People'. *Guardian*, 10 November. https://www.theguardian.com/fashion/2022/nov/09/blackbird-spyplane-newsletter-jonah-weiner-interview.

Coleman, R. 2009. *The Becoming of Bodies: Girls, Images, Experience*. Manchester: Manchester University Press.

Colomb, C. 2012. 'Pushing the Urban Frontier: Temporary Uses of Space, City Marketing, and the Creative City Discourses in 2000's Berlin'. *Journal of Urban Affairs* 34 (2): 131–152.

Conor, B., Gill, R., and Taylor, S. (eds). 2015. *Gender and Creative Labour*. Oxford: Wiley-Blackwell.

Cooper, M. 2017. *Family Values: Between Neoliberalism and the New Social Conservatism.* Cambridge, MA: MIT Press.

Cowie, C., and Lees, S. 1981. 'Slags or Drags'. *Feminist Review* 9 (1).

Cox, A. M. 2015. *Shapeshifters: Black Girls and the Choreography of Citizenship.* Durham, NC: Duke University Press.

Crenshaw, K., Ocen, P., and Nanda, J. 2015. 'Black Girls Matter: Pushed Out, Overpoliced and Underprotected'. *African American Policy Forum and Centre for Intersectionality and Social Policy Studies.* https://scholarship.law.columbia.edu/faculty_scholarship/3227.

Curran-Troop, H., Gill, R., and Littler, J. 2023 'Freelance Feminism'. *European Journal of Cultural Studies 13* (April), special issue.

Darkwah, A. 2022. 'Ethical Fashion Initiatives in Ghana: The Case of Studio 189'. Paper delivered at *Global Fashion and Social Change Conference*, Loughborough University, London Campus, 6 July.

Davis, A. Y. 1991. *Blues Legacies and Black Feminism: Gertrude Ma Rainey, Bessie Smith and Billie Holliday.* New York: Vintage Books.

Deleuze, G. 2009. *Foucault.* New York: Continuum Books.

Denise, L. 2019. 'The Afterlife of Aretha Franklin's "Rock Steady:" A Case Study in DJ Scholarship'. *Black Scholar* 49 (3): 62–72.

Donzelot, J. 1979. *The Policing of Families.* Basingstoke: Macmillan.

Dorfman, A. 1983. *The Empire's Old Clothes.* London: Pluto Press.

Dowling, E. 2021. *The Care Crisis.* London: Verso.

Driscoll, C. 2002. *Girls: Feminine Adolescence in Popular Culture and Cultural Theory.* New York: Columbia University Press.

Driscoll, C. 2008 'Girls Today: Girls, Girl Culture and Girl Studies'. *Girlhood Studies* 1 (1).

Duffy, B.E. 2017. *(Not) Getting Paid to Do What You Love: Gender and Aspirational Labor in the Social Media Economy.* New Haven, CT: Yale University Press.

Du Gay, P., and Hall, S. 1997. *Doing Cultural Studies: The Story of the Sony Walkman.* London: Sage.

Enninful, E. 2022. *A Visible Man.* London: Bloomsbury.

Evans, A. 2017. *Technologies of Sexiness.* London: Routledge.

Feldman-Barrett, C. 2021. *A Woman's History of The Beatles.* Bloomsbury: London.

Foucault, M. 1987. *The History of Sexuality.* Vol 1. London: Penguin.

Frith, S. 1978. *The Sociology of Rock.* London: Constable.

Gelder, K., and Thornton, S. 1997. *The Subcultures Reader.* London: Routledge.

Gill, R. 2007. *Gender and the Media*. London: Routledge.

Gill, R., and Orgad, S. 2018. 'The Confidence Culture.' *Australian Feminist Studies* 30 (86).

Gilroy, P. 1987. *There Ain't No Black in the Union Jack*. London: Routledge.

Gilroy, P. 2000. *The Black Atlantic*. New Haven, CT: Yale University Press.

Goh, A., and Thompson, M. 2019. 'Sonic Cyberfeminisms: Introduction.' *Feminist Review* 127: 1–12.

Gramsci, A. 1974/2021. *Selections from the Prison Notebooks*. London: NLB/Verso.

Grant, C., and Waxman, L. (eds). 2011. *Girls! Girls! Girls! In Contemporary Art*. Bristol: Intellect Books.

Gürbüz, T. S. 2021. 'Revisiting Early Punk Cinema.' *Punk and Post-Punk Journal* 10 (1): 45–62.

Halberstam, J. 2005. *In a Queer Time and Place: Transgender Bodies and Subcultural Lives*. New York: New York University Press.

Hall, S. 1973. 'The Determinations of News Photographs.' *Working Papers in Cultural Studies* 2. Birmingham: Birmingham University.

Hall, S. 1980. 'Cultural Studies: Two Paradigms.' *Media Culture and Society* 2 (3).

Hall, S. 1988. *The Hard Road to Renewal: Thatcherism and the Crisis of the Left*. London: Lawrence and Wishart.

Hall, S. 1992/1996. 'What's This Black in Black Popular Culture?.' In Morley, D., and Chen, K.-H. (eds), *Stuart Hall Critical Dialogues in Cultural Studies*. London: Routledge.

Hall, S. 1997/2013. 'The Spectacle of the Other.' In Evans, J., and Nixon, S. (eds), *Representation*, 2nd. ed. London: Sage.

Hall, S., Critcher, C., Jefferson, T., Clarke, J., and Roberts, B. 1978. *Policing the Crisis: Mugging, the State and Law and Order*. London: Routledge.

Hall, S., and Jefferson, T. (eds). 1975. *Resistance through Rituals*. London: Routledge.

Halliday, A. S. 2020. 'Twerk Sumn!: Theorizing Black Girl Epistemology in the Body.' *Cultural Studies* 34 (6).

Harris, A. 2004. *Future Girl: Young Women in the 20th Century*. London: Routledge.

Hartman, S. 2021. *Wayward Lives, Beautiful Experiments: Intimate Histories of Riotous Black Girls, Troublesome Women and Queer Radicals*. London: Profile Books.

Harvey, D. 2005. *A Brief History of Neoliberalism*. Oxford: Oxford University Press.

Hebdige, R. 1978. *Subculture: The Meaning of Style*. London: Methuen.

Henriques, J. 2021. Sound System Outernational. https://www.gold.ac.uk/sound-system-outernational.

Hermes, J. 1995. *Reading Women's Magazines.* Cambridge: Polity Press.

Hill, B. (dir). 2011. *Feltham Sings.* London: Channel 4 Production Company. https://www. youtube.com/watch?v=yzTIvajQq-0.

Hobson, D. 1982. *Crossroads: Drama of a Soap Opera.* London: Methuen.

Hoggart, R. 1957. *The Uses of Literacy.* Harmondsworth: Penguin.

hooks, b. 1981. *Ain't I a Woman? Black Women and Feminism.* Boston: South End Press.

hooks, b. 1990. *Yearning: Race, Gender and Cultural Politics.* Boston: South End Press.

hooks, b. 1992. *Black Looks: Race and Representation.* Boston: South End Press.

hooks, b. 1996. *Killing Rage: Ending Racism.* London: Penguin.

hooks, b. 1997. *Bone Black: Memories of Girlhood.* London: Women's Press.

James, R. 2021. 'Sonic Cyberfeminisms Perceptual Coding and 'Phonographic' Compression'. *Feminist Review.*

Julien, I. (dir). 1983. *Who Killed Colin Roach?* London: Sankofa Productions.

Julien, I. (dir). 1991. *Young Soul Rebels.* London: Sankofa Productions.

Kanai, A. 2018. 'From Can Do Girl to Insecure and Angry: Affective Dissonances in Young Women's Post-recessional Media'. *Feminist Media Studies* 19 (6).

Kearney, M.C. 2006. *Girls Make Media.* London: Routledge.

Klein, N. 2000. *No Logo: Taking Aim at the Brand Bullies.* New York: Harper Collins.

Kneese, T., and Palm, M. 2020. 'Brick-and-Platform: Listing Labor in the Digital Vintage Economy'. *Social Media + Society* (July–September): 1–11.

Kollewe, J. 2023. 'Almost 50 UK Shops Closed for Good Every Day in 2022'. *Guardian*, 2 January. https://www.theguardian.com/business/2023/jan/02/almost-50-uk-shops-closed-for-good-every-day-in-2022-says-report.

Lewis, G. 2000. *Race, Gender, Social Welfare: Encounters in a Postcolonial Society.* Cambridge: Polity Press.

Le Zotte, J. 2017. *From Goodwill to Grunge: A History of Secondhand Styles and Alternative Economies.* Chapel Hill: University of North Carolina Press.

Littler, J. 2017. *Against Meritocracy: Culture, Power and Myths of Mobility.* London: Routledge.

Livingston, J. (dir). 1990. *Paris Is Burning.* Off White Productions.

Lloyd, R. 2006. *The Neo-Bohemians.* Chicago: University of Chicago Press.

Markham, A., and Baym, N. (eds). 2009. *Internet Inquiry: Conversations about Methods.* London: Sage.

Martin, D. 2003. 'Pepper LaBeija Queen of Harlem Is Dead.' *New York Times*, 26 May. https://www.nytimes.com/2003/05/26/arts/pepper-labeija-queen-of-harlem-drag-balls-is-dead-at-53.html.

Mattelart, A., and Dorfman, A. 1975. *How to Read Donald Duck*. London: Penguin.

McKittrick, K., and Weheliye, A.G. 2017. '808s and Heartbreak.' *Propter Nos* 2 (1).

McRobbie, A. 1976/1982. 'Jackie: An Ideology of Adolescent Femininity.' CCCS Stencilled Paper. Reprinted in Bennett, T., et al. (eds), *Popular Culture Past and Present*. London: Routledge.

McRobbie, A. 2001/2016. 'Club to Company.' In *Be Creative: Making a Living in the New Culture Industries*. Cambridge: Polity Press.

McRobbie, A. 2005. *The Uses of Cultural Studies*. London: Sage.

McRobbie, A. 2008. *The Aftermath of Feminism*. London: Sage.

McRobbie, A. 2020. *Feminism and the Politics of Resilience*. Cambridge: Polity Press.

McRobbie, A., and Garber, J. 1975. 'Girls and Subcultures.' In Hall, S., and Jefferson, T. (eds), *Resistance through Rituals*. London: Routledge.

Mirza, H.S. 1992. *Young, Female and Black*, London: Routledge.

Mitchell, C., and Reid-Walsh, J. (eds). 2007. *Girl Culture: An Encyclopedia*. Vols. 1–2. New York: Greenwood.

Moran, C. 2011. *How to be a Woman*. London: Penguin.

Moran, C. 2020. *More Than a Woman*. London: Penguin.

Morley, D. 1980. *The Nationwide Audience*. London: BFI.

Mulvey, L. 1975/1999. 'Visual Pleasure and Narrative Cinema.' In Brandy, L., and Cohen, M. (eds), *Film Theory and Criticism: Introductory Readings*. Oxford: Oxford University Press.

Munoz, J. 1999. *Disidentifications: Queers of Color and the Performance of Politics*. Minneapolis: University of Minnesota Press.

Nava, M. 1982. ' "Everybody's Views Were Just Broadened": A Girls Project and Some Responses to Lesbianism.' *Feminist Review* 10 (Spring).

Negus, K. 1992. *Producing Pop*. London: Edward Arnold.

Norris, L. 2012. 'Trade and Transformations of Second-Hand Clothing: Introduction.' *Textile: Cloth and Culture* 10 (2).

Parsons, P. R. 1988. 'The Changing Expectations of Women Executives in the Recording Industry.' *Popular Music and Society* 12 (4).

Payson, A. 2021. 'Makeover Welfare: Mary, Queen of Charity Shops, Reality TV and Real Secondhand Politics.' Paper delivered at Conference on Second Hand Cultures (online).

Phoenix, A. 1991. *Young Mothers*. Cambridge: Polity Press.

Phoenix, A. 2004. 'Neoliberalism and Masculinity: Racialization and the Contradictions of Schooling for 11–14 Year Olds'. *Youth and Society* 36 (2).

Quinn, B. 2022. 'Racism Cited as Factor as Young Girl, 15, Strip Searched at School'. *Guardian*, 15 March. https://www.theguardian.com/uk-news/2022/mar/15/black-girl-racism-police-strip-search-london-school-hackney.

Riley, D. 1992. 'Citizenship and the Welfare State'. In Allen, J., et al. (eds), *Political and Economic Forms of Modernity*. Cambridge: Polity Press.

Ringrose, J. 2015. *Children, Sexuality, Sexualisation*. London: Routledge.

Rocamora, A. 2017. 'Mediatization and Digital Media in the Field of Fashion'. *Fashion Theory* 21 (5).

Rocamora, A., and Smelik, A. 2016. *Thinking through Fashion: A Guide to Key Theorists*. London: I.B. Tauris.

Rose, J. 1986. *Sexuality in the Field of Vision*. London: Verso.

Rose, T. 1994. *Black Noise: Rap Music and Black Culture in Contemporary America*. Middletown, CT: Wesleyan University Press.

Rottenberg, C. 2018. *The Rise of Neoliberal Feminism*. Oxford: Oxford University Press.

Sandberg, S. 2012. *Lean In: Women, Work and the Will to Lead*. New York: Knopf.

Satenstein, L. 2020. 'This 22-Year-Old is Paying for College by Selling Rare Vintage on Depop'. *Vogue*, 23 December. https://www.vogue.co.uk/miss-vogue/article/olivia-haroutounian-depop.

Savier, M., and Wildt, C. 1978. *Mädchen: Zwischen Anpassung und Widerstand [Girls: Between passivity and resistance]*. Munich: Frauenoffensive.

Shilliam, R. 2018. *Race and the Undeserving Poor*. Bristol: Policy Press.

Skeggs, B. 1987. *Formations of Class and Gender: Becoming Respectable*. London: Sage.

Sobande, F. 2020. *The Digital Lives of Black Women*. Basingstoke: Palgrave.

Spillers, H.J. 1987. 'Mama's Baby, Papa's Maybe: An American Grammar Book'. *Diacritics* 17 (2).

Square, J.M. 2020. 'How Enslaved People Helped Shape Fashion History'. *Guernica*, 14 December. https://www.guernicamag.com/how-enslaved-people-helped-shape-fashion-history/.

Taylor, H. 2023. 'Call for Inquiry into Surrey School after Black Pupil Attacked'. *Guardian*, 9 February. https://www.theguardian.com/uk-news/2023/feb/09/call-for-investigation-into-surrey-school-after-black-pupil-suffers-racist-assault.

Thomas, M.E. 2011. *Multicultural Girlhoods: Racism, Sexuality and the Conflicted Spaces of American Education*. Philadelphia: Temple University Press.

Thomas, M. 2018. 'Nappily Ever After Review: Relatable but Not Revolutionary'. *gal-dem*, 9 October. https://gal-dem.com/nappily-ever-after-review/.

Thompson E.P. 1978. *The Poverty of Theory*. New York: Monthly Review Press.

Thornton, S. 1995. *Club Cultures*. Cambridge: Polity Press.

Wacquant, L. 2009. *Punishing the Poor: The Neoliberal Government of Social Insecurity*. Durham, NC: Duke University Press.

Welsh, I. 2001. *Trainspotting*. London: Faber.

White, C.L. 1970. *Women's Magazines 1693–1968*. London: Penguin.

White, J. 2020. *Terraformed: Young Black Lives in the Inner City*. London: Repeater Books.

White, J., and Gilroy, P. 2020. 'SPRC Short Takes: Terraformed: Young Black Lives in the Inner City'. Sarah Parker Remond Centre, UCL London. https://www.ucl.ac.uk/racism-racialisation/transcript-terraformed-young-black-lives-inner-city.

Whyte, W.F. 1943/1993. *Street Corner Society*. Chicago: University of Chicago Press.

Williams, R. 1957. *Culture and Society*. London: Allen and Unwin.

Williamson, J. 1978. *Decoding Advertisements*. London: Methuen.

Willis, P. 1978. *Learning to Labour*. Wolverhampton: Saxon House.

Wilson, E. 1985. *Adorned in Dreams: Fashion and Modernity*. London: Virago.

Wilson, K. 2015. 'Towards a Radical Reappropriation: Gender, Development and Neoliberal Feminism'. *Development and Change* 46 (4).

Winch, A. 2014. 'Brand Intimacy, Female Friendship and Digital Surveillance Networks'. *New Formations* 84–85.

Winship, J. 1985. 'A Girl Needs to Get Street Wise: Magazines for the 1980s'. *Feminist Review* 21.

Wollen, P. 2003. 'The Concept of Fashion in *The Arcades Project*'. *boundary 2: An International Journal of Literature and Culture* 30 (1): 131–142.

Yates-Richard, M. 2021. 'Hell You Talmbout?': Janelle Monáe's Black Cyberfeminist Sonic Aesthetics'. *Feminist Review* 127.

Young, L. 2000. 'How Do We Look? Unfixing the Singular Black (Female) Subject'. In Gilroy, P., Grossberg, L., and McRobbie, A. (eds), *Without Guarantees: In Honour of Stuart Hall*. London: Verso.

Zukin, S. 2012. *Landscapes of Power*. New York: Columbia University Press.

Index